A CALL INTO HIS PRESENCE
When the Spirit Prays
Volume 1

By Evelyn A. Johnson

Copyright © 2009 by Evelyn A. Johnson

A Call Into His Presence
When the Spirit Prays Volume 1
by Evelyn A. Johnson

Printed in the United States of America

ISBN 978-1-61579-093-7

All rights reserved solely by the author. The author guarantees all contents are original and do not infringe upon the legal rights of any other person or work. No part of this book may be reproduced in any form without the permission of the author. The views expressed in this book are not necessarily those of the publisher.

Unless otherwise indicated, Bible quotations are taken from
   KJV.
   NLT. Copyright © 1997 by Tybdale House Publishers, Inc.
   NIV. Copyright © 1996 by Zondervan Corporation.

www.xulonpress.com

Table of Contents

Introduction xiii
✈ Day 1 ~ The Humility of Man Gives You an Audience
          with the King 21
Day 2 ~ The Lord Speaks To Us in a Small Still Voice 33
Day 3 ~ Faith Will Take You to Your Fruit 39
Day 4 ~ Another Spirit 57
Day 5 ~ Lord, Let Your Favor Compass Us like a Shield 71
Day 6 ~ Six the Number of Man 81
Day 7 ~ God's Perfect Number 93
Day 8 ~ New Beginning & Resurrection 103
🕊Day 9 ~ Wisdom 119
Day 10 ~ We Are Disciples of Christ 137
Day 11 ~ The Number 11 Means Disruption & Disorder 155
Day 12 ~ The Words of the Lord Are Pure 167
Day 13 ~ The Spirit of Disbelief & Doubt 177
Day 14 ~ I Must Cross Over 191
Day 15 ~ God Is In Communication with You 209
Day 16 ~ Seven Times A Day Will I Praise, Thee 225
Day 17 ~ The Price of Salvation Is Priceless 239
Day 18 ~ I Love You, Oh, Lord, with All of Who I Am 261
Day 19 ~ Stay On the Wall, the Wall of Faith & Belief 279
Day 20 ~ Spirit of the Living God, Fall Fresh On Me 287

Dedication

I dedicate this book to my husband, C. Charles Johnson Jr., my friend and my Lion. He is my Pastor; a man who has given over to the suffering of prayer that souls would be changed all over the world. My Abraham, who sold out and left everything to go to a place he knew nothing of to do the Will of his God. I love you and I am so thankful to God for creating you to be who you are and especially making you for me.
Your wife,
Evelyn

INTRODUCTION

There is a difference in the phrases 'to Seek' and
'to be 'Called'

It's another story when we seek God for His PRESENCE versus God Himself calling us into His PRESENCE.

The Call was A Request—a Demand was made to come into His **PRESENCE**. Our Pastor answered and said "Yes" and we followed!

The Call Into His **PRESENCE** was a 40 days journey where one-step took us one day. With each step, it brought about a new experience in that day; a day in which we had never seen before or knew what challenges we would encounter. This book is for everyone who desires to go into a place in God where no Human Being can take them! The prayers contained in the following pages are actual recordings of our cries out to God. It is our desire that God would use them to inspire and uplift you as you enter into THE **PRESENCE** OF GOD. Come with us during these 40 days, and you will climb the mountain with intense, sincere and uninterrupted dedicated prayer, which will take you into the **PRESENCE** of God!

Dear Reader,
While reading this book, I pray that you will join in with us and experience the prayer, which was prayed through the Holy Spirit. I firmly feel in my spirit that you will experience a life-changing occurrence in prayer. This experience will change the very core of your soul.

<u>I pray this book will inspire you to take a stand against the flesh and say:</u>
- I will pray beyond the human mind, understanding and logic
- I will pray until my mind, body and Soul is united as one in the Holy Spirit
- I will pray until my Soul clings to God

Jesus is our example because He prayed so fervently, sweat dropped off him like blood! We want to pray everything that is not like Jesus will fall off drop by drop! We also want to pray until every dark place in us is taken out so we will shine as lights in this dark and corrupted world.

<u>This book is non-fiction. Our Pastor, through the influence and power of the Holy Spirit, prayed all of the prayers. I have written this book to the best of my ability to help you understand what we were feeling and how we were blessed in the **PRESENCE** of God. Therefore, in the actual prayers there may not always be correct grammar and punctuation. Some days may not have an opening or closing remarks due to our Pastor being led by the unction of</u>

the Holy Spirit to enter directly into prayer. I would like to deeply express that the emphasis of this book is "when the Spirit prays." The focus is not on our Pastor, although he prayed the prayers, nor is it on the church, it's on the Holy Spirit. It takes the all knowing Spirit of God to be able to intercede and know what to pray for each individual, every situation and the world. Man can only go but so far; it is the Holy Spirit that takes us to the beyond! Additionally, some individual's names have been changed to protect their privacy. I firmly believe you will find a prayer which will fit your personal situations in one of these 40 days of prayer. We pray this book will be another tool to help you in your prayer life just as it has helped us! We love you!

PREPARING FOR PRAYER:

The day that was to begin the first day of the 40 days of prayer, I could not wait until prayer began. I knew we had just left church from New Year Watch Service but there was a panting in my soul and a yearning to get to church! My heart was beating rapidly because I knew God was going to meet us and I could not wait for His arrival!

When we pulled up to the church, every step had a heartbeat. The closer I got to the door, the louder my heart cried out, "Lord, I love you." It was at that moment I knew I had an audience with the King! I felt as if I would faint because my soul was about to burst out proclaiming,

<u>"Oh, my God, how I love you! Oh, how I love you with all of my being, with all of my might, with all of my strength, with all of my heart, with all of my soul, and with all my understanding of who You are! Take me, God! Take me to a place in you where I will experience Your Glory and Your PRESENCE to a degree that will stain my heart and soul forever!"</u>

My God! It happened. 7:30 pm! The first day of prayer and Pastor uttered his first words, "**<u>God was waiting for us</u>**." His **PRESENCE** was so great in the place! Right then in front of all of us, our Pastor stepped out of the natural and into the supernatural! His body was there because we saw him, but his spirit was taken to a place for preparation that he would be able to lead us into the **PRESENCE** of God for 40 days. **Spirit of the Living God, fall fresh on me!**

THE CALL: EXODUS 24:12-18 (KJV)
"And the Lord said unto Moses, Come up to me into the mount, and be there: and I will give thee tables of stone, and a law, and commandments which I have written, that thou mayest teach them. And Moses rose up, and his servant, Joshua: and Moses went up into the mount of God. And he said unto the elders, Tarry ye here for us, until we come again unto you: and, behold, Aaron and Hur are with you: if any man have any matters to do, let him come unto them. And Moses went up into the mount, and a cloud covered the mount, and the glory of the Lord abode upon Mount Sinai, and the cloud covered it six days: he called unto Moses out of the midst of the cloud. And the sight of the glory of the Lord was like devouring fire on the top of the mount in the eyes of the children of Israel. And Moses went into the midst of the cloud, and got up into mount: and Moses was in the mount forty days and forty nights."

This passage of Scripture is the foundation for this prayer. God has called our leader, our Pastor, to come up just as He called Moses to get the instructions for the lives of His people. If you read the whole chapter in Exodus 24, you will find that verse two says "**And Moses alone shall come near the Lord; but they shall not come near; neither shall the people go up with him**."

There comes a time in the ministry where the leader has to go to God alone. There is also a time in our individual lives when we must go to God alone to hear and receive what God has for us. Prayer really is personal. This is a great sacrifice to give up our daily routines and put life on hold to seek God. The question was asked, "How bad do you want it? How bad do you want God or a change in your life?" We wanted it just that bad to give up everything for 40 days just to be in His **PRESENCE**!

WE ARE SOLDIERS ON THE FRONT LINE OF PRAYER
We are climbing the mountain for 40 days to hear from our God. We are determined to make it to the top! Everything will be placed on

hold until we hear from God. Pastor Johnson started out by saying, "Trouble has to travel a long way to find us in church." This is God's church and even the sinner has to admit God is here. This prayer is to seek God for instructions and directions for our daily lives. We are praying for the wisdom of God, for He is all knowing and He is everywhere; for He is God alone, and there is no one else.

EQUIP US FOR BATTLE, GOD!
Before you can go into prayer for this length of time, you have to be equipped. Let us not think the Devil is not going to fight us and try to get us off focus. The thing about Satan is that he knows God. He believes in God and he knows God's power. God has all power and created Satan himself. Satan's fight is not to let you get to know God for who He really is. If he can stop or hinder us from believing and receiving God then he wins, but if we have the greater one inside of us, which is Christ Jesus, then he loses!

Every solider has a uniform. God clothed and equipped us by showering us in His anointing, dressing us in determination, strapping on Faith, booting us up with the Word, filling our backpacks with strength and we armed ourselves with praise. Now we were ready to go into prayer. The war was on!

THE CLOUD FILLED THE TEMPLE
As soon as the Pastor began to read the Scriptures, the power of God fell even greater in the place. Tears were streaming down my face like a broken faucet! <u>Can a soul take any more?</u> I felt the explosion and I knew at that point, I was BROKEN. I fell out on the floor and the floor felt as if it wasn't there. I could not contain my emotions as my soul, my spirit, and my deadened flesh was yielded over to God and His will. Oh, if I can only express to you what took place on that night! The cloud of glory filled the Temple! The fire fell and there was a praise that went up which shook every brick and door in the church! We knew as a congregation God had called this prayer and a call was made to come into His **PRESENCE**!

Personal Note:

The Pastor strongly believes in the last statement: that once again, when God called for the prayer, he said, "YES!" We are a praying ministry so prayer is no stranger to us. What we need God to do, there is no way we can be disobedient. The only One who can help us is God because He is the only one who can do this, so we owe everything to Him!

After Pastor explained to us the seriousness of what we were getting ready to embark on, (a war we would not fight against flesh and blood but against spirits and wickedness in high places) we enlisted and said, "United we stand. Divided we fall!" We all fell to our knees and corporately prayed.

It is so wonderful during this day and time that we live in to find a Pastor who is sold out to prayer. I encourage every Pastor who may read this book, if you don't have a prayer life, make it a priority. If you do have one, make it a greater one. Our Pastor is a Prayer Warrior. The Lord gave him to name the church Temple Of Prayer because it would be a place where prayer is one of the stronger attributes in the ministry. We are a prayer center! We love praying and communicating with God! God has conditioned Pastor Johnson for warfare to lead us up the mountain **INTO HIS PRESENCE. Come go with me INTO HIS PRESENCE!** ~ *Evelyn*

STEP 1/DAY 1, MONDAY

"The Humility of Man Gives You an Audience with the King"

Personal Note:

Today was the first day of prayer. As the people gathered themselves to enter into sanctuary, there was little or no talking. Everybody's soul was in suspense waiting, believing, and expecting but not knowing how God's glory or **PRESENCE** would show up. There was a calmness in the atmosphere. It was cold outside as we layered ourselves with extra clothing and coats. The sanctuary looked different. The room was extra bright and there was a sweet smelling aroma in the place. The children were there but they were quite as if they knew God was going to reveal Himself even to them. As we sat still, the anointing began to fall softly like snowflakes into our souls. Tears fell from my face as I knew God was there waiting for us saying, "I love you my children." It was at that moment that our souls were arrested by the power of the Holy Spirit to take us to place in God that eyes have not seen, ears have not heard what God was going to reveal to us. Come journey for 40 days "Into His Presence."
~ *Evelyn*

DAY 1 PRAYER SERVICE BEGINS

Opening Remarks: Mountain Climbing Instructions

"The Lord has given us to pray for 40 days. The Lord called and I yielded to it as I prepared myself to go the mount. I pray that God would send His cloud to cover the mountain, to show a sign the Lord and His glory was there. I pray that the Lord illustrate Himself as fire, showing us signs and wonders while we wait to hear the call from God to come up to receive instructions on what to do for our church and for our family in this year. Each individual's house, family, head of each home, and personal situation should be like a type of Moses listening for God to call you up to give you instructions for you and your household. During these 40 days, if God does not give instructions, the fault and failure would not lie with God. There is no way on earth if we present ourselves like Moses did and pray every day for 40 days, that God would not give us instructions for our lives and for this year."

Let Us Pray:

Oh, God, we come into this place out of obedience, Lord. We come out of a need for instruction and desire to be instructed. We come for strength that we will be able to be consistent and follow the instructions you will give us, and the instruction you have already given. We come with thanksgiving thanking You, God, for even speaking to us and allowing us to hear the call for prayer. So many people, God, are not hearing the call. We thank you, Lord God, for the instructions and encouragement through the Word which gives us examples, and grant us to know You still speak to Your people even in this year as You did with Moses.

You have called us, Lord God, to come for 40 days and this is day one. Father God, we come consecrating ourselves believing You will speak and instruct us. Give us Your commandments, laws and precepts for this year that our homes will be in better conditions. We come that our lives and our minds will be in better conditions. We prayer for stability, we pray for our needs to be met, we pray for health, we pray for so many things, God, but we are asking on today as we open ourselves up completely to Thee, You speak to us. Speak to us and have Your way, Lord God, in our lives. We yield ourselves to Thee completely.

Father God, we ask now for those who have not sanctified themselves or consecrated themselves for this time for 40 days of prayer. Those who have not asked for forgiveness out of their souls and truly repented, You would touch them that they would repent and ask for forgiveness.

We ask now, Lord God, for this church for the disobedience that was shown last year that it would end and not move over into this year. We will not be a disobedient church. We will be an obedient church and follow the instruction You have given us. God, we want to take the flame of fire up again and do what You have told us to do: to invite seven souls a week. We want to share the love of God. We want to share Your goodness and testimonies of what You have done for us. God, we ask now, the commandment You have give us through the Word, we should pray and not faint. Help us, Lord God, to pray this year like we have never prayed before. God, we don't want to ever appear to be ashamed of calling on the Name of Jesus. God, there is no other name that You have given to man to call upon except that Name, and that Name is Jesus! God, if we have to be a church which will be popular or one that draws much hatred for sticking with the simplicity of the Word and prayer, so let it be. We declare that there is only one God: the God of the Bible and Jesus is Lord!

We declare, Lord God, we are vessels who are willing and available to be used by Thee for this entire year, and for the rest of our lives rather it be one more day or rather it be one thousand years. We are not going to fall short in our minds and in our desire. We are not going to fall short in our souls, God, because we can do all things through Christ that strengthen us.

God, we pray now for the moving of your Spirit in this place and in our souls. God, even in my soul, and even in my flesh that I would not pray out of a natural sense of what I feel, or what I think or what I believe or what I know as a need. Nevertheless, I would pray out of my soul, God, by the moving of your Spirit, Lord Jesus, under the unction of the Holy Ghost; for when we do not know how to pray for ourselves as we ought, to, the Holy Spirit itself will make intercession for us with groans and utterings that no man can understand. Only you, God, can decipher and translate the meaning of those audible sounds; sounds which are not understandable because they are not in any type of language.

I pray now, Lord, You would allow this church during these 40 days to experience what the children of Israel experienced. In that Scripture, God, they saw the cloud of glory cover the top of Mount Sinai. They saw the devouring fire sit upon the top of the mountain. Moses heard the call to come into Your **PRESENCE**. God, help us not to be in a rush. Help us not to feel forced or to be anxious, God, as we wait for You to speak and move in this dispensation. Forty days, God, bless us to live. Bless us, God, to see You move. Bless us to hear Your voice during these 40 days. Bless us, God, in our frailty of human being to see signs and wonders during these 40 days. Bring about restoration; bring about a pause that has transpired in our lives God. We ask, Lord God, for a deferment during these 40 days in everything. All the trouble, all the pain, all the tribulation that followed us into the year, make them stop! Father, You stopped the sun for Joshua. God, stop these problems for 40 days! Give us a release, God, until we hear from You.

God, 40 days as we wait for You to move. Forty days as we believe You will trouble the waters of our souls. Hallelujah! Help us, God; help us not to rely on our logic. Help us not to rely on our minds and intellect. Help us not even to rely on our experiences we have had in the past during the magnificent time of prayer and devotions, consecration and re-dedication. Help us, God, to come freshly into this situation waiting for a fresh anointing from You to pour out Your oil like never before. Waiting for Your deliverance to come, God. Waiting for the moving of the Holy Ghost like never before! Waiting for You, Lord God, to do something for us that has never been done in our lives! Hallelujah! Thank you, Jesus.

God, we ask now, Lord God, You would move and remove anything in us which is ungodly, sinful, lustful, nasty, hateful, vindictive, envious jealous, pride, a haughty spirit, high-minded, spirit of control, lying, deceit, anything sinful, God. Remove it, Lord God, in the Name of Jesus! We don't want anything to hinder us from hearing You when You call us to come into Your **PRESENCE**. We don't want anything, Lord God, to make us miss what You will have for us. For we believe there is a blessing in these 40 days of prayer, being innumerable which no one can stop us but ourselves from receiving from You.

God, this church declares Jesus Is Lord. We declare this is Your church. This church bows itself down before Thy throne, Hallelujah, and we say have Your way and use us! Anyway, You so deem, anyway You see fit! God, we submit our wills and our desires and thoughts to Thee. Oh, God, shake the very foundation of this ministry, God! Shake the very foundations of our souls! From the youngest child, the youngest baby who has just been born in this church family, to the eldest person in this place. Hallelujah. To the sick and afflicted who cannot come out, God. Shake us like never before, God! Let Your fire, the devouring fire of the Holy Ghost, come now! Sit upon the top of our minds, God, and burn up everything not like You in the minds, God. Bring about a spirit of yielding, a spirit of obedience, God, in the Name of Jesus!

Let the thunderous voice be heard out of every soul in this church. Let Your thunderous voice be heard out of every soul who is taking time during the hours of 7:30-8:30 p.m. to pray. God, somewhere during the time of praying with us in the spirit, they ask You for Your help, Lord God. We need You now, Lord Jesus! We need You now, God! We need you right now!

Perilous times have come upon us, God, and we live in a society where murder is commonplace. We exist in a church world where the people of God hate each other instead of loving one another, God; for the people of God are fighting against one another instead of fighting against the Devil. The people of God will not help or support one another, God, but will tear each other down and be happy about it. We live in a time, God, where people will not obey the leaders in the church like they use to, God. They won't obey the Prophets, the Pastors, Lord God, the Teachers, the Evangelists, God, like they did in the Bible days when great success was wrought in the church and evangelized in the world, God. Hallelujah.

The world needs evangelism like never before, God, and we need help! Help, God! Help this church! Look now, God, on one of the Elders from the church now who is in Africa, God. Protect his life from every demonic force that comes against him. We bind it now. The death angel, God, is lurking over his soul. We bind it now and rebuke it in the Name of Jesus and we speak life! We speak life, God! We speak life! We speak life, God! We take the Blood of Jesus and we place it over the doorpost of his home, his children, and his wife in this country, God. We take the Blood of Jesus and place it over the doorpost of every home, God, which is represented here in this place. We take the Blood of Jesus and place it on the doorpost of every member of this church, God. Let the death angel pass us by once again for another year, God! Hallelujah, God!

We ask, now for your mercy to be shown once again, God. Give us a chance to live to be obedient to do Thy will and to do Thy work! Jesus, even doing these 40 days, send the souls. Send the souls which once were connected and now that are disconnected because they have been hurt and abused by dirty, nasty, hurtful things members in this church have said to them, God. People outside of this church have told lies and said things, which are not true, God, Hallelujah! Remove the hurt, pain and bitterness and let them find their way back to the House of Prayer, God, that they would join with us during these 40 days as we intercede and pray. Lord, we ask for the moving of Your Spirit and Your will in this place, in this church, in this ministry, in every department, in every department head, in every leader, in every lay member, in every child, and in every visitor who walks through those doors, God! For in this year, they would experience the move of the Holy Ghost like they have never experienced in their life and that they would be able to see the very God of Peace! Move in this place through healings, deliverances, and removing addictive spirits, God.

Casting out every spirit of devilment in the Name of Jesus! The sick being healed, God. Move in the minds of those who have been attacked mentally, God. We bind the nervous breakdown! We bind the spirit of paranoia and depression! We bind the spirit of anything, which is not of God! We cast it out by the root and send it back to the dry places! Let it wander no more, protect, and cover us under the Blood of Jesus! Cover us under the Blood of Jesus!

Save, God. Save in our families and remember the prayers we have prayed for years. Not just the prayers from last year, but prayers we have prayed for many years. God, we will continue to pray for deliverance in our own families; for our cousins, uncles, aunts, brothers, sisters, children, mothers, fathers, grandparents, save now in the name of Jesus! I don't care if they are in Alaska; Hawaii; or London, England. Save if they are in China. Save, God, if they are in Quake, Afghanistan, or Iraq. Save in the name of Jesus!

Help us, God, help us, God, help us God! We present ourselves as a living sacrifice holy and acceptable unto Thee, which is our reasonable service. On this night, the first night, we consecrate this prayer, God. Don't let anyone faint as we wait for the moving of your Spirit like we have never experience before. We know Your **PRESENCE** is in this place even now, but we ask for the greater. We ask to experience You in a way like we have never seen. We ask to experience something we have never experienced. We are asking for a Bible experience. We ask for an experience where we hear God's voice calling us higher! Hallelujah.

As a church, God, some individuals in this room have heard the voice of our God, You, God, speaking and saying come higher in prayer, come higher in service, come higher in your commitment, and You will speak to us. God, but everyone in this church, everybody who is a part of this church family has not heard Your voice. God, they have not yielded to the voice of God and the call to a higher commitment in service and prayer. Some people, God, think it is a game. Some people think You are a light switch they can turn on or off, God, but we cannot turn you on and off. We have no control over what You do. We have no control over who You say You are. For You, are God and You alone! You are the King of Kings and the Lord of Lords. God, we make the declaration in this room before every living creature, rather it is a human being or a spirit, God! Rather it is an Angel or a Demon we make the declaration Jesus is Lord! That our God is the God of all flesh! Hallelujah! Hallelujah! Hallelujah!

We give You praise and we honor You. We give You glory! We are not telling You how to do it; we just believe You will do it. We are not telling You when to do it; we are just asking You would expedite for mercy sake. For the sake of our Lord and Savior Jesus Christ who is making intercession for us right now, even at the right hand of Your throne God. He is interceding and asking that You would look down upon the Saints of the Temple Of Prayer, God, and You would help them and You would hear their prayers. He is ushering in our prayers before Your **PRESENCE**! Oh, Bless His Name! Bless Your Name, God! Our lives are on the line. The life of this church is on the line. My life is on the line.

Moses, God, for six days he had to wait before You called him into Your **PRESENCE**. Six days of purification and sanctification; getting his mind right; his thoughts right; his words right, for he did not want to come before Your **PRESENCE** and offend Thee because it would cost him his life. God, on this night let these people know in this room, they have to get their minds right. We don't want to come before Thy **PRESENCE** into Thy sacred place, God, and offend Thee for it might cost us our lives! It's just that serious, God, and we believe it to be so. For Your Word never changes. Jesus Christ the same today, yesterday, and forevermore. The Word never changes and what You did for Moses, You can do for me. What You did for Moses, You can do for anybody in this room. What you did for the children of Israel, You can do for this church. You were their God, You protected them, and You met their needs. You forgave them and had mercy on them, God. We need You to protect us. We need You to meet our needs. We need You to have mercy upon us and we need you to wipe out our enemies. God, rather it is coming from a demonic force or human forces, we believe no weapon formed against us can prosper!

We pray now for a clear path in this year. We pray for a clear path, God. Please give us a clear path this year. Oh, Lord, oh, Lord, shower us with Your **PRESENCE** the more! God, every day we live, let us look forward to meeting You, God, Hallelujah! Every day we live, Lord God, let us be glad for that day. Let us look for the glory of the Lord! Open up the eyes even on tonight, God, and prepare those who do not believe that they can see the cloud of glory! Yea, God! In our souls, God, open up our understanding! Open up the stopped up ears, God, so we can hear Your voice when You speak! Do it, God, for we believe so therefore we pray.

Now, God, the sacrifice we have brought on tonight, in comparison to what You have done is nothing. The sacrifice of our time on a holiday, a man made holiday, is not much. Nevertheless, we bring it to you sincerely and truthfully as we have started this prayer on this first day of this year. We ask, God, You would look at the sincerity of the sacrifice and the humbleness in which we bring before Thy throne that You would not reject it, and You would accept the gifts we have brought along with the praises and the prayers we have brought on tonight.

God, we ask now, as we prepare to close this first day of prayer, You, Your **PRESENCE**, and Your glory would not leave this building and Your glory would not leave from inside of us. Even when we go home, bring the illumination of the cloud in our homes, God, for 40 days, in our homes, God, for 40 days, in homes, God, for 40 days, in us, God, for 40 days. Forty days, Lord God, of true submission in our souls to Thee. Only focusing on, Hallelujah, hearing from You, and Your instruction on what You are saying. Not concerning ourselves on what we face, but having the faith to believe You have called us for this time and this season of prayer.

Forty-days for 40 years, 40 days for 40 years. If we yield ourselves, God for 40 days, we won't have to go through 40 years of wilderness experience and we thank You, God. We thank You for the victory. We thank You for the opportunity to see birth. We thank You, God, for giving us a mind and willingness to be obedient and understand You, we are in reverence to You. Without You, God, we can do nothing, like a body without a soul. We need You and we are not ashamed to say it. We love you and we are not ashamed to say it. We will serve You and we are not ashamed to say it. We will obey You and we are glad to say it. Hallelujah! Hallelujah! Hallelujah! Be it done now, we pray these prayers. Thank You, God, for giving us the opportunity to come before Your **PRESENCE** with prayers. We are asking, God, you would speak to us throughout these 40 days. The cloud of glory, which represents Your **PRESENCE**, would be in this place and Your devouring fire would manifest itself before these people and, God, You would do for us like You did for Moses and the children of Israel: speak and instruct us. We will be obedient with the help of the Lord. This we pray, in Jesus' Name. In Jesus Name, people of God say Amen. Amen.

Closing Scripture: Exodus 4 (KJV)

"And Moses answered and said, But, behold, they will not believe me, nor hearken unto my voice: for they will say, The LORD hath not appeared unto thee. And the LORD said unto him, What is that in thine hand? And he said, A rod. And he said, Cast it on the ground. And he cast it on the ground, and it became a serpent; and Moses fled from before it. And the LORD said unto Moses, Put forth thine hand, and take it by the tail. And he put forth his hand, and caught it, and it became a rod in his hand: That they may believe that the LORD God of their fathers, the God of Abraham, the God of Isaac, and the God of Jacob, hath appeared unto thee. And the LORD said furthermore unto him, Put now thine hand into thy bosom. And he put his hand into his bosom: and when he took it out, behold, his hand was leprous as snow. And he said, Put thine hand into thy bosom again. And he put his hand into his bosom again; and plucked it out of his bosom, and, behold, it was turned again as his other flesh. And it shall come to pass, if they will not believe thee, neither hearken to the voice of the first sign, that they will believe the voice of the latter sign. And it shall come to pass, if they will not believe also these two signs, neither hearken unto thy voice, that thou shalt take of the water of the river, and pour it upon the dry land: and the water which thou takest out of the river shall become blood upon the dry land. And Moses said unto the LORD, O my Lord, I am not eloquent, neither heretofore, nor since thou hast spoken unto thy servant: but I am slow of speech, and of a slow tongue. And the LORD said unto him, Who hath made man's mouth? or who maketh the dumb, or deaf, or the seeing, or the blind? have not I the LORD? Now therefore go, and I will be with thy mouth, and teach thee what thou shalt say. And he said, O my Lord, send, I pray thee, by the hand of him whom thou wilt send. And the anger of the LORD was kindled against Moses, and he said, Is not Aaron the Levite thy brother? I know that he can speak well. And also, behold, he cometh forth to meet thee: and when he seeth thee, he will be glad in his heart. And thou shalt speak unto him, and put words in his mouth: and I will be with thy mouth, and with his mouth, and will teach you what ye shall do. And he shall be thy spokesman unto the people: and he shall be, even he shall be to thee instead of a mouth, and thou shalt be to him

instead of God. And thou shalt take this rod in thine hand, wherewith thou shalt do signs. And Moses went and returned to Jethro his father in law, and said unto him, Let me go, I pray thee, and return unto my brethren which are in Egypt, and see whether they be yet alive. And Jethro said to Moses, Go in peace. And the LORD said unto Moses in Midian, Go, return into Egypt: for all the men are dead which sought thy life. And Moses took his wife and his sons, and set them upon an ass, and he returned to the land of Egypt: and Moses took the rod of God in his hand. And the LORD said unto Moses, When thou goest to return into Egypt, see that thou do all those wonders before Pharaoh, which I have put in thine hand: but I will harden his heart, that he shall not let the people go. And thou shalt say unto Pharaoh, Thus saith the LORD, Israel is my son, even my firstborn: And I say unto thee, Let my son go, that he may serve me: and if thou refuse to let him go, behold, I will slay thy son, even thy firstborn. And it came to pass by the way in the inn, that the LORD met him, and sought to kill him. Then Zipporah took a sharp stone, and cut off the foreskin of her son, and cast it at his feet, and said, Surely a bloody husband art thou to me. So he let him go: then she said, A bloody husband thou art, because of the circumcision. And the LORD said to Aaron, Go into the wilderness to meet Moses. And he went, and met him in the mount of God, and kissed him. And Moses told Aaron all the words of the LORD who had sent him, and all the signs which he had commanded him. And Moses and Aaron went and gathered together all the elders of the children of Israel: And Aaron spake all the words which the LORD had spoken unto Moses, and did the signs in the sight of the people. And the people believed: and when they heard that the LORD had visited the children of Israel, and that he had looked upon their affliction, then they bowed their heads and worshipped."

END OF DAY 1 PRAYER SERVICE

Personal Note:

We thank God for the first day of prayer. As Pastor uttered his closing remarks, we captured each one in the purse of our souls. I looked at him as he sat there in his chair not moving or talking

because the anointing was so great upon him. I knew without any doubt that God had taken him and sanctified him for that time. I released him as my husband in the natural sense, turned him over to God, and handled him from that moment forward as a called out holy man of God who was set apart for 40 days to suffer in prayer for God's people. We left that place but not God's **PRESENCE**. As we drove home, the assigned Angels of the Lord flew in front, behind and on the side of the car making sure that nothing in the natural or supernatural harmed our leader or stopped him from fulfilling his purpose to pray.
~ *Evelyn*

STEP 2/DAY 2, TUESDAY

"The Lord Speaks to Us in a Small Still Voice"

DAY 2 PRAYER SERVICE BEGINS

Opening Scripture: 1 Kings 19:4-21 (KJV)

" *But he himself went a day's journey into the wilderness, and came and sat down under a juniper tree: and he requested for himself that he might die; and said, It is enough; now, O LORD, take away my life; for I am not better than my fathers. And as he lay and slept under a juniper tree, behold, then an angel touched him, and said unto him, Arise and eat. And he looked, and, behold, there was a cake baken on the coals, and a cruse of water at his head. And he did eat and drink, and laid him down again. And the angel of the LORD came again the second time, and touched him, and said, Arise and eat; because the journey is too great for thee. And he arose, and did eat and drink, and went in the strength of that meat forty days and forty nights unto Horeb the mount of God. And he came thither unto a cave, and lodged there; and, behold, the word of the LORD came to him, and he said unto him, What doest thou here, Elijah? And he said, I have been every jealous for the LORD God of hosts: for the children of Israel have forsaken thy covenant, thrown down thine altars, and slain thy prophets with the sword; and I, even I only, am left; and they seek my life, to take it away. And he said, Go forth, and stand upon the mount before the LORD. And, behold, the LORD passed by, and a great and strong wind rent the mountains, and brake in pieces the rocks before the LORD; but the LORD was not in the wind: and after the wind an earthquake; but the LORD was not in the earthquake: And after the earthquake a fire; but the LORD was not in the fire: and after the fire a still small voice. And it was so, when Elijah heard it, that he wrapped his face in his mantle, and went out, and stood in the entering in of the cave. And, behold, there came a voice unto him, and said, What doest thou here, Elijah? And he said, I have been very jealous for the LORD God of hosts: because the children of Israel have forsaken thy covenant, thrown down thine altars, and slain thy prophets with the sword; and I, even I only, am left; and they seek my life, to take it away. And the LORD said unto him, Go, return on thy way to the wilderness of Damascus: and when thou comest, anoint Hazael to be king over Syria: And Jehu the son of Nimshi shalt thou anoint to be king over Israel: and Elisha the son of Shaphat of Abelmeholah shalt thou anoint to be prophet in thy room. And it shall come to pass, that him that escapeth the sword of Hazael shall Jehu slay: and him that escapeth from the sword of Jehu shall Elisha slay. Yet I have left me seven thousand in Israel, all the knees which have not bowed unto Baal, and every mouth which hath not kissed him. So he departed thence, and found Elisha the son of Shaphat, who was plowing with twelve yoke of oxen before him, and he with the twelfth: and Elijah passed by him, and cast his mantle upon him. And he left the oxen, and ran after Elijah, and said, Let me, I pray thee, kiss my father and my mother, and then I will follow thee. And he said unto him, Go back again: for what have I done to thee? And he returned back from him, and took a yoke of oxen, and slew them, and boiled their flesh with the instruments of the oxen, and gave unto the people, and they did eat. Then he arose, and went after Elijah, and ministered unto him."*

Insight As We Prepared for Prayer:
We are building up the Kingdom of Heaven in our lives. There is no way on earth or in Heaven where God will ever leave us or forsake us when things get tough. When things were tough in Elijah's

time, he felt like he had failed after all the work that he had done. He wanted to die but God loved him enough to feed him and provided so much for him, he was able to make it to where God had called him without eating while on a 40 day journey. **"God never calls us to go down; He always calls us to go up!"**

In the two narratives from Exodus 4 and 1 Kings 19, Moses and Elijah were called to a mountain to go up. They were not instructed to dig a hole to go underneath the mountain but to climb it and go up. Climbing a mountain is not easy; furthermore, it is a whole lot harder than walking on straight level ground or on a decline. It's an incline and it will take some effort. It will take some effort in these 40 days of prayer to go up spiritually where you will be able to hear the voice of God. The reason God calls us to go up, not only because He is up, but what He has for us is at a higher plain or at a higher level. It requires a greater sacrifice. The problems we are facing and currently involved with cannot follow us up God's mountain. The Devil cannot follow you up the mountain and he can only go so far. Demons can only go so far because there is a secret place in God where only those who believe can go. The benefits of being a child of God are wonderful. God rewards those who diligently seek Him. God will reward us for making that effort of going up! Are you willing to go up in prayer?

Let Us Pray:
Magnificent God and King, Father, as we read the Scripture on tonight, we come to You as individuals. Some are sick right now, God, some people could not make it. Some people are feeling the way Elijah felt in that moment when Elijah had done all he knew to do, he yet felt like as if he had failed. Elijah felt isolated and alone ready to die, but You loved him so much, God, You didn't let him die. You fed him natural food, which brought supernatural strength. That lets us know, God, we are not alone and You will feed us naturally and meet every need to bring about supernatural results. This year, God, we come before Your **PRESENCE** on this second night of 40 days of prayer saying we cannot make it for the rest of these days in our own strength. Not only do we acknowledge that, but we cannot make it for the rest of this year or the rest of our lives in our

own strength. Therefore, we ask, God, You will feed us, this local assembly, feed us and meet the needs.

Feed our natural needs and let it bring about supernatural strength for the journey, which lies ahead of us for the rest of these 40 days of prayer and for the rest of the days of our lives as we pray. We believe just as You met the needs of Elijah, You will meet every need of every believer in this place and every family, which is represented, every member of this church, every member of the body of Christ who is calling upon Your Name. Some Christian, even right now is praying, wherever the location throughout this world might be, is asking You to meet every need. Somebody else is praying the same time we are, in this world, and we join in and ask, God, just like the 7,000 who did not give into Baal, we pray the body of Christ would be strong everywhere and not give into the Devil or his devices. God, the Christians are being pressured for standing up and saying, "I am saved. I am a Christian, a Saint, a holy and righteous person of God. I am a child of the King!" We call for the strength of God now in the Name of Jesus!

We pray now, God, we be included in the prayers of the Saints everywhere, like we include them in our prayers. We might not know them by name, just like they don't know us by name, God, but we know if we touch and agree in the spirit, knowing there are saved people everywhere who have not given into the wiles and trick of our adversary, You will hear and answer all of us. Lord God, we ask now, for the same spirit Elijah had: one of obedience, willing to travel to the mount, willing to go in a cave to be observant, patient and having a discerning spirit. So many of us, God, we jump out at the first sign or first thing which appears to be You moving, and we leave from where safety is, not receiving instruction on what to do. We don't want to be like that, God. We want to be like Elijah, who waited until You spoke, and You did not speak in a dramatic fashion in that case. You spoke in a small still voice, one that was understandable.

We ask now, Lord God, for those who are in this place that falls into the conditions of Elijah: waiting to hear from You. We pray for those in this membership and in leadership who falls in the conditions of Elijah who might not recognize You, God. We ask You keep it simple for our sake. Speak to us in a voice we can recognize. Let us have an ear, which is attentive to Your voice, a spirit that is willing to be obedient to do whatever You direct us to do in our lives. Regardless, God, of how hard the task may seem, You appoint us to do it. We are saying, "Yes, in our souls," God, and we will obey and commit our wills to You whatever You instruct us to do this year, God we will do it! Even if it's unpopular, we will do it! Even if it brings us criticism and disrespect, we will do it, God! Even if it brings alienation and isolation from our family and friends, we will do it, God! Lord, call us into the clouds where we may be hidden in Thee. As we climb up the mountain, the devil cannot follow us! He cannot go but so far! We want to reach Heaven! God never calls us to go down but to go up! Take us up out of ourselves! Take us up away from doubt and fear. Take us up, Lord, away from negativity and from the things that bring us down. Father, we will not take another step without You! God, we pray that You kill the 'I' in us! Kill our flesh, our wills, and our ways! Father, it must be Your Will. Kill our flesh as we bring ourselves to Your altar as a living sacrifice. Let the death of flesh take place now in the Name of Jesus! We cannot do anything in our own strength. We cannot do Kingdom work with human power! God, we need You! Take us over! Be in control of our lives now and forever more we pray. Manifest yourself, God, to us who brings about a natural occurrence that will bring about a supernatural strength! Flood us with Your power, Your Holy Spirit, to take us on this 40 day journey to be in your **PRESENCE**, which will change the very core, the essence, of who we are. This we pray all these prayers in Jesus Name. Amen.

Closing Scripture: John 14:12-29 (NLT)

"I tell you the truth, anyone who believes in me will do the same works I have done, and even greater works, because I am going to be with the Father. You can ask for anything in my name, and I will do it, so that the Son can bring glory to the Father. Yes, ask me for anything in my name, and I will do it! "If you love me, obey my commandments. And I will ask the Father, and he will give you another Advocate, who will never leave you. He is the Holy Spirit, who leads into all truth. The world cannot receive him, because it

isn't looking for him and doesn't recognize him. But you know him, because he lives with you now and later will be in you. No, I will not abandon you as orphans—I will come to you. Soon the world will no longer see me, but you will see me. Since I live, you also will live. When I am raised to life again, you will know that I am in my Father, and you are in me, and I am in you. Those who accept my commandments and obey them are the ones who love me. And because they love me, my Father will love them. And I will love them and reveal myself to each of them." Judas (not Judas Iscariot, but the other disciple with that name) said to him, "Lord, why are you going to reveal yourself only to us and not to the world at large?" Jesus replied, "All who love me will do what I say. My Father will love them, and we will come and make our home with each of them. Anyone who doesn't love me will not obey me. And remember, my words are not my own. What I am telling you is from the Father who sent me. I am telling you these things now while I am still with you. But when the Father sends the Advocate as my representative—that is, the Holy Spirit—he will teach you everything and will remind you of everything I have told you. "I am leaving you with a gift—peace of mind and heart. And the peace I give is a gift the world cannot give. So don't be troubled or afraid. Remember what I told you: I am going away, but I will come back to you again. If you really loved me, you would be happy that I am going to the Father, who is greater than I am. I have told you these things before they happen so that when they do happen, you will believe."

END OF DAY 2 PRAYER SERVICE

STEP 3/DAY 3, WEDNESDAY

"Faith Will Take Us to Our Fruit"

DAY 3 PRAYER SERVICE BEGINS

Opening Remarks:

Many things are happening in our city and we acknowledge God is the only one who can protect us. Envision something like a force field, on the Star Track Enterprise movies where they put up the shields to keep the Klingons from penetrating. We are praying and asking God in these 40 days to be our protective shield. If we are bombarded and penetrated by the weapons of the enemies, it is hard to focus, concentrate, and hear what God has to say.

The number 40 is an extremely significant number. It is the number of probation, trial and testing. God gave people different times, whether 40 days or 40 years: Noah was in the Ark for 40 days. David reigned for 40 years. Moses went his first 40 years trying to find out who he was. He went his second 40 years after he left Egypt discovering he was a nobody. No longer, a Prince of Egypt; his title didn't mean anything from the social status where he came from. While with a slave class of people, he discovered it was time for him to actually hear the call of God. In the last 40 years of his life, the people were freed. He took them out of Egypt, they wandered in the wilderness, and discovered God was everything they would ever need. An eleven-day journey took 40 years. We don't want to make the same mistake.

The Lord gives us an opportunity to be tried during a time of testing. Jesus was tempted for 40 days in the wilderness as He fasted and sought the will of God. There is something about the number 40, so let us not look over the significance of this number. God gave us to start the year off with the first 40 days dedicated in prayer and consecration. These 40 days of prayer are different than any of the other 40 days of prayer, because we never actually started it on the first day of the year. This made it easy to keep up with the calendar days of prayer. This is the third day of prayer and the third day of this year.

Opening Scriptures: Numbers 13:17- 33 (KJV)
*"And Moses sent them to spy out the land of Canaan, and said unto them, Get you up this way [into the Negev], and go up into the mountain, And see the land, what it is; and the people who dwell therein, whether they are strong or weak, few or many; And what the land is that they dwell in, whether it is good or bad; and what cities they are that they dwell in, whether in [camps], or in strongholds; And what the land is whether it is fat or lean, whether there is wood therein, or not. And be ye of good courage, and bring of the fruit of the land. Now the time was the time of the first-ripe grapes. So they went up and searched the land from the wilderness of Zin unto Rehob, as men come to Hamath. And they ascended by the [Negev], and came unto Hebron, where Ahiman, Sheshai, and Talmai, the children of Anak were. (Now Hebron was built seven years before Zoan in Egypt.) And they came to unto the brook of Eshcol, and cut down from there a branch with one cluster of grapes, and they bore it between two upon a staff; and they brought of the pomegranates, and of the figs. The place was called the Brook Eshcol, because of the luster of grapes which the children of Israel cut down from there. And they returned from searching of the land after **forty days.** And they went and came to Moses, and to Aaron, and to all the congregation of the children of Israel, unto the wilderness of Paran, to Kadesh; and brought back word unto them, and unto all the congregation, and showed them the fruit of the land. And they told him, and said, We came unto the land to which thou sentest us, and surely it floweth with milk and honey; and this is the fruit of it. Nevertheless,*

the people are strong that dwell in the land, and the cities are walled, and very great: and, moreover, we saw the children of Anak there. The Amalekites dwell in the land of the [Negev]; and the Hittites, and the Jebusites, and the Amorites, dwell in the mountains; and the Canaanites dwell by the sea, and by the [edge] of the Jordan. And Caleb, stilled the people before Moses, and said, Let us go up at once, and possess it; for we are well able to overcome it. But the men that went up with him said, We are not able to go up against the people; for they are stronger than we. And they brought up an evil report of the land, which they had searched, unto the children of Israel, saying, The land, through which we have gone to search it, is a land that eateth up the inhabitants thereof; and all the people that we saw in it are men of great stature. And there we saw the giants, the sons of Anak, who come of the giants; and we were in our own sight as grasshoppers, and so we were in their sight."

Insight As We Prepared For Prayer:

In this reading of the Scripture, as we prepare to go into prayer, we should consider this: each head of every family in this church talks about how they want to be like Moses in the Scriptures and read Exodus 24 for their inspiration; they further state how they would like to be like Elijah, to discern when God speaks. God doesn't speak the same way all the time, but when He speaks, we want to make sure we are obedient.

On this third night, let us pray for a spirit like Caleb and Joshua. As every head of household, we need to understand that we are spying out the land God has for us during these 40 days of prayer. We exhort that if everyone in this church, if we all had the mind of Caleb, we would be able to do great things because we would have done great things, so it is obvious we all don't have that mind.

When God gives us a refresher, it is almost like getting on the web of the internet. When you hit refresh, you get a refreshed webpage of the current page you are on. God is giving us an opportunity and we don't need anybody to be like the ten of the twelve. Even though we understand that, we would have people who will say, "It's too great. We cannot do it. We won't achieve it. We can't make it," but we will press forward. If the people who felt that way concerning what

God had told us to do in this church, then they wouldn't see results in their lives. As a man thinks, so is he. And if you think that way, guess what? You won't make it.

We can only accomplish and do great things when we have the right spirit. We told the church that after we have spent 40 days in prayer, we want to come back with a good report like Caleb. When they brought those clusters of grapes back, they were huge, large, delicious, enchanting and encouraging. The land was truly a land flowing with plenty. The following is a record of the message I gave to the church:

> "I am going to pray and ask those who have the faith, if they would pray with me on tonight, that God gives us a cluster of grapes during these 40 days of prayer. I pray that God would give us something to let us know where we are heading is full of plenty. There is enough spiritually and naturally to take care of every member of this church and every family which is a part of this church. Will you give the Lord a hand clap offering for your land?"

The cities are great and we face a giant. The children of Anak were giants. We have the Hittites, Jebusites, Amorites and Canaanites; we are surrounded by nothing but trouble. However, Caleb said, "Let us go up at once, let's not think about it. Let's just go and let's do it." Somebody say "Right now!" (Right now!) If you don't have a right now spirit, then you are going to miss out on an opportunity.

I am not looking at what I have and what I don't have. I am not looking at what the church has and what the church doesn't' have, because whatever we don't have, God has to make a way because He is the only One who can make a way. If it's a shortage of people, then that means God has to send in the people. If it's a shortage of people who don't have the right frame of mind to do whatever God says to do, then God will send the right people in as we have seen in these Scriptures. We don't need the majority of right thinking people to do great things. You just need two. The Bible says, "where two or three are gathered in His Name. and God will do great things." There are more than two or three of us in this place.

Once again, on tonight out of those who are here, there is somebody in the room who really does believe the Bible to be the inspired and only infallible written Word of God. If God said it in the Word, it can be done. I want to be in a place spiritually where the milk and honey and the blessings of God are flowing so my spiritual life can prosper. I cannot prosper naturally according to the Scriptures, "I desire that you prosper and be in good health, as your soul prospers." Therefore, if my soul, my spirit is not prospering then I am not prospering from any other aspect of living. Even if I had all the money on the planet, I still would not be in a prosperous state. I want to be in a prosperous state of being that can only come from the Lord fattening my soul. I hope and think the rest of us would consider those words, reevaluate, maybe make some readjustments in our goals and reprioritize some things and put God first on tonight, the rest of this year, and the rest of our lives.

Let Us Pray: Singing (My soul loves Jesus)
Let us go to God in prayer on tonight asking God to help us in our lives and that we not only hear Him, but also see His works, believing God without doubt for we believe His Word.

We thank you, Lord God. Oh, God, You are a wonder in our souls and we love You. Thank You for another day, Lord God, for You have kept us and You have allowed us to make it back to the House of Prayer once again. During this time of consecration, Lord God, we thank You for our lives, our families, our material things, our souls saved this year. We ask, Lord God, for two specific things leading up to this night and now, we include something else in prayer. We want, Lord, to have a mind and spirit like Caleb, like Joshua. One of courage, one of faith so we may see the territory, the land, which is laid out before us in our lives. We believe we heard the promises You have given us through the Word that the victory is ours and we are more than conquerors through Him that loved us. We believe that we can do all things through Christ that strengthens us. But God, we need the courage, the faith these two patriots had to make a bold statement, God, which the land is available and ready to be taken regardless of what we see.

With Your blessings and promises, what You have given us permission to acquire seems to be fortified by all types of demonic activity, walls and barriers have been set before us. Famine, nakedness, peril, sword, or death, You said nothing could separate us from Your love. We want to experience Your love, Your power, and the anointing of God to a degree we have never experienced before in our lives. We are not asking You to do it again this year, we are asking for a new experience.

Eight is a sign of new beginnings and resurrection. Eight. Resurrect something inside of us, God, You planted in us before we were placed in our mother's womb or born. Resurrect something in us that no Demon can stifle. Resurrect in us a mind, boldness, a holy boldness, God, which we will serve You with gladness, and serve You, God, with an urgent spirit and a willingness, God, to reach souls that are dying. We are willing, God, to stand in a society that doesn't believe in the Bible anymore, or the truths of the Bible. God, they have explained away the miracles the Bible said happened. They have even tried to explain the birth of Christ away. They have tried to explain His Deity away, God, but He is God. You said He was with You from the beginning. Father God, we make these declarations to reaffirm our faith and boldness by calling on the Name Jesus that we would be saved. Not just from our sins, but from everything that is ungodly; saved from ourselves and our fears.

We don't want to be like the ten spies who were afraid or felt Moses had led them down a dark dead end alley, God. We don't want to be like those spies who felt there was another way of negotiation, God, when You have explained to us in Your Word we have to expand the Kingdom of Heaven by force. We have to be obedient and do whatever You said do regardless of how painful the experience might be for others or even ourselves.

We are saying on tonight, God, we are looking in the mirror of self-examination through the Word. As we find us, show us. We are looking with the microscope of the Spirit. We want to detect; we want to find any errors in our lives. We want to find the shortcomings. We want to find the weak areas. We want to find areas of sin. We want to find the areas which have weighted us down, and we want those areas removed. We don't want anything that would hinder us in this year. We want to experience the greatest year of our lives, God. Even if we are two years old, we want this to be better than the first year. If we are two hundred years old, we want it to be the best year of the last one hundred and ninety-nine years. Father, this is the year we are alive. We cannot relive 1950, we cannot relive 1989, and we cannot relive 2002. We can only live for today, God.

We need your help right now, in other words, God. We need Your instructions right now. We need some fruit, God, and we want some grapes! Oh, God, Moses instructed them to go up on the mountain to look. We are going up the mountain to look, to see what is ours, and then to receive instructions on how to go possess it and, God, we are declaring whatever You instruct us to do we will do it! Whatever is necessary to possess what You said we could have in this year, God, we will do it regardless, Lord God, if we are unpopular. If it means being stoned to death, we will do it, God. If we lose our lives, we want to lose ourselves in Your Will. We want to lose the desire for our wants and our selfish needs in Your Word, God, wash us under the Blood of your Lamb once again. Cleanse us from all filthiness of the flesh and unrighteousness, God; cleanse us from murmuring, complaining, and a doubting spirit God. Help us, Lord God, to not only attain but also retain a spirit that is willing, a spirit of obedience, God, not just for today, but also for the rest of our days, God, throughout eternity.

God we want to say yes to Your Will. We want to obey You in every instruction You give. As a church, Lord God, we need Your help. As a people, we need Your help. As families, we need Your help. As individuals, we need Your help. As children, we need Your help. As parents, we need Your help. As adults, we need Your help, God. As husbands and wives, we need Your help, God. We just need Your help, God, and we are not ashamed to say it. Oh, God, we thank You for Your Spirit residing in this place. We thank You for Your **PRESENCE** and Your glory, God, being with us always for You have promised us through Your Son Jesus that You would never leave us nor forsake us.

We even pray that this year, You teach us how to pray and how to be more fervent in our prayers. We desire to know how to be effective in our prayers and how to pray in Thy Will, God. Not pray amiss from Thy Will, and not pray a prayer that troubles You, God; but a prayer that pleases You, God. Not a prayer that is selfish, God, but a prayer that praises You, God. Not a prayer of complaints God, but a prayer of thanksgiving. A prayer that gives You honor and glory for You truly are God and there is no one else. God, we ask now as You have said in Your Bible, not one jot or tittle would pass away from Your Word; it would stand forever. Heaven and earth and everything connected to man would pass away first before Your Word. God, Your Word is true and forever settled! We stand on the truth and in the power of Your Word, God, You bring these things to pass.

When we pray as we are led under the unction of the Holy Spirit to pray these prayers, God, You said we can cast all our cares upon You for You carest for us. We care for our families, God, we care for our children, God, we care for our loved ones, God, we care for the jobs, God, and we care for the material things You have given us.

> Thank You Lord God for the feelings! We know life is not built on feelings, salvation is not built upon feelings, but, God, You have manifested Yourself in many, many ways to the people.

We care for the souls that are going to come! We care for the souls that are already here. We care for those who are weak and poor in spirit. God, we care enough for the sick and afflicted to pray and ask divine healing. We pray that supernatural encouragement will come, God, as we reflect on the joy of the Lord that is our strength. Oh, God, bring forth much joy in the saddened heart. Bring forth much strength God that we would praise Thee with gladness. Oh, God, as we praise You even in our prayers all during the day, and all through this whole year.

This year is only three days old, God, but we haven't complained and we haven't murmured, yet we give You glory for these three days. We give You our prayer and praises for these three days. We have acknowledged You, God, in all of our goings and we give You honor. We are adoring You, extolling You, lifting You up for these three days God. Three days of sacrifice out of 40, waiting, God, eagerly for each day of this year, each day of this prayer, each moment and each second that goes by! We wait for the move of You, God, in only a way You can move!

Thank You Lord God for the feelings! We know life is not built on feelings, salvation is not built upon feelings, but God, You have manifested Yourself in many, many ways to the people, Your chosen people, God, to the Gentiles, to the people who were heathens. You have shown Yourself to the world in other words, God, and we thank You for showing Yourself to the Body of Christ.

We thank You for allowing us to feel Your **PRESENCE** to know You are here not just by faith. You are looking past our humanity and letting us be touched by Your mercy, and letting us be touched by Your grace. Thank You, Lord, for allowing us to be filled by Your Spirit, the same Holy Spirit that sat upon the 120, God, Hallelujah. The same Holy Spirit that sat upon each one of them like fire, God, is the same Holy Spirit here even now! God, Your Spirit, Your Holy Spirit, we read last night about who You would send in Jesus Name. The same Holy Spirit would comfort us when we felt comfortless. The same Holy Spirit will not leave us, God, but will be with us everywhere we go! The same Holy Spirit that said He would abide in us. The same Holy Spirit, God, will pick us up when our heads are down. We thank You that Your Spirit dwells inside of the believer and we can feel the move of Your Spirit right now!

We can feel the very **PRESENCE** and essence of Your glory in this place! God, I simply ask, God, as even in that Scripture we read, Lord God, in Numbers, Hallelujah, the people would see You move, God. They would see Your **PRESENCE**, God, like never before! Open up their eyes, God, which they might see the Promised Land that lies before them. Take them up higher in the Spirit, God that they can get a panoramic view, God, of all the manifold blessings You have placed before them. Then give the people a mind to go do it, God, to go quickly, God, to move quickly, God, to be obedient God in this year, God.

You have already given us insight on dealing with the number seven. God, if we would, the church, would just simply be obedient and invite seven souls every week, we would see the outcome that comes with being obedient. God, we cannot say as a church we have done that. God, we thank You for forgiveness. Through forgiveness, we say thank You for a new beginning this year starting this week. Every member has an opportunity, God, to invite their seven! Let us try You and see if You are God. I have no doubt that You are

A Call Into His Presence

God, but somebody in this church, somebody in this membership doesn't believe, God. Oh, God, we pray You touch and deliver in their minds! Bind the disobedient spirit and cast it out! We loose the obedient spirit that everyone would invite seven souls and get past their excuses. Get past their excuses, God, get past the lying, God, past the laziness, God, past the lack of faith, God, and simply do as You have instructed. If we would be obedient, God, we would not only possess the land, God, we would not have to wait 40 years to do it. We wouldn't have to wait 40 months to do it, God. We wouldn't have to wait 40 more days to do it, God, if we would just be obedient, make a declaration, and commit. A wholehearted commitment of being obedient to You, God; and if we do that, there is nothing You would withhold from us if we would just walk up rightly, hold on to Your commandments and obey them with a grateful heart.

God, help us now to look past the circumstances of our trials and tribulations. God, we ask You put the force field up. Put up the protection of Your Angels; put the protection of Your Holy Ghost around our homes. We plead the Blood of Jesus. We plead the Blood of Jesus to cover us, cover us, cover us! Cover our loved ones. Cover our loved ones, God, cover our children, cover us, God, in the Name of Jesus! We plead the Blood of Jesus to cover us now! Cover us under the Blood. Protect us God; protect us from supernatural demonic attacks! Protect us from the natural attacks that come forth as people want to rob, rape, maim, set fires, shoot and murder! God, protect us from those who want to do character assassination, lie on us, God, and pull us down. God, we pray for every family, for every member, God, for every lie that will be told on them. Give them the strength to stand for every discouraging word or remark that will be given to them and give them the strength to stand on Your Word, God. For every word of discouragement, God, and negativity that comes into their ears, let it not stay, God. Remove it now even before the seed is planted. Oh, God, let the power of the Holy Ghost rise up inside every believer.

God, if there is anybody not saved in this church, in this membership, save in this year! Save God, save God, save, save, save, save, save, save, save now, God. Go into our homes and save! For the unsaved love ones who are not here, we are praying for God's move now. Move every obstacle, God, move every obstacle, God.

Bind the temptations that come against the mind and the body, God. Give them the strength they need to be honest with themselves and realize they are not happy in their sins. Sin brings about death and degradation. Sin brings about depression, doom, God; it brings about a spiritual dehydration. **It drains the very spirit of life out of the sinner until spiritual death takes place.**

But, oh, ooooh, God, the God of heaven! The God of Moses! The God of Caleb! The God of Joshua! The God of the Children of Israel! I call for that God, and if there are grapes there must be some water where the grapes live by. I call for the rain of the Spirit of God to rain on every dehydrated Soul in this church, in this membership, and in our families! Let the anointed rainfall and bring life, and bring life! Let us be little clouds filled with the anointed rain of God. We pray that the words we speak would be words of life! The words we speak would bring life. The words we speak would bring deliverance. The words we speak would bring salvation. Do it now in the Name of Jesus, I pray! Hallelujah, Hallelujah, Hallelujah, Hallelujah, Hallelujah, Hallelujah, Hallelujah, thank You, God! Thank You, God, thank You, God!

We are going to praise You in advance. We are going to thank You for today. We are going to give You glory for the right now! We are in the land of the living and a living dog is better than a dead lion! We are glad to be alive! We are glad our children are alive! We are glad our families are living in our homes, God. We bless Your name, bless Your name! Thank You for a mind to pray! Thank You for willingness to yield ourselves. Thank You for allowing us to be sanctified and set apart for Your use. Thank You for washing and cleansing us. Thank You for forgiveness of sin, God! Thank You for allowing us to lay ourselves as a sacrifice on Your altar, yea, God, and live in and experience the Old Testament worship. God, You sent the fire of the Holy Ghost to light the altar. God, we ask You light the altar of our heart as we give ourselves as a sacrifice. Burn up everything that is not like You! God, we give You a burnt offering. We give You a fat offering, and a peace offering. We give You heave offering's as we lift up our voices, as we heave up the praises in this place!

The Lord is good! The Lord is great! He is greatly to be praised! He is worthy! I thank You for the grapes, Hallelujah! We might not be in the Promised Land yet, but the grapes are here. Thank You for the grapes! Thank You for the grapes, the sign to let us know the land is rich with milk and honey. The land has been blessed and no one can curse it! Your Promise Land no one can keep You out of but Yourself! Hallelujah, and Self be crucified that God be glorified, that we be validated by our faith and faith takes us to the promise! **Faith takes us to the fruit!** Where is your faith? If you have it, you can have your fruit, thank You, Jesus! Thank You for the cluster of grapes, God, Hallelujah, Hallelujah, Hallelujah, Hallelujah!

Now, God, there was no mercy, no prayer for mercy for the Hittites, Jebusites, the Amalekites, or Canaanites. There was no mercy no prayer of mercy, no prayer of negotiation prayed from them. You simply said go and posses the land. Now, God, we are praying against every enemy. We are praying against every spiritual demonic enemy, the principalities and the wickedness in high places. The spirits are in the people, God, who has placed themselves against You, because when they place themselves against us they have placed themselves against You. God, we are asking You give us the strength to go up and posses the land by any means necessary. Whatever You tell us to do, we will do. Whatever You tell us to do for our homes, our children and love ones, and for we ourselves that we would be saved, we will do that, so that no one would be lost because it's just that serious! Now help us, God, not to have a spirit like Lot's wife to turn back from what we have declared. We are not going to turn back! We want to make it, God, we need to make it. We need You in order to be successful because we cannot make it without You. These prayers we have prayed in Jesus Name, the people of God say Amen and Amen.

Closing Scripture: Numbers 14 (KJV)
"And the congregation lifted up their voices, and cried; and the people wept that night. And all the children of Israel murmured against Moses and against Aaron: and the whole congregation said unto them, Would God that we had died in the land of Egypt! Or would God we had died in this wilderness! And wherefore have the Lord brought us unto this land, to fall by the sword, that our wives and our children should be a prey? Were it not better for us to return

into Egypt? And they said one to another, Let us make a captain, and let us return into Egypt. Then Moses and Aaron fell on their faces before all the assembly of the congregation of the children of Israel. And Joshua, the son of Nun, and Caleb, the son of Jephunneh, who were of them that searched the land, [tore] their clothes; And they spoke unto all the company of the children of Israel, saying, The land, which we passed through to search it, is [a very] good land. If the Lord delights in us, then he will bring us into this land, and give it to us: a land which floweth with milk and honey. Only rebel not ye against the Lord, neither fear ye the people of the land; for they are bread for us; their defense is departed from them not. But all the congregation [demanded to] stone them with stones. And the glory of the Lord appeared in the tabernacle of the congregation before all the children of Israel. And the Lord said unto Moses, How long will this people provoke me? And how long will it be [before] they believe me, for all the signs which I have shown among them? I will smite them with the pestilence, and disinherit them, and will make of thee a greater nation and mightier than they. And Moses said unto the Lord, Then the Egyptians shall hear it (for thou broughtest up this people in thy might from among them), And they will tell it to the inhabitants of this land; for they have heard that thou, Lord, art among this people, that thou, Lord art seen face to face, and that thy cloud standeth over them, and that thou goest before them, by daytime in a pillar of a cloud, and in a pillar of fire by night. Now if thou shalt kill all this people as one man, then the nations which have heard the fame of thee will speak, saying, Because the Lord was not able to bring this people into the land which he swore to give unto them, therefore he hath slain them in the wilderness. And now, I beseech thee, let the power of my Lord be great, according as thou hast spoken, saying, The Lord is long-suffering, and of great mercy, forgiving iniquity and transgression, and by no means clearing the guilty, visiting the iniquity of fathers upon the children the third and fourth generation. Pardon, I beseech thee, the iniquity of this people according unto the greatness of thy mercy, and as thou hast forgiven this people, from Egypt even until now. And the Lord said, I have pardoned according to thy word; But as truly as I live, all the earth shall be filled with the glory of the Lord. Because all those men who *have seen my glory, and my miracles, which I did in Egypt and in the wilderness, and have [put me to the test] now these ten times, and have not hearkened to my voice; Surely they shall not see the land which I swore to give unto their fathers, neither shall any of them that provoked me see it. But my servant, Caleb, because he had **another spirit with him**, and hath followed me fully, him will I bring into the land where into he went; and his seed shall possess it. (Now the Amalekites and the Canaanites dwelt in the valley.) Tomorrow turn you, and get you into the wilderness by the way of the Rea Sea. And the Lord spoke unto Moses and unto Aaron, saying, How long shall I bear with this evil congregation, who murmur against me? I have heard the murmurings of the children of Israel, which they murmur against me. Say unto them, As truly as I live, saith the Lord, as ye have spoken in mine ears, so will I do to you. Your carcasses shall fall in this wilderness; and all who were numbered of you, according to your whole number, from twenty years old and upward, who have murmured against me, Doubtless ye shall not come into the land, concerning which I swore to make you dwell therein, except Caleb, the son of Jepunneh, and Joshua, the son of Nun. But your little ones, whom ye said should be a prey, them will I bring in, and they shall know the land which ye have despised. But as for you, your carcasses, they shall fall in this wilderness. And your children shall wander in the wilderness forty years, and bear your [harlotries], until your carcasses be wasted in the wilderness. After the number of the days in which ye searched the land, even forty days, each day for a year, shall ye bear your iniquities, even forty years, and ye shall know my breach of promise. I, the Lord, have said, I will surely do it unto all this evil congregation, who are gathered together against me: in this wilderness they shall be consumed, and there they shall die. And the men, whom Moses sent to search the land, who returned and made all the congregation to murmur against him, by bringing up a slander upon the land, Even those men who did bring up the evil report unpin the land, died by the plague before the Lord. But Joshua, the son of Nun, and Caleb, the son of Jephunneh, who were of the men who went to search the land, lived still. And Moses told these sayings unto all the children of Israel; and the people mourned greatly. And they rose up early* *in the morning, and [went] up into the top of the mountain, saying, Lo, we are here, and will go up unto the place which the Lord hath promised; for we have sinned. And Moses said, Wherefore now do ye transgress the commandment of the Lord? But it shall not prosper. Go not up, for the Lord is not among you; that ye be not smitten before your enemies. For the Amalekites and the Canaanites are there before you, and ye shall fall by the sword; because ye are turned away from the Lord, therefore the Lord will not be with you. But they presumed to go up unto the hilltop; nevertheless the ark of the covenant of the Lord, and Moses, departed not out of the camp. Then the Amalekites came down, and the Canaanites who dwelt in that hill, and smote them, and [routed] them, even unto Hormah."*

Closing Remarks:

I suggest you read this chapter over again for a greater understanding. When God said to do something, the people murmured and complained. They brought slander against God and wanted to stone Joshua and Caleb. They lied on the land and God said the land was flowing with milk and honey. They said the land would eat them up. I have news just in case someone doesn't know, which it needs to be said: realize God knows your thoughts are far off according to Psalms 139:1-2 (O Lord, thou hast searched me, and known me. Thou knowest my downsitting and mine uprising; thou understandest my thought afar off). Now, you read it for yourself. I did instruct the members of the church to invite seven souls a week, and some people say inviting seven souls a week is silly, simple, stupid, and don't make any sense, but I know the Lord told me to instruct this congregation to do it. If you have murmured or said to yourself, or your thoughts are to be disobedient, it is not against the leader or that individual the leader has delegated, it's against God.

After the people heard what God said He was going to do, they were at the Promised Land. The spies had led them to the Promised Land and God told Moses to take the people back to the Red Sea through the wilderness. After he took them back through the wilderness, it took them 40 years to get back to the Promise Land again! They wandered again for 40 years: for every day the spies spent in the land, God added a year for every day.

We don't often hear about the children of Israel wandering for 40 years. Many times that is not brought out that they were already at the Promise Land. All they had to do was go and possess it, but because they said it was not the thing to do and giants were in the land. They wanted to stone God's servants and they said Moses had brought them there so the men could die and the wives and children would be prey for these nations. God reversed it and said, "I am going to let them possess the land, but you and everyone 20 years and older will not enter into the Land."

What does that mean for the Temple of Prayer? Very simple. Some people in here, some people who have joined this church are going to sit in church and do the same things they've been doing for years. In our case, they will come into the new building and just as they did at the old location: murmur, complain, be disobedient and inconsistent in their service. They will not have an opportunity to be a part of the ministry. Being a part of the ministry is not being a part of the Temple of Prayer Ministries or just being a part of any church's ministry. Being a part of ministry is being a part of God's ministry. You cannot be a part of God's ministry and not be obedient. Plain and simple. Guess what that means? Spiritual increase and growth will not manifest in the life of an individual who is disobedient.

The Bible says a righteous man will scarcely make it in, so if a person who is doing all that they know to do, and they still barely make it in, where does that leave everybody else? Sometimes they are saved for six months living all for Christ, then the next six-months they are not. What if God caught you during the six months you stopped living for Christ and you die? You are in trouble. Sin separates us from God. Who wants to play Russian roulette with their soul? I don't. I have been there and I have done that. It's a scary thing to get caught outside the will of God. That has happened to me. It's a scary thing to almost die in sin. I have been there and have learned from that experience.

A new year brings us the opportunity to do what we have never done, be obedient. Simply just do what God says to do without questioning, without complaining. Is that too simple or too hard? Just do it. The only way to get 100% guaranteed results is we have to be obedient 100% to the instructions and directions to the all knowing

God who all ready knows the beginning of YOU and everything life will bring because He is already at your ENDING! Why not trust him? **"JUST BELIEVE"**

END OF DAY 3 PRAYER SERVICE

Personal Note:
Praise the Lord for His Word! All we have to do is just believe! Thank you Lord! Pastor asked for at least twelve people who were attending this prayer to be a representative of the twelve spies. The difference being that all of these spies would be like Joshua and Caleb and bring back a good report, positive thinking, knowing we can do all things through Christ that strengthen us. Go and bring back the grapes! Grapes signified through souls, love, peace and joy! Grapes demonstrated through a godly life, which is pleasing to God. The grapes will display that we bring a good report, believing what God has promised.

<u>Lord manifest Yourself to us to bring about a natural occurrence that will bring about a super-natural strength to continue to climb this mountain</u>.

Pastor Johnson asked at least twelve people to attend the 40 days of prayer representing the twelve spies but the difference being that all twelve have a "another spirit" like Caleb and Joshua. He is praying that we bring back a good report and some grapes!
~ Evelyn

<u>"Your land is waiting for you, go and posses it for the Lord thy God is with thee wherever you go!"</u>

STEP 4/DAY 4, THURSDAY

"Another Spirit"

DAY 4 PRAYER SERVICE BEGINS

Opening Remarks:

We thank God for making it back for the fourth day of prayer. We, the church, with a greater determination than yesterday to hear from God, we enter with excitement as we prepare to make our prayer and evening oblations unto the God of all gods knowing that He is in this place and in heaven at the same time sitting on His throne. Looking all over the World and the Saints prayers are being ushered up before his **PRESENCE**. We want our prayers to be included in the prayers that God sees coming up before Him. We believe the Lord takes those prayers and intercedes for us because the Scripture encourages us that Jesus, even now, is at the right hand of God making intercession for us. Saints, we need that intercession. Thursday is our normal night of intercessory prayer. As we were in our 40 days of prayer, every night was a night of intercession for ourselves, for our families, for our church, our community, our state and even the world.

If you turn on the news, you hear about murders and the bodies which have been found in Kentucky and other parts of the country. Car accidents take innocent people's lives, yet the Lord has been kind to us to let us live. The Bible says, "<u>Take no thought for tomorrow, for tomorrow is not promised to you</u>," and we understand that. At the same time, we go before God for directions. If it be God's will for us to live this year, we want to go in the direction He wants us to go in. So we pray, and in our prayers we exhibit faith believing God is going to bless us to live, and if He is going to let us live, we are going to need His directions and His assistance in everything we do.

"But my servant, Caleb, because he had another spirit with him, and hath followed me fully, him will I bring into the land where into he went; and his seed shall posses it." Numbers 14:24

Physically, as well as spiritually, during these 40 days, I want to encourage you to physically do some things, as well as prayerfully. By entering in to a consecrated time of prayer, we are spiritually saying "yes" to God that we will go into deeper realms in Him even if it's only for a day or two out of the 40 days. We need Him give us some foresight into where we should be in the spirit and not in our imagination. Sometimes, God can give you things in the Spirit. Things, which are visual, and people will say, "That's just your imagination. You are just dreaming."

In this Scripture, Caleb was one of the two spies who actually went into the Promised Land, saw what was there, and brought back a report. During these times, the remaining 40 days of prayer, continue to pray for the items on your heart and for what you desire. I encourage you physically: If you are praying for a house, make an appointment and physically go into the house. If it's a job, go to that place and take a tour. Walk around the place before you get the application. Don't just get the application and walk out the door without spying out the land. Go look and see what is happening, ask questions. If someone desires to go to college, then you need to write the school you desire to attend to and have them send you some information, and also send you a package about the school. By faith by doing these things, we are saying we have "another spirit" like Caleb.

I have prayed and I have shared this before as I passed by other churches in the city, and I asked the Lord a question, "Why can't we do that? And I said I believe we can, but how?" Then God told me, "You need another people." I have shared this with our congregation before. Another people are a people with a mind that is different than what everybody else is thinking. This goes back to the early messages from a previous year about thinking outside of the box and getting outside of the box.

Your prayers during these 40 days have to be one that is outside of the box if you want outside of the box results. If we stay in the box and never venture outside of the box, how will we ever know what is outside of the box? The only reference point we have is what we have experienced inside of the box. If no one ever sends anyone outside of the box, or somebody comes from the outside and gets into the box, how else will we ever know what is outside of the box? We will never know, so we need God. We can be like Caleb and have "another spirit" as God sends us outside the box, then we will see what is outside of the box. It is going to be greater then what is inside of the box, because if it wasn't, it would be inside of the box! Am I making any sense?

Therefore, we need another people. We need people with another spirit, another mind. In this year, which is the beginning of another year of ministry, it is a new beginning. When God gives us a fresh start, we can be the same person but that doesn't mean we are the same person, because technically we are not the same person as last year. We are not the same, we are four days older than what we were in last year, so we should be four days closer to God than what we were. Am I still making sense? Therefore, people who have the same mind because there were some people who came and crossed over with the same mind), will not receive and they will not understand according to 1 Corinthians 2:10-14:

> *But God hath revealed them unto us by his Spirit; for the Spirit searcheth all things, yea, the deep things of God. For what man knoweth the things of a man, [except] the spirit of man which is in him? Even so the things of God knoweth no man, but the Spirit of God. Now we have received, not the spirit of the world, but the Spirit who is of God; that we might know the things that are freely given to us of God. Which*

things also we speak, not in the words which man's wisdom teacheth, but which the Holy [Spirit] teacheth, comparing spiritual things with spiritual. But the natural man receiveth not the things of the Spirit of God; for they are foolishness unto him, neither can he know them, because they are spiritually discerned.

Those carnal things, carnal minded people cannot understand the spiritual things God has in his Word, therefore, He speaks through His men and women to instruct us on what to do concerning our lives. Everybody is not going to grab hold to that, but some people are going to grab hold and they are going to do things.

If you don't have a car and are walking, we can go by what the Scriptures have taught us from Ecclesiastes 9:4 "<u>For to him that is joined to all the living there is hope; for a living dog is better than a dead lion.</u>" In other words, "something is better than nothing" which is basically, what this Scripture means when it says, "<u>a living dog is better than a dead lion.</u>" Therefore, if a person does not have a car, they should not be down at a Rolls Royce Dealership trying to get a Bentley, because there is a difference between Faith, Foolishness and Presumption. But although you have to start somewhere, common sense should tell us we should not be at car lot test-driving a car with no job, no credit and not a dime in our pocket. A baby doesn't jump out of the womb running like Carl Lewis winning gold medals. A baby has to crawl first.

The history of our church as well as the history of other churches has proven that no church just jumps out and buys a one or five million dollar building and build a twenty million dollar ministry from scratch. If you ever listen to the testimonies from other ministries, it takes years along with time. However, if we never take the initiative to get out of the box then we can forget about the Bentley's and Rolls Royce's. In other words, we can forget about getting the greater in life and what God has already said we can have. If we don't have enough faith to believe God for a common cold and a headache, how can we have enough faith for God to heal us from cancer?

We have to start from somewhere and our box should continue to get bigger and bigger for the rest of our lives. Once you step out of the box and acquire which was outside of your box, what was inside of your original box has been disbanded and you now have a new box. Your new box might be a 12 by 12, but sooner or later you are going to want something outside of that box and once the new box is obtained, you will be in a 14 by 14, and it keeps getting bigger and bigger. As your faith continues to grow and God uses you more, this leads to you pleasing Him more.

God wants us to get out of the box so He can bless us. It's not just for us to be blessed while here on earth, but God has a reward for us that is eternal. God is going to reward those who please Him and have stepped out of the box as He instructs here on this earth. He loves us so much He said, "There is no good thing that He would wit hold from them that walk uprightly." It's not just for my house, my job, my school, my this, my clothes, my bank account, or my that. It's for the more permanent things God has for us because He knows it is far better than any house, any amount of money you can have in your bank, or any kind of car you could ever drive. God knows He has something that will blow our minds!

He loves us so much that He set these situations up. Trials and tribulations only bring us closer to God. You cannot gain patience unless you go through tribulations. You cannot gain experience unless you go through those things, which leads to hope. Let us not ever be ashamed of our relationship and testimony of faith about how we got out of the box. Sometimes God challenges us like the eagle that takes the eaglets, dumps them out, and says, "Either you are going to fly, or you are going to die." If you are a real eagle, you are going to fly! Sometimes God says, "I love you so much but you can't stay up in here in this nest, because what is outside of this nest is where your blessings are." He takes us through trials and tribulations, which will force us in many cases, to step out of our comfortable box.

This is the year we should say we are going to pray more and we are going to be uncomfortable. I don't want to be comfortable. If I am comfortable, I have the tendencies to stay inside of the box. There is no way on earth we want to be like the ten spies who God cursed, because they lied on the land, they murmured and they mocked Him. If God says, something is a blessing, who can say it is a curse? We cannot let people tell us what is a curse in our lives. Don't let anybody do that! If God said it is a blessing, it is a blessing. Therefore, what, you don't have it now? God lets you see your blessing. He is not letting you see your blessing for you not to acquire it.

When we pray from this moment forward, every night we want to add something to help us in the formation of our prayers. Not for this year, but from here on we will pray in a different way. Add something to our prayers and be more serious and more fervent. Have more faith in our prayers. Believe if God answers and says this is yours, then it's yours.

It is only a matter of His time before we will acquire what we pray will be manifested in our lives. Just because it doesn't happen right now, doesn't mean it is not going to happen. After we have read the Numbers 14, we will go home, pray, and maybe the Lord will allow us to highlight some other areas of concern to pray. Not just for ourselves, because we are not selfish, but to pray for your church and the members. Give your church "another spirit" that invites souls to Christ. Get in your spirit that you have to do this! Then let us all thank God for another spirit.

Church, can we image, if everyone would be obedient just on this week! We have an opportunity. God has given us a new slate this year, and come Sunday when I ask, "How many people invited and evangelized this week?" everybody who has been coming to prayer should be able to raise their hand. The whole church should be able say, "I invited my seven." Do know how excited God would be? If we would be obedient and take the brakes off of Him, He would give us what He has promised this church. Somebody say "Supernatural increase." Supernatural increase means God is going to put it in your spirit whatever He has already placed inside of you before time begin shall come to pass. If it is to make money, be prosperous, or be a blessing, God is going to stir that thing up and show it to you. Then it will be up to you to go quickly and possess your land!

The past is the past. We want to include in our prayers, and put an emphasis on God to forgive and clean us as we consecrate ourselves for six days, because on the seventh day, God can bless us within the seven days or better yet within these 40 days. When He gave them a taste of the land, He gave them the grapes. They brought back a cluster, an abundance of the best grapes, to say that the land had everything they needed and more! Now, all we have to do is just go take it. In our cities we have everything we need! What we need are some people who really believe what God has for us, is right here! I don't have to go to Paris, France, I don't have to go to New York or move somewhere else to do ministry. God has planted you right where you are. Say to yourself, this is where I am going to work and believe God is going to give an increase in the harvest! Hallelujah, Hallelujah, Hallelujah!

Opening Scripture: Isaiah 6 (KJV)
"In the year the King Uzziah died, I saw also the Lord sitting upon a throne, high and lifted up, and his train filled the temple. Above it stood the seraphim: each one had six wings: with [two] he covered his face, and with [two] he covered his feet, and with [two] he did fly. And one cried unto another, and said, Holy, holy, holy, is the Lord of hosts; the whole earth is full of this glory. And the post of the door moved at the voice of him who cried, and the house was filled with smoke. Then said I, Woe is me! For I am undone, because I am a man of unclean lips, and I dwell in the midst of a people of unclean lips; for mine eyes have seen the King, the Lord of hosts. Then flew one the seraphim unto me, having a live coal in his hand, which he had taken with the tongs from off the altar. And he laid it upon my mouth, and said, Lo, this hath touched thy lips, and thine iniquity is taken away, and thy sin purged. Also I heard the voice of the Lord, saying, Whom shall I send, and who will go for us? Then said I, Here am I; send me. And he said, Go, and tell this people, Hear ye indeed, but understand not; and see ye indeed, but perceive not. Make the heart of this people fat, and make their ears heavy, and shut their eyes; lest they see with their eyes, and hear with their ears, and understand with their heart, and [be converted], and be healed. Then said I, Lord, how long? And he answered, Until the cities be wasted without inhabitant, and the houses without man, and the land utterly desolate, And the Lord have removed men far

away, and there be a great forsaking in the midst of the land. But yet in it shall be a tenth, and it shall return, and shall be eaten; as a teil tree, and as an oak, whose substance is in them, when they cast their leaves, so they holy seed shall be the substance of it."

Insight as We Prepared for Prayer

God had an assignment for a man who had enough sense to realize he was a sinner. He said, "Woe is me, I am undone. I dwell among unclean people and some of them have rubbed on me and I am unclean myself." God cleansed and purified him with the fire from the coal that came off the altar.

We have prayed, and for those who have been here for the first three days have heard me say, "Lord, we have sacrificed. We are the sacrifice and we put ourselves on the altar." I asked on last night that God would send the Holy Ghost down like He did in Old Testament worship and the fire of God would come and lick the sacrifice up. We want God to come with His fire and lick, take it, do whatever He wants to do with us! Cleanse us up because the call we have is like Isaiah's, it is great! We have a great call to do here on this earth. The encouraging thing about this Scripture is, did you know God already knew Isaiah was not worthy? He didn't clean Isaiah up with His tongue first. He let him see something first, see His glory; see His train fill the Temple. That is the same smoke and the same cloud the children of Israel saw in Exodus 14:19-24, which we read the first night. It's the same God, it's the same glory, and it's the same pillar of cloud, which was the smoke by day. On tonight in your prayers, you should also include "Lord let me see. Open up my spirit. Open me up to the spirit realm and let me see Your glory on tonight!" And if you do, I guarantee you, God will let you see His glory on tonight. Hallelujah, bless Him, bless Him, bless Him, bless Him, bless Him, bless Him!

Let Us Pray:

Let us go to God in prayer believing the Scripture. God is God and He is going to do it.

(The atmosphere tonight is pure praise! The people are praising and worshipping God, Pastor can hardly begin to pray! I hear a lot of shouting and screaming coming out from the souls giving God their all. People are crying and wailing. The train of God has filled the Temple!)

Bless Him, bless Him, Hallelujah, thank You, thank You, God, thank You. Bless Your Name, bless Your Name, bless Your Name, God, Hallelujah, Hallelujah bless Him, bless Him all day. Father God, we thank You for this night. We thank You, God, for allowing us the opportunity for a new beginning. We thank You, Lord God, for giving us a mind, an understanding and a revelation of the Word. God, we pray on this night, as we have done on the previous nights, You forgive us of all of our sins, cleanse us from all unrighteousness. Remove the spirit of disobedience, complacency and mediocrity from us. Give us another spirit like Caleb, God; give us another mind of willing obedience, God, gleeful, joyful, obedient, and glad to be obedient. Help us now, God, because we see our land. Some of us have seen. For those who have not seen, open up their understanding, God, spiritually to get a glimpse of things You are promising by faith, God, and that it is okay to go and get what You have promised us, Lord God. They don't have to be afraid of how big the obstacles or task, but to go get it. Oh, in the Name of Jesus, we also ask, Lord God, You give us a mind like Isaiah as we are in Your Temple, God. Open up the spirit realm inside of us that we might see Your glory. We might see Your train even here now in the room. Now the smoke is even here now!

The earth is full of Your glory. The Temple of Prayer church is located in the earth, so this church is full of Your glory, God! Make Your glory known before these men and women, boys and girls in this place. We thank You, God, we thank You, we thank You even now, Hallelujah, for the expanding of our souls. For taking us outside of the box of conformity, God, and complacency and confinement that we have existed in before, God, but no longer will we stay inside of the box! No longer, God, will we allow people to chain us, bind us, put us in bondage, God, to keep us from doing what You have called us to do: be great soul winners for Christ! Be great prayer warriors in this church, God. Raise up a prayer warrior army of Saints in this church, God, for when the Saints get together, touch and agree, there is nothing You wouldn't do because of the great faith these people have exhibited in You. God, by personally stepping outside of their boxes in their own homes, God, on their jobs, wherever they might be, God, give them faith to rebuke the Devil in Jesus Name.

Satan, the Lord rebukes you! We don't have any power, but there is power in the Name of Jesus! We are not ashamed, God, to come into this place and call on the Name of Jesus! We have something Isaiah didn't have. Yes, he saw the seraphim. Yes, he saw them flying. We might never see the seraphim on this side of time, God, until we step into eternity, but we still have something Isaiah didn't have. We have something Caleb, Moses, and Joshua didn't have. We have a Name we can call on. The Name of JESUS! The power that comes with that Name, we can call upon Thy Son's Name, the Name of Jesus. Knowing things are going to change, things are going to happen, and Your Will must be done! Everything ungodly must cease when we call upon the Name of our Lord and Savior, Jesus Christ!

God, we pray for the sick and afflicted every night. We pray for those who have requested prayer. We bind the strep throat now, God. We bind the flu in the Name of Jesus. God, set them free in their bodies. God, if there are any in the room who is sick and afflicted, touch us all. God, heal and deliver from our youngest to the eldest. God, for those who are a part of the church who are not here and are sick and afflicted, touch and deliver now, God.

Let the cloud of glory cover over us as we leave this place. As we go into our homes, even on tonight, when we have an encounter with our families, they will know something is different about us from the last time they saw us. Even if we don't say a word, they will be able to know by the countenance of our faces, we have been with God! We have been taken to the high place! We have been taken to the Holies of Holies on tonight! We have gone beyond the Veil into the secret place into Thy **PRESENCE**, God, Hallelujah! Bless Your Name, bless Your Name, bless Your Name God!

Take the hot tongs, God, off Your altar in heaven and send the fire of the Holy Ghost! Burn up everything in our minds, in our mouths, in our bellies, even in our spirits! In our souls what is not like Thee, burn it up, God, so we might invite seven souls to Thee! Burn it up so the unsaved would come! Burn it up so the sick and the afflicted from everywhere would fill this church! Those who are diseased with the addictions of alcohol, drugs or whatever the addictions might be; those with a mind and whoredom spirit, God, whatever it is let them come! We make a call now, God. Send the souls this way! We can pray a prayer of faith and they would be delivered, healed and set free in the Name of Jesus! Our desire, our desire is to serve Thee, God. Our desire, God, yes, Lord, yes, Lord we are grateful, thank You for our trials and tribulations. We might not understand them fully but we believe the Word and we know that all things work together for the good to them that love God, to them who are the called according to his purpose.

You have tried to push us out, God, so we would soar like the eagle. You tried to push us out because the eagle is like a leader. The eagle separates itself from the rest of the birds and animals, Hallelujah. His nest is sometimes 10,000 feet high up in the sky in some mountain. It makes it hard for prey to get to it, God, and prey on the eaglets. God, we want You to lift us up high in the spirit!

As we climb the mountain of prayer during these 40 days to be like Moses to come into Thy **PRESENCE**! We want to be like Elijah and hear from You, God. We want to be like Isaiah and be in the Temple, the sacred place of God! To see the wondrous works of the Almighty magnificent God! Oh, God, take us up higher where these trivial problems in life will not stop us, God, from moving forward now! I speak to breach in the minds, the minds that have been broken and separated. I speak unification of mind, body and soul be thine set free in the Name of Jesus!

We rebuke the Devil. I call for peace in the mind! I call for peace in the home! I call for peace in our children! I call for peace in the spouses! I call for peace for every head of the home whether they be a single woman or a single man. This is a new day, God, this is a new beginning, God, and we want to walk in the newness of life! If any man be in Christ, he is a new creation! We are new, God, for we are not the same! We are not the same, God. Four days of holiness. Thank You, God for this year! Four days of being free from sin, thank You! Four days of prayer, God. Thank You for this year!

The significance of the number four, God, is on the fourth day, You created the earth Hallelujah! Thank You, God, thank You, thank You, thank You for creation in us! Thank You, God, for

A Call Into His Presence

creation in our souls! Thank You, God, for creation in our minds. We are stepping out by faith, God, we are walking by faith, God, now lead us in the path of righteousness for Thy sake, God! Let our steps be ordered by the Lord with good men and women, with good boys and girls because we belong to You! Isaiah belonged to You. He was good enough to see Your glory, and then You purged him. Let us see Your glory because we pray a prayer of purging first! God, let us see Your glory on tonight! In the souls of these people let Your glory be revealed now in this church as we give You praise, Hallelujah!

Hallelujah, Hallelujah, Hallelujah out of your soul, give Him praise! God inhabits the praise of His people. Praise Him, a new praise, not like you did on last year, but step out of the box on tonight and praise Him! If you never lifted your hands before, lift them up! If you never lifted your voice to a scream, shout out the praise of victory! Hallelujah, Hallelujah. If you have never clapped your hands, clap them for God! Clap your hands all ye people shout unto God with a voice of triumph! There is victory in here! There is victory in here! There is victory in this place! There is victory in this place; shout it out "Victory, victory, victory!" Open up your mouths. Saints shout it out "Victory, victory in Jesus!"

Hallelujah, bless Him, bless Him, bless God, bless Jesus, bless the Holy Ghost, bless Him, bless Him, bless Him, bless Him!!! Thank You for another spirit! Thank You for another mind! The mind of God be in this church, lead this church, sit on the throne of this church, Jesus! This is your church, Hallelujah! Sit on the throne of each and every believer. Yes, God, yes, God, have Your way! Have Your way, have Your way, have Your way!

Now, God nothing is impossible to them that believe. Move, send your glory to room 23 in the nursing home right now and strengthen my mother! Touch her body, yea, God, and send forth the cloud, Hallelujah, to Florida. Touch my other mother, my mother-in-law. Touch her body, God, and strengthen her now in her spirit. Add to her life, Jesus! I send now the spirit of God to Darfur, Africa touch our Elder. Keep him alive! Give him supernatural manifestation, insight into the future, yea, God, Hallelujah! Bless God!

He is worthy, His glory is here! His glory is here; His train is filling the Temple! Will you let Him fill yours? Do you want Him to fill your Temple? Do you want Him to fill your soul? You have a chance for a real experience out of the Bible on tonight, but it is up to you! Will you step out of the box?! Will you step out of the box?! Will you step out of your box on tonight, on this fourth night?! Will you step out of the box! Glory, glory, glory, glory, gloooorrrryyyyyy, glory to the Lamb of God, glory! This glory is in all the earth, give Him glory!

Glory, glory, give Him glory, Hallelujah, Hallelujah, Hallelujah, Hallelujah, bless Him, bless Him. Will you help me bless Him?! Will you help me bless Him?! Will you help me bless Him, bless Him?! Bless Him, yeeeesssss, bless Him, Hallelujah, Hallelujah thank You, God, thank You, God, yeeeeeaah! Oh Sweet Wonder, Hallelujah, we love You, God, we love You, God, we love You, God, and we love You, God! Yea, Lord, yea, Lord, we love You, God!

That's it. Step out of your box. What you need and what you want for your life is not in your box. You have to step out of your box. We thank You and we magnify You for Your Spirit moving in this place. You are God and You alone. We stand on Your Word, God, not on our own understanding, but on the Word. Now speak to our minds, our hearts and our understanding, and our spirits. Our ears are open to Your voice; our ears are open to Your voice. Lead us into the path of righteousness, always we pray. Answer the prayers of Your people, God, for they depend on You. Help this church for we are Your church. We need Your instruction and guidance for this year in our lives, in this church, and as individuals. We need You, God, we praise You and we love You. We do have another spirit, another mind yea, God, yea, God. Be it done now in Jesus Name, and the people of God say Amen and Amen. **Give the Lord some praise!**

Closing Scripture: Psalms 4 (KJV)
"Hear me when I call, O God of my righteousness. Thou hast enlarged me when I was in distress; have mercy upon me, and hear my prayer. O ye sons of men, how long will ye turn my glory into shame? How long will ye love vanity, and seek after [falsehood]? But know that the Lord hath set apart him who is godly for himself;

the Lord will hear when I call unto him. Stand in awe, and sin not; commune with your own heart upon your bed, and be still. Offer the sacrifices of righteousness, and put your trust in the Lord. There are many that say, Who will show us any good? Lord, lift thou up the light of thy countenance upon us. Thou hast put gladness in my heart, more than in the time that their [grain] and their wine increased. I will both [lie] down in peace, and sleep; for thou, Lord, only makest me dwell in safety."

Thus said the Word of the Lord. Those who receive it will be blessed and benefit by it.

Closing Remarks:

Four is a significant number in the numeric principal and the importance of number 4 in Scripture. On the 4th day, all material creation was finished. There are 4 seasons. As the material things on earth were finished, God did not add anything else to the earth from the material side. Everything was all ready placed inside; there was something that was not shown, gold, silver and things of that nature. Coal and metal things that was in the earth would take some digging to find. Diamonds are also in the earth it took some digging to get those things out too.

Even though this is only the fourth day out of 40, we declared that we would have the opportunity to testify on what we believed God has already finished. We must step out of the box to go, retrieve, and dig to bring those things back. And we want to bring so much back that we don't have room in our old box…we need a new box, because it won't be room enough in the old box to be able to hold the blessings and answers to prayers, and the souls that will be saved. We declared that we didn't want this box, our church building, to be able to hold the souls that would come. We want God to expand us because there are souls out there that needs to come into the safety and House of God!

END OF DAY 4 PRAYER SERVICE

STEP 5/DAY 5 FRIDAY

"Lord, Let Your Favor Compass Us Like a Shield"

DAY 5 PRAYER SERVICE BEGINS

Opening Remarks:

We need to come up! How can we tell our children to be holy and live a life for Christ if we are not? We cannot go to God any kind of way. Lord, we hear the call. Do we want to go up the mountain? Do we really want to see God; if we do, then we must go up the right way. We want to hear the Lord say "Come in," not only just come up the mountain, but we want to go in. Lord, we want to see Your glory on this earth! If God can call Moses into his **PRESENCE**, why can't He call us to come? How can we go up into the **PRESENCE** of God without praise and worship?

Opening Scripture: Exodus 24:12-18 (KJV)
"And the Lord said unto Moses, Come up to me into the mount, and be there; and I will give thee tables of stone, and a law, and commandments which I have written, that thou mayest teach them. And Moses rose up, and his [servant], Joshua; and Moses went up into the mount of God. And he said unto the elders, Tarry ye here for us, until we come again unto you: and, behold, Aaron and Hur are with you; if any man have any matters to do, let him come unto

them. *And Moses went up into the mount, and a cloud covered the mount. And the glory of the Lord abode upon Mount Sinai, and the cloud covered it six days; and the seventh day he called unto Moses out of the midst of the cloud. And the sight of the glory of the Lord was life devouring fire on the top of the mount in the eyes of the children of Israel. And Moses went into the midst of the cloud, and got up into the mount; and Moses was in the mount forty days and forty nights."*

Insight As We Prepared for Prayer:

<u>There is not a friend like the lowly Jesus</u>
<u>No not one.</u>
<u>He will guide until the day is done,</u>
<u>There is not a friend like the lowly Jesus,</u>
<u>No not one, no not one.</u>

We thank God we understand to a greater degree than we did on yesterday, that the truth is, there is not a friend like the lowly Jesus, and truly He has been our friend and our guide. This day is a day we are privileged to see than some others have not seen. For in the society we live in, people have set fires and killed their family members. That is not good, but we thank God the Lord has blessed us to be in our right minds; we are not doing anything in that manner and have not done anything like that, and we don't allow those thoughts to cross our minds and stay in our hearts as we ask God to remove anything that is not like Him. Whether iniquity hidden or not hidden out of our hearts, minds we might come before His **PRESENCE** with thanksgiving and we might be honest in our prayers, and worship our God and our King.

<u>Additional Scripture: Psalm 5 (KJV)</u>

"Give ear to my words, O Lord, consider my meditation. Hearken unto the voice of my cry, my King, and my God; for unto thee will I pray. My voice shalt thou hear in the morning, O Lord; in the morning will I direct my prayer unto thee, and will look up. For thou art not a God who hath pleasure in wickedness; neither shall evil

dwell with thee. The foolish shall not stand in thy sight; thou hatest all workers of iniquity. Thou shalt destroy those who speak [falsehood]; the Lord will abhor the bloody and deceitful man. But as for me, I will come I into thy house in the multitude of thy mercy; and in thy fear will I worship toward thy holy temple. Lead me, O Lord, in thy righteousness because of mine enemies; make thy way straight before my face. For there is no faithfulness in their mouth; their throat is an open sepulcher; they flatter with their tongue. Destroy thou them, O God; let them fall by their own counsels; cast them out in the multitude of their transgressions; for they have rebelled against thee. But let all those who put their trust in thee rejoices, let them ever shout for joy, because thou defendest them; let those all who love thy name be joyful in thee. For thou, Lord, wilt bless the righteous; with favor wilt thou compass him as with a shield."

We thank God for the reading of the Scripture. Let us receive it considering it in our prayers. We want God's favor to compass us as a shield. Give the Lord some praise. Let us go to God in prayer believing God is going to compass us about with his favor.

Let Us Pray: Singing "Oh, Sweet Wonder"
Hallelujah, Oh, bless Your name, sweet wonder, sweet wonder, sweet wonder, Hallelujah, glory to Your Name, God, glory to Your Name, glory to Your Name, God. Oh, God, we thank You for this fifth day. We thank You for this fifth day of this year; we thank You for this fifth day of this month. We thank You for the fifth day of this prayer, God, a new beginning in this year Hallelujah. Oh, God, five is the number of grace and favor. We ask now, Lord God, You would compass us about with Your favor as a shield and Your favor protect us as David prayed that prayer, we include it in our prayers on tonight. Not just us, Lord God, but we ask Your favor would compass about everyone in this church and every member of this church. Let Your favor be compassed about in our families, God, to the body of Christ everywhere. We call upon You once again, Lord God, as we go higher as we have been climbing up this mountain of prayer into Thy glory Lord into Thy **PRESENCE** before thee.

We come with a grateful heart, God, a mind of sanctification separating everything not like You out of our minds. Separating ourselves from those things, God, fleshly things, human things, and carnal things, which bring us down in the Spirit. We need You, Lord God, to sustain us and keep us above all the Devil has dug: many holes and many pitfalls for us to fall in, but this is the year, Lord God, we are standing strong and saying, "No, not this year, not today, not now." We are not going down into the pit, Lord God. We are not going to have a mind of lowliness of thought, Lord God and doubts, fears in comparison to what You said You could do, and how You can lift up the bowed down head. How You can mend the broken hearted. We thank You, God, for Your mending and Your lifting of our heads for You are the lifter of our heads and we are grateful.

We ask now, Lord God, as we have come into this place to keep our covenant of prayer, Lord God. We ask that You would bind every evil spirit, every demonic force, which comes against every family and every individual, Lord God, of this church membership. We are praying for deliverance God. We are praying for deliverance God. We lift our children up, if they are adults, we are praying for deliverance in their minds. If our children are teenagers, we are praying for deliverance in their minds. If our children are little, small or in between, we are praying for deliverance in their minds.

Move now, in the Name of Jesus, have Your way and destroy every yoke now, we pray, God. Oh, God, bless us, bless us, bless us, bless us as we bless You. Bless us as we praise You. Bless us as we glorify You. Bless us as we make our request known before Your throne, Lord God. We need You. You are God and there is none else! You are God and there is no other God. You are the King of Kings and the Lord of Lords. God, let our enemies be consumed in their unrighteousness, Lord God, if they continue to refuse to turn to Jesus the Christ, the Savior of the World.

God we are praying now for the strength of the church, Lord God. We are praying for the deliverance for the church, Lord God. We are praying for the deliverance of Your people everywhere. Lord God, bring about deliverance now in the Name of Jesus. Deliver, deliver, deliver, deliver in the bodies, Lord God, Hallelujah, touch and heal. Touch and heal as only You can, Lord God. Bless us with favor in our bones, Lord God, the very bones that ache, God, they would ache no more.

Come now and make Thy **PRESENCE** known as You have done these previous nights of these 40 days of prayer. You have made Your glory known in this place; You have even made Your glory known in our minds and our thoughts. God, You have given us an end, Lord God, an end to the situations we are involved in, God. The visions and dreams You have allowed us to dream and see, Lord God, as the Bible says, "In the last days You would pour out Your Spirit upon all flesh. There would be people that would dream dreams and see visions Lord God, speaking in new tongues." God, we ask now that You would unleash now the tongue, the tied down tongue that they would praise You. We ask, Lord God, for those who have never been baptized in the Holy Ghost, You would baptize them in Your Holy Ghost. We ask now for those who need a refilling, You refill on this night. Whatever the need is, Lord God, we are saying here we are, Lord God. Here is our cup and we need a refilling now, God, we need a refilling now. Pour out Your anointing, for the anointing destroys the yoke. Destroy every yoke now.

Teach us in this place, God, by Your Spirit how to pray. God, teach us not to rely on words of eloquence, Lord God, not to rely on words other people pray, but teach us how to pray a prayer of a sincere heart. Out of a sincere heart and a broken and contrite spirit, teach us how to pray a prayer of obedience and willingness. Teach us how to pray a prayer of self-sacrifice. Teach us how to pray a prayer and in that prayer we would ask for the crucifixion of self to take place on a daily basis, as Paul has said, "I must die daily." God, let the 'I' in us die! Let the Christ in us live! Live forever more in our souls, God, live-forever more in our desires, God, live forever more in our will, God, let our wills be Your Will, God.

Thy Will be done as it is in heaven. Thy Will be done in our homes as it is in heaven. Thy Will be done in this church as it is in heaven. Thy Will be done in every department of this church as it is in heaven. Thy Will be done in our children as it is in heaven! Thy Will be done in husbands and wives as it is in heaven, the parents as parents as it is in heaven. Thy Will be done everywhere! Everywhere all over this World, God, Your Will be done! Open up the Saints understanding, God, to let us know we are not alone for the Spirit of God is with us, Hallelujah. Jesus is still Lord. He is the Savior. He sits on the throne of every believer's heart and, God, we thank You for letting Your Son sit upon the throne of our hearts. We thank You for letting Him sit upon the throne, God, of this church, for He is the King of everything in this place. This is God's Church. This is Christ's Church. He gave His life for the church, God, Hallelujah, and now we offer up the sacrifice of praise in this place! Hallelujah, we worship the Lord in the beauty of holiness! We lift the Name of Jesus up higher, higher than any sin! Higher than any shameful act or deed for the Blood of Jesus cleanses, washes, and renews and brings about reconciliation and regeneration.

God, we pray now, Lord God, with an earnest heart and out of faith the size of a grain of a mustard seed, that every mountain in our way, God, we speak to every mountain now and say be thou removed! We are not going to face the mountain of trials and tribulations and be fearful, but we are going to be authoritative in the Name of Jesus! Will you call upon His Name Jesus? Will you call upon His Name Jesus, on tonight? Do you not know there is power in the Name of Jesus? All power is in that Name. Only in that Name: Jesus, Jesus, Jesus, Jesus, Jesus, Wonderful Savior Jesus! Magnificent Lord, Jesus the only King, Jesus! The true and living God, Jesus! The Bishop of our souls, Jesus! The Savior of the World, Jesus! The only Sacrifice accepted by God. Jesus, the one who shed His Blood on Calvary. Will You help me lift up the Name Jesus until every Demon has to leave out of this place as we call on the Name of Jesus? There is real power, true power, Holy Ghost power in the Name of Jesus. Will you help me call on the Name of Jesus? Are You ashamed of that Name? I am not ashamed of the Name Jesus for there is no other Name in Heaven or on Earth, which Man can call upon to be saved. I call upon the Name of my God and my King, my Savior and my Lord! His Name is Jesus! Send Your favor down on this fifth night. Send Your favor down as it is in the 5th Psalms, God, covers us like a shield with Your favor. With Your favor God, send the favor of God upon every family. Make a way that every bill be paid in every household, in the Name of Jesus.

A Call Into His Presence

Jeeeeeeeeuuusssssss. There is something about calling on that Name. Maybe it doesn't do anything for You, but I feel better when I call upon that Name Jesus. The power of the Lord begins to strengthen me when I call upon the Name of Jesus and give Him the high praise Hallelujah, Hallelujah, Hallelujah, bless us, bless us, God, bless us, God, with Your favor! Bless us, God, with Your favor! Bless us with Your glory! Let Your train fill the Temple and take us higher! Higher, take us higher in Thee! Take us to the top of the mount of glory and praise! Take us to the top of the mountain of prayer and supplication. Take us, God, where no Demon can go! Take us, God, where no problem can go! Take us beyond the flesh in the Spirit realm. Take us, God, all the way to Thee, Hallelujah!

Hallelujah, Hallelujah, bless Him, bless Him, bless Him, bless Him! I will bless the Lord; will you bless Him at all times? Is there a praise in your mouth? Is there a continuous praise in your mouth? If you want an out of the box result, you have to get out of the box on tonight and give God an out of the box praise!

Get out of your flesh. I rebuke tiredness! Get out of your flesh. I rebuke worry! Get out of your flesh. I rebuke the bad minds! Get out of your flesh. I rebuke the pain in the body in the Name of Jesus! Jeeeeeesus, Jeeeeeesus we give Him glory! We give Him glory in this place! Give Him glory, give Him glory, give Him glory, give Him glory! Glory, glory, glory, glory, give Him glory in this place, in your soul bless Him. In your soul bless Him, bless the Lord, oh, my soul and all that is within me, bless His Holy Name.

Bless the Lord, oh, my soul and forget not all His benefits. Has He been good to you? That's a benefit! Has He blessed you to see another day? That's a benefit! Are your children still alive? That's a benefit! Do you have a place to stay? That's a benefit! Has He heard and answered your prayer? That's a benefit! He is our God and we are His children, the sheep of His pasture, that's a benefit, yessssssss!!!! Do you have the Holy Ghost burning inside of you? That's a benefit. Yea, thank You for Your benefits! Are you saved? That's a benefit! If You call on Him in the midnight hour, that's a benefit! Can you call Him in the morning? That's a benefit! Have you ever called Him in the noonday? That's another benefit and don't forget the evening time, that's another benefit!

He is worthy, worthy, worthy, He is God, He is God, He is God!!! Bless Him, bless Him, bless Him, Hallelujah, Hallelujah, Hallelujah, Hallelujah, we thank You, God, we do thank You and we love You. We appreciate You; we worship You in the beauty of holiness. God, we know in our own righteousness we are not worthy to come before Thee with any prayer request, but because of the Blood of Jesus that was shed on Calvary for the remission of our sins, we must be washed in that Blood. You said we could come boldly before Thy throne and make our prayer request known to You. Therefore, on this fifth day of prayer, we have come once again and on this day, we ask for Thy favor. We ask for Thy favor, we ask for Thy favor, God, to compass us like a shield. Favor, God, grace, and unmerited favor. We don't desire it, we cannot earn it, but we can praise You for it and believe You, God, when You said You will bless us with Your favor.

Oh, God, oh, God, thank You, Jesus, thank You, Jesus, thank You, Jesus! Now, God, we are not only praying for favor for this church, for the members of this church, the people in this church, our families, but we are praying for the Saints everywhere all over the world. There is somebody who needs Your favor more than we do. Their life is on the line and they need a miracle just to live. We are praying for those families who are crowded around a bedside calling on the Name of Jesus right now for the life of that love one. We are praying for the families huddled together somewhere in some dark place somewhere around the world and bullets are being shot everywhere and bombs are being dropped! They are not calling on a strange God, they are not calling on another God, but they are Christians and they are calling on the Name of the Lord Jesus and they expect for You to do something miraculous! God, even if it means their life must be given. Take them swiftly that there will be no suffering in their bodies.

God, I pray for the young women these mass murders, rapists and molesters, Lord God, not just here in America, but things that are done far worse than what we know about in this country, and out of this country. These soldiers and brutal forces have some young girl tied down. God, take her life now as she is praying to die. Don't let her live through that situation, God. We are praying for the man who is getting ready to get shot in the back of the head because he refuses to denounce Christ! Oh, God, receive His soul, ooooh, in the Name of Jesus.

    We have so much to be grateful for in this country where we can openly call upon the Name of our God! We can openly praise You and we even ask for more favor. Open up our eyes that we might see the favor You have already blessed us with. If You never bless us with anything else, we have more than enough to praise You for the rest of our lives, God and on this night, we want to tell You thank You for Your favor!!! Thank You for what You have already done! Thank You how You have kept us alive! Thank You how nobody has been raped! Thank You nobody has been burned or shot because they called upon the Name of the Lord! Thank You God for giving us a building to worship You in! Hallelujah, Hallelujah, Hallelujah, Hallelujah, bless You, God, bless You, God, bless You, God.

    Now we ask, Lord God, we ask for Your favor to be continued in our service. Give us a mind to praise You, God, like we were already in heaven with the rest of the Heavenly Host lifting and magnifying Your glory. Help us to do that on this night and not to hold back. Help us to let go and let You have Your way. Help us to give You all the glory, not some of the glory, but all the glory, all the glory. You are worthy of all the glory. For we wrestle not against flesh and blood. This is a spiritual warfare and in our spirits, we say yes! Yes to God, yes to God, yes to His Will. Give us a yes Lord Spirit. We say yes on tonight, God, not holding back! We say yes on tonight, God. Thank You for another day! We say yes on tonight. God, thank You for another day of prayer. We say yes on tonight. God, thank You for making a way for another day. We say yes on tonight. Yes in our souls. This service is a yes Lord Service on tonight! We are not going to hold back, we are not going to hold back. We are going to give God all the praise! Out of our souls, we say yes! Satan, the Lord rebuke you, and we thank You Lord for the victory! We thank God for the victory! We thank God for the victory! We thank Him for the victory! We praise Him for the victory! We thank God for the victory in Jesus Name, in Jesus Name, we pray and the people of God say Amen and Amen. Will you give the Lord some praise!?!

Closing Scripture: Isaiah 12 (KJV)

"And in that day thou shalt say, O Lord, I will praise thee; though thou wast angry with me, thine anger is turned away, and thou comfortedst me. Behold, God is my salvation; I will trust, and not be afraid; for the Lord, even [the Lord], is my strength and my song; he also is become my salvation. Therefore, with joy shall ye draw water out of the wells of salvation. And in that day shall ye say, Praise the LORD, call upon his name, declare his doings among the people, make mention that his name is exalted. Sing unto the Lord; for he hath done excellent things. This is known in all the earth. Cry out and shout, thou inhabitant of Zion; for great is the Holy One of Israel in the midst of thee."

Closing Remarks:

Thank God for the reading of the Word. To everyone who will be obedient to the Word of God, you shall be blessed. Will you cry out, "Oh, Zion, for great is the Holy One of Israel!" Will you cry out, "Hallelujah!" Will you cry out, "Hallelujah!" And the people of God be blessed.

END OF DAY 5 PRAYER SERVICE

STEP 6/DAY 6, SATURDAY

"Six is the Number of Man"

DAY 6 PRAYER SERVICE BEGINS

Opening Remarks:

On the sixth day of the year, we give God praise and we thank Him for another day of life! Can you imagine what this world would be like if everyone stopped praying? I don't want to ever experience that. The Lord is blessing us to spread the word of prayer; to encourage everybody to pray more this year than we did on last year. If more Christians prayed, we would see more of an effect in the world. We know if we do pray, the effects from it would be a positive one. We need God to continue to give us an increase in our prayer life not just for our benefit, but for the future of our children and their children. Children are the future of this world and we want them to be able to have a chance to have a decent life. Through prayer, they will be strengthened and they will realize whatever decision they would have to make, they can go to God and ask Him to help them and He would help them.

We thank God for His kindness and His mercy on the sixth day. Six is the number of man and that is not always a good thing. Because in the examples that have been given in the Bible, I have looked up the significance of the number six and I have come to find out it points to the failure of man. How societies have built up and have become confident in knowledge in their ways and when there was a great fall, they had to turn to God. Think back to Moses. God wanted to help Moses' mind to be more spiritual. In case you didn't know, Moses was a man with a bad temper, a very bad temper. His temper caused him to kill someone. When you made Moses angry, he got upset, So, maybe that was one of the reasons why God had to wait until six days before bringing Moses into His **PRESENCE**.

God has blessed us these six days, but the seventh day, the day of completion, we can actually say, "Thank God for one whole week of this and being alive! One whole week of prayer and one whole week of a better life, yes a better life!" In our lives, we have gone through trials and tribulations, like last year, but we made it through. We cannot go back and relive the past, good or bad. On our sixth day, by faith, we spoke a better life and we believed God to bless us to have a wonderful celebration!

In Psalms 51 David ask God for forgiveness, to give him his joy back and to hide his face from sin and purge him. I hope and pray as we grow as a church, and as kingdom citizens, we never get to the point where we feel like we don't have to ask God to forgive us anymore. Every day we should ask God to forgive us of our sins. Jesus even said, "Forgive us of our trespasses as we forgive those who trespass against us."

We leave with great expectations waiting for something unbelievable to happen tomorrow night. Something words Cannot describe: some miracle, some deliverance, some prayer being answered, some yoke being destroyed. Something we have been praying for six days. We are going to ask God for some grapes. We want God to do something within theses 40 days that will be great! Something we will never forget! Something that will blow our minds that even after the 40 days of prayer we will be so encouraged and our faith increased to the max that anything we go through this year, the Lord can handle or do!

Opening Scripture: Psalm 51 (KJV)

"Have mercy upon me, O God according to thy loving-kindness; according unto the multitude of thy tender mercies blot out my transgressions. Wash me [thoroughly] from mine iniquity, and cleanse me from my sin. For I acknowledge my transgressions, and my sin is ever

*before me. Against thee, thee only, have I sinned, and done this evil in thy sight, that thou mightest be justified when thou speakest, and be clear when thou judgest. Behold, I was shaped in iniquity, and in sin did my mother conceive me. Behold, thou desirest truth in the inward parts, and in the hidden part thou shalt make me know wisdom. Purge me with hyssop, and I shall be clean; wash me, and I shall be whiter than snow. Make me hear joy and gladness, that the bones which thou hast broken may rejoice. Hide thy face from my sins, and blot out all mine iniquities. Create in me a clean heart, O God, and renew a right spirit within me. Cast me not away from thy **PRESENCE**, and take not thy Holy Spirit from me. Restore unto me the joy of thy salvation, and uphold me with a [willing] spirit. Then will I teach transgressors thy ways, and sinners shall be converted unto thee. Deliver me from bloodguiltiness, O God, thou God of my salvation, and my tongue shall sing aloud of thy righteousness. O Lord, open thou my lips, and my mouth shall show forth thy praise. For thou desirest not sacrifice, else would I give it; thou delightest not in burnt offering. The sacrifices of God are a broken spirit; a broken and a contrite heart, O God, thou wilt not despise. Do good in thy good pleasure unto Zion; build thou the walls of Jerusalem. Then shalt thou be pleased with the sacrifices of righteousness, with burnt offering and whole burnt offering; then shall they offer bullocks upon thine altar."*

Insight As We Prepared For Prayer:

Thank God for the reading of the Scripture and we prayed the Lord heard us as we included this prayer of David in our prayer. I have no doubt that God will forgive us of our sins. Once we realize and know God forgives us of our sins, washes us and cleanses us and gives us His Holy Spirit, the Scripture says, "After that then we can teach transgressors thy ways (God's ways) and sinners shall be converted unto thee."

Once we are converted, Temple of Prayer members were to invite seven souls a week for the rest of this year with the expectation they will come and not only join the church, but will be converted, saved and become a part of the Body of Christ. We will not let our past hinder our future. We will not be ashamed. We will be a witness for Christ, be able to relate to people after reading these Scriptures, and

A Call Into His Presence

not judge them. A person can say, "I am struggling with this" and we can say, "I struggled with something and God forgave me, saved me and delivered me." That is a whole lot better than, "You are going to hell and I am better than you." We cannot have that type of attitude but go way out of our way to let people know, yes we are saved and maybe they are not saved, but all of us are human and God sent Jesus for every human being.

Anyone who asks God for forgiveness, and means it from their heart, God will forgive them. We can be a living example for them. Tell people, "I was pretty bad (you don't have to go into details) and wasn't exactly the best human being on the planet but I am still working on it. I have given my life to Christ and I am saved." I have been convinced, and I believe without a shadow of a doubt no one can convince me no other way, that if I die I am going to heaven because God promised me that. He said, "If any man believed that Jesus Christ, He is the Savior and ask God to forgive them of their sins, they would be saved," and that means we get to go to heaven!

We had many things we were praying for... a whole list. In fact, we couldn't wait to get to the next list, but the first thing on the list should always be, I want my life to please God and I want to go to heaven. That's why we go to church to learn more about God. We say we want to be in the place where there is no more suffering, no more bills, no more stress, no more headaches, no more jobs, no more paying car insurance, and no more of those kinds of things. Wow, heaven is going to be great! We have peace because of the investment we made here on this earth. We have invested our greatest treasure, which is our Souls in the Bank of Eternity called Heaven, just by giving our lives to Christ! Why not today if you haven't made that investment? Think about this, if people can go out and share information with people about all kinds of ways to make money, then why can we not share information about how to make the best investment a human being could ever make by giving their lives to Christ? We are asking God to have mercy upon them according to His loving kindness, according to his tender mercies.

God will blot out and erase our past. The blood of Jesus gets rid of all sin. So when we pray, it leads us back to we don't have to have a guilty conscience in our prayers. Because we ask God to forgive us every time we pray, we ask God to forgive us and we are good to go! Now that is comfort, which is a stress reliever that helps me to wait a little bit longer when I am saying to myself, "I cannot wait any longer, God. I need an answer now." I may need an answer now but I know I can wait just a little bit longer because I know the biggest concern I should have is if my sins are forgiven, and if the answer is yes, then I can wait. I can wait. It might be a little tense but I can wait because if all else fails and I lose my life, I won't lose my eternal life because Paul said, "If you lose your life you gain it." Therefore, if I lose my life waiting on God, He just gave me eternal life quicker than I thought I was going to get it. Either way we get the victory! Let us praise God for life everlasting!

Let Us Pray: Singing "I need Thee"

Let us go to God in prayer thanking him for having mercy on us and asking God on this sixth day to give us an anointing as we invite seven souls a week who will not only come to church, but they will be converted from a sinner to a Saint!

Hallelujah, bless Your Name, You are worthy of the praise, You are worthy of the praise! Lord, oh, God, we thank You for this sixth day; we thank You for this sixth day! We thank You, God, You have kept us alive six days of this year. People have died between yesterday's prayer and today, God, and You have been kind to us. There is someone who is sick today who was well on yesterday, God, who was rushed to the emergency room, but You have been kind to us. We have come, God, on this day, the sixth day, the day You created man. The sixth day, God, the number of man. The history of man has not been good, God. When things have gone well we begin to rely on our own wisdom and strength. Our own ideology, our own way of thinking and we have turned from You historically. Even on today, this sixth day, we pray that history does not repeat itself in our lives. We come before Your **PRESENCE,** God, with a very humble mind and humble Spirit on this night. You have been mighty in this place. God, Your glory has been revealed in our hearts and minds.

On tonight, God, we ask You would extend Your mercy to each and every one of us in this room and to our families, to this church family, to the Body of Christ, everybody who is crying out for Your mercy on today. Extend Your mercy toward us in a way David asked according to Thy tender mercy and Your loving kindness. Blot out all of our transgression. Forgive us of all of our sins. Forgive us for the disobedience, which took place on last year. We thank You, God, for forgiving us and letting us know sin cannot follow us over into this year. We thank, God, we thank You, Lord God, for a renewed mind and spirit to be obedient to Your Word this year. We thank You, God, for letting us hear the call to come to pray. We thank You for even giving us a mind to repent and ask for forgiveness of our sins, God, because there are many in this world who feel what they are doing is not wrong and they are not asking for forgiveness. They don't even believe in You, God, to know to ask for forgiveness, but You promised us, Lord, if we would just believe on Jesus and repent of our sins, we would be saved.

You loved this world so much, You gave Your only begotten Son and we believe. Therefore, God, not only do we pray, but we ask You wash us. Wash us with hyssop and renew in us a right spirit. Create in us a clean heart that we might be able to teach, not so much in a lesson or sermon, but just by the words, we share of encouragement in our prayers and in the life, we live before our families and people in our circles, God. They would see Christ in us, and we would be able to lead them to Christ and lead them to salvation. Allow them the opportunity to share in eternal life that You have for everyone who comes before Your throne asking for forgiveness and accepting Jesus as Savior.

We pray a very desperate and humble prayer on this night, God, because we believe You will allow us to live to see tomorrow. Tomorrow is going to be a great day, not just, because it's going to be another day of life, but because it is the seventh day! Lord God, something unusual about the seventh day falling on a Sunday, God. The seventh day, being the actual seventh day of prayer, believing in what the Word teaches us about the number seven being a perfect number; a number of completeness, God. We completed one week, if we live to see tomorrow for this year, we want this first week, to be a part of what we are sowing into our own future. God, this year, this week has gone by and already we have had some hard times and some up's and down's, but You have blessed us, God, to make it through. Lord, if You blessed us this week, then we know You will bless us for the rest of this year. We make that statement by faith and we believe it to be done in Jesus Name.

We ask now, God, self-examination take place and we look within our hearts and within our souls and examine ourselves by Your Word through the Spirit. If there are any areas, God, which have hidden iniquity somewhere deep, rooted seeded somewhere that we really don't want to face or deal with, we ask now, that You would open up our eyes to the sins in our own lives. Open our eyes to the weights and things that are holding us back. It might not be a sin, but You said, "Lay aside every weight and sin that so easily beset us and run this race with patience." We thank You, God, for the patience we have learned from all the trials and tribulations we have gone through.

We ask, God, for a time of resting, a sabbatical time, Lord God, of not having to go through any more trials and tribulations for a period. We a for a time where we can build our spirits up, where we can build our bodies up, where we can build our homes up, where we can build our finances up, where we can build our joy up, where we can build our services to You up. Give us an opportunity to build our momentum up in this year, God; we know if we live, there are many storms that are going to be waiting. We ask now You let the storms stop now, God, and give us a time during these 40 days of prayer to build up our faith, God, to build up our prayer life. Give us a time to build up our joy, spiritual positive thinking, knowing we can do all things through Christ not through ourselves, not because we come out to prayer, but all things through Christ that strengthen us. We are trying our very best to live according to Your Word, God.

You said to examine ourselves and Paul said we die daily. God, everyday, we have to examine ourselves and ask that self be crucified the more so we can become more like the image of Christ, our Lord and Savior. God, we are practicing this ministry as Paul also said we are practicing because one day we will be just like Christ, literally, God, our bodies will be just like He is. We will be in heaven, we will be able to sit and sing and be in front of our God. We will be able to be with all the rest of the Angels and Heavenly Host and all the Saints who have died before us, God, and the Saints who will come after us, we will all be able to be together and worship You around Your throne. We are practicing for those days now, here on this earth and, God.

We want to be encouraged that if You have given us to invite 7 souls, it is nothing more than being obedient to the Scriptures to go out to the world to compel men and women to come to Christ. Time is running out, Lord God, time is running out in this world. We do not know when the Savior will come back and rapture the Church, God. We don't know, it can be today, a few hours from now, it can be this year, we don't know, God, but we want to be ready when Jesus comes! We want to be ready, God, we want to be ready. We don't want to have any sin hidden in our hearts, God, Hallelujah, Hallelujah and, God, we are not ashamed to call unto You and say, "Lord, forgive us." We are not ashamed to call on You and say, "Lord, help us!" We are not ashamed to call on You and say, "Make us like Thy Son." We are not ashamed to say, "The perfect One is inside of us; we can not only hear the great call, but we do the great call!"

We can be great soul winners for Jesus this year, God, we really, Lord Jesus, just want to be obedient. We want to be obedient, God. We want You to fill this church up where there is no room, God, Hallelujah! We want You to fill this church up with people who will have the same mind to pray one for another. We want people to come into this place not with a big attitude that they are great, but they will come in with the same attitude we have on this year, Lord God, without You we are nothing and we need You. God, everyone we come in contact will know whatever we have and whatever we have been blessed with, it has been because You have been kind and extended Your mercy into our lives and we are grateful.

In that Psalms, David said, "He would give You praise and he would thank You for forgiving him." He would thank You, God, for using him. He would thank You, God, for giving him another chance. We want to praise You and thank You on this sixth day for giving us another chance this year and for keeping us alive, God. For making a way for us, God, even though the way might seem dark. It might seem cloudy, it might seem dreary but we know if the S-O-N is anywhere around, we know, God, deliverance must take place! Therefore, God, it is imperative and important, every day we pray a prayer of forgiveness so there will be nothing in the way that will stop You from blessing us. Nothing in the way that will stop You from filling our souls more with Your glory and giving us a revelation on how to win souls and a revelation on how to live a victorious life! God, give us a revelation on healing and deliverance, a revelation on salvation, a revelation on peace in our minds, God, Hallelujah!

If You have forgiven us of our sins, then we know the Bible says, "You are faithful and just to forgive us and cleans us from all unrighteousness." If that Word is true, God, then there is no reason why we should be worrying about anything on this earth God because what is greater than salvation? What should be more important to us than our souls and going to heaven? That's the most important thing, God, and You have already made a way so we look to You by faith! God, we don't know how You are going to do it. We don't know how You are going to help us. We cannot understand how You forgive us. Your love and mercy cannot be explained. We cannot understand how You washed us and purged us and cleaned us up. We just receive it by faith it has been done in Jesus Name. You have washed us in the Blood of the Lamb! We are clean. We are the righteousness of God, we are pure, we are sanctified in our minds. We are growing, we are not shrinking, God, but our Spirit Man is striving to please You. Our desires to serve You are increasing, God; we are walking by faith and not by sight. We know it is impossible to please You without faith so they that come to You must first believe that You are God and You are a rewarder of them that diligently seek You.

We are seeking You during this sixth day of these 40 days, if You bless us to live; we are going to seek You the more every day. Even if we live after 40 days, we're going to continue to seek You. The testimonies in this church have gone forth and the prayer request. Open up our ear that we can hear You! Open up our eyes that we can see You! Open up our understanding that we can receive Your revelations! Remove disobedience, and fear and doubt, God, so that we will be bold through the power of the Holy Ghost to do whatever You command us to do on this year. Let us receive the love, God, You have given and shared with us. Let us know we have not received Your love by our works, God, but by being obedient and giving our best efforts every day. I don't care how hard the Devil kicks us, every day is a day of thanksgiving! Every day is a day of thanksgiving and we are going to praise You for forgiveness! We are going to praise You for making us whole! We are going to praise You for giving us a fresh start. We are going to praise You for salvation, God; we are going to praise You for the Holy Ghost! We are going to praise You for filling us. You are going to praise You.

Lord, I believe You are going to baptize some people, God, even during these 40 days. God, You are going to refill during these 40 days, God, and we are going to thank You for the wisdom, which comes through the Holy Ghost that we won't make the same mistakes we made last year! This is a new day! This is a new era! This is a new dawning, the light of God be shined on our countenance as David said in Psalms and let Your favor compass us about as a shield. Hallelujah, bless Him, bless Him, bless Him!

We thank You, God, because You answered the prayer! We thank You because there are prayer requests like David, whatever You do, whatever the punishment might be, do not take Your Holy Spirit away from us! We need the Spirit of God, we need the Holy Ghost! We cannot make it without Your leadership inside of us. The Comforter inside of us, the Guider inside of us, the Revelator inside of us! The Eliminator inside of us, the Empowered inside of us, we need dunamis power! Dynamite power exposed in our souls!

With compassion exposed in our souls with long-suffering and mercy, God, and kindness as we encounter people every day, we will let them feel the explosion of love. The explosion of compassion, the explosion of kindness we are not on this earth to judge! We are not on this earth to be critical and criticize people. We are not on this earth to be negative. Let us live that we can share the Gospel of Jesus Christ! This church is saying thank You for letting us be sharers! Thank You for letting us be witnesses. Thank You for the light, which has been revealed in our souls! We are the light of the World, Hallelujah, bless You, bless You, bless You, bless You, bless His Holy Name!!!

God, I don't know what You are going to do, but 40 hours are counting down, it's going to end on tomorrow, God, and somebody is going to receive a miracle in this place on Sunday! On the seventh day, somebody is going to be delivered! Somebody is going to be set free! You are going to add to somebody's life! Somebody's household is going to be put back together. Somebody is going to get a better job. Money is going to come, healing and deliverance, peace, joy, happiness all in the Holy Ghost! Supernatural power is going to come inside somebody's life for 40 hours Hallelujah! The grapes of the Promise Land, Hallelujah, we give You the highest praise Hallelujah!

Thank You, Jesus, thank You, Jesus! Thank You, Jesus, thank You, Jesus, thank You, Jesus, wonderful Savior! We praise You, we exalt You! We lift You up, we give You the glory! We worship You in the beauty of holiness! With outstretched arms, we give You a wave offering, Hallelujah, Hallelujah, and in our wave, God, we are trying to get Your attention that You would stop by every individual and pour out some more of Your mercy! Pour out some more of Your goodness! Pour out some more of Your glory! Pour out some more of Your love! Pour out some more of Your power! Pour out some more of salvation! Pour out some more of deliverance! Pour out some more of Your Holy Ghost! Pour out some more of Your fresh rain! Pour out some more of Your anointing, Hallelujah! Anoint us to be vessels of praise that we would praise You on tomorrow! We will praise You in the midnight of tonight! We will praise You in the wee hours of the morning! We will praise You all day because You are worthy! You are worthy, worthy, worthy of all the praise! Thank You, Jesus, thank You, Jesus, thank You, Jesus, thank You, Jesus, thank You, Jesus, thank You, Jesus, thank You for a new dimension, Hallelujah! Thank You for higher heights and deeper depths! Thank You for Your **PRESENCE** inside of this place, Hallelujah! Thank You for Your Angels protecting our loved ones! Thank You for watching over us all night long, bless Him, bless Him, bless Him, bless Him, bless Him. Will You bless the Lord?! Will You bless Him, Hallelujah!!! Thank You for another mind, thank You for another Spirit, thank You for another people because we are no longer the same, Hallelujah. We are not the same, we are new like a new year, because we are in the New Year. We are in the newness of God, a new experience, a greater experience! Hallelujah, as we give a new commitment, a greater commitment to serve You, to live for You, yea, God, yeaaaaaaaa, God!

Now we give You the praise the glory and honor. Thank You for forgiving us and cleansing us while our consciences are clear. No one, not even the Devil himself, who is the accuser of the brethren, can accuse us of anything because the Blood of Jesus covers us everywhere, all over, Hallelujah. We expect miracles by faith and we expect it to be done in Jesus Name and the people of God say, "Lord I thank You for Your mercy." Give Him some praise in this place! Give God some praise in this place! Give God some praise in this place! Hallelujah, for He is worthy of the praise!

Closing Scripture: Psalms 106:1-12 (KJV)

"PRAISE ye the Lord. Oh give thanks unto the Lord, for he is good; for his mercy endureth forever. Who can utter the mighty acts of the Lord? Who can show forth all his praise? Blessed are they that [observe justice], and he that doeth righteousness at all times. Remember me, O Lord, with the favor that thou bearest unto thy people; oh, visit me with thy salvation, That I may see the good of thy chosen, that I may rejoice in the gladness of they nation, that I may glory with thine inheritance. We have sinned with our fathers, we have committed iniquity, we have done wickedly. Our fathers understood not thy wonders in Egypt; they remembered not the multitude of thy mercies, but provoked him at the sea, even at the Red Sea. Nevertheless, he saved them for his name's sake, that he might make his mighty power to be known. He rebuked the Red Sea also, and it was dried up; so he led them through the depths, as through the wilderness. And he saved them from the hand of him that hated them, and redeemed them from the hand of the enemy. And the waters covered their enemies; there was not one of them left. Then believed they his words; they sang his praise."

Closing Remarks:

Thank God for these encouraging Scriptures. We are not going to forget. We are going to remember what God has done, and we are going to sing His praise. What an encouraging Scripture. God saved Israel for His name's sake and for His power to be known, and God got rid of all of their enemies. God is going to save us for His name's sake and He is going to get rid of all our enemies! He is going to do something so great for us if we believe His Word. Amen!

END OF DAY 6 PRAYER SERVICE

STEP 7/DAY 7, SUNDAY

"God's Prefect Number"

DAY 7 PRAYER SERVICE BEGINS

Opening Remarks:

The Lord has blessed us to come out for seven days. Seven days of this year we have come to prayer and God is worthy of the praise. Isn't it a wonderful thing when we give God all the praise and glory knowing He is the life giver, health provider and the strength maker! Where would we be without him? What would we do without him?

Our Scripture Psalm 7, is a very powerful Psalm, especially with what God is going to deal with us on this seventh night. We are spiritually energized believing God to bless us, and asking God to do this Scripture for us and to keep on doing this Scripture for us and it will be a great, great testimony.

Opening Scripture: Psalms 7 (KJV)

"O Lord my God, in thee do I put my trust; save me from all those who persecute me, and deliver me, Lest he tear my soul like a lion, rending it in pieces, while there is none to deliver. O Lord my God, if I have done this, if there be iniquity in my hands, If I have rewarded evil unto him who was at peace with me (yea, I have delivered him who without cause is mine enemy), Let the enemy persecute my soul, and take it; yea, let him tread down my life upon the earth, and lay

mine honor in the dust. Arise, O Lord, in thine anger; lift up thyself because of the rage of mine enemies: and awake for me to the judgment that thou hast commanded. 7. So shall the congregation of the peoples compass thee about; for their sakes, therefore, return thou on high. The Lord shall judge the peoples; judge me, O Lord, according to my righteousness, and according to mine integrity that is in me. Oh, let the wickedness of the wicked come to an end, but establish the just; for the righteous God [testeth] the [minds and hearts]. My defense is with God, who saveth the upright in heart. God judgeth the righteous, and God is angry with the wicked every day. If he turn not, he will whet his sword; he hath bent his bow, and made it ready. He hath also prepared for him the instruments of death; he ordaineth his arrows against the persecutors. Behold, he travaileth with iniquity, and hath conceived mischief, and brought forth falsehood. He made a pit, and digged it, and is fallen into the ditch which he made. His mischief shall return upon his own head, and his violent dealing shall come down upon his own pate. I will praise the Lord according to his righteousness, and will sing praise to the name of the Lord most high."

Insight As We Prepared For Prayer:

This is a wonderful Psalms especially when you feel like your enemies, and people are against you, and life is giving you a hard time. This is a wonderful Psalm to read especially in that tenth verse, "My defense is with God, who saveth the upright in heart." Who is our defense? It is God, who can protect us? It is God, who is going to fight for us. It is God. Even if God instructs us to stand up and be strong, we are not standing in our own strength; we are standing in God's strength. Let us be encouraged on this seventh day as we go into prayer believing God for something miraculous to take place even on this night in this place. I don't know where your prayer and concerns might be but you might have someone in Iraq or you can have someone in California who you are praying for, but God is powerful enough that he can send his deliverance anywhere around the world.

Let Us Pray:
Let us go to God in prayer believing that God is our defense. He is going to help us, he is going to strengthen us, he is going to continue to save us if we put our trust in him.

Hallelujah, thank You, God, thank You, Lord, for this seventh day of prayer. Thank You God for letting us come seven days. The seventh day of this year, You have blessed us to make it for this number. God, we ask now as we come to Thee with a prayer David wrote. We ask, Lord God, as we have put our trust in You, that You would save us from our enemies. Save us, God, from those who mean us no good. Save us from those, God, who are trying desperately to put an end to the dream You have given us; to try to stop us from achieving a goal You have set before us. You have given us a mission to move forward and we have said yes in our souls we will move forward as a church. As families within the church, God, as individuals, God, we are saying yes we are going to move forward.

We need Your help, Lord; we need Your help on tonight. We need Your strength, we need Your guidance, we need Your wisdom, and we need deliverance in our minds, God, that all fear will be removed. Any doubt would be removed and we put our confidence solely in Thee. God, we ask now this would be a time of resting from fear. Not a time of resting from work, but times of resting from fear. A time of ease from our sorrows, trials and tribulations, the hurts and bruises which come along with just being alive, Lord God. We are not complaining and we are not asking You make everything so easy and wonderful we never have a struggle in life, but we are asking, God, You strengthen us for every struggle. That no struggle would overcome us, God, but we would overcome any area of struggle in our lives. Help us now we pray, Lord, help us now we pray in the Name of Jesus, to have a mind of an over comer.

God, we need Your help. We are saying we are willing to work, but we need Your help spiritually, Lord God, to fight these battles. We put our trust in Thee. Everyone who has dug a ditch, let them fall into their own ditch according to this Scripture in Psalms 7. Lord God, make a way of protection for Your people for we trust You, God, and we have placed our lives in Your hands. We need You, God, even on this day of prayer, we are saying in our prayers we need You, and we also are making a declaration we are not going to say it just for today. We are not going to say it for these 40 days. We made a declaration in our souls every day we live, we wake up, we will admit, we will verbalize, we will think about it, we will mediate on the fact we need You and we want You, God. We love You, God. We want to serve You. We want to please You. We want to learn more about You. We want to be used by You. We want You to have Your way in our lives. We want to be healed. We want to be delivered. We want to be used so others can be healed and delivered. We want to share the power which comes through the love of Christ. The power of the Holy Ghost with any and everyone who is willing, God, who is willing to give us a few moments of their time, to let them know there is a better way for living, and that way comes through Jesus the Savior.

We ask now You honor the Scripture as it has been written in the seventh Psalms, Lord God, as we continue on in this service, continue on in these prayers for these next 40 days. Oh, God, we have thirty-three days left if You allow us to live and within that time, God, we believe You are going to do something great! You are going to finalize some things, God, which has been left open in our minds. You are going to finalize some things, God, we have been thinking about for years but never had the faith or boldness to step out and make it a reality. As You give us instructions on what to do, how to do, when to do it, where to do it, how to go and come among people, God, as if we have been educated at that level all along. God, You are going to give us the wisdom on how to be around people who have a whole lot more than what we have at this particular time from a materialistic stand point. Maybe from an educational standpoint, even in a spiritual standpoint, God, we want to be around people who will sow seeds into us, God, which can flourish into a great harvest. Then we want to take those seeds and sow into others so they can flourish into a great harvest.

God, we just want to be a part of the Kingdom building, which is going on here on this earth. Help us, God, as we have consecrated ourselves for these six days and on the seventh day, You called Moses into Thine **PRESENCE**. God, You called us and have allowed us to go into Thy **PRESENCE** on this seventh day.

And after Moses came off the mount, he had instructions on what the people were to do and how they were to govern their lives. God, as we come out of this seventh day of prayer, we ask for instructions, which will govern us on what to do, how to go about, how to help families make it, and how to make it ourselves. We desire to know how to instruct others on how to love You, serve You, how to pray with a sincere heart, how to offer up the sacrificial praise, and how to get rid of everything that is junkie and messy. Everything that is not like You, God, we want You to clean our souls out, Hallelujah! We want to have room only for You. We want only the Holy Ghost to dwell inside of us. We don't want any other thing to dwell inside of us: no unclean thoughts, no unclean thoughts, no unclean thoughts, we bind it now!

We don't want sickness in our bodies, God. We speak health to the body, God. We don't want any sickness in our homes. Keep our children healthy, God. We want them alive and not dead. We bind death itself through the power that is in the Name of Jesus! We know man is appointed a time to die but, God, this is not our time we believe. Let us live for we have a mind to work! We want to work for You, Lord God. We want to work, we want to work, we really want to work, Give us an opportunity that people might see the glory of God, which dwells within our souls. The glory of God which dwells over our homes. The glory of God which dwells over this Ministry God. We can do great things through Christ that strengthens us, Hallelujah!

Bring about a separation, God. Let our enemies be made known before our very eyes, God, and separate them from us. Put a hedge of protection around us, God, so that they can't put their hands on us. We can't let their words be effective to cause us to cease, God, cause us to quit, cause us to be discouraged or depressed. We bind every attack of the enemy, every wayward word spoken against us, God. We curse it and speak against it! We speak life to everyone who speaks death to our situation. We don't receive the death sentence. We receive the sentence of life through the grace and mercy of our Lord and Savior Jesus Christ. Help us now, God, as we pour out of our souls! Help us to look to Thee to Thy throne in Heaven for our help. All of our help comes from You! Help us to look towards the hills, the Holy Mount of God. Help us now in the Name of Jesus to crucify the flesh!

Even on tonight, if there is tiredness in this place, if there is tiredness in the bodies and minds, if people have been weary in their souls, we speak the joy of the Lord to come now to be our strength. We speak the power of praise to take over as we offer You the high praise, God. Pour out Your anointing of strength inside of us that we can make it the rest of this week God! Pour out Your strength inside of us that we can make it the rest of this year. Pour Your strength inside of us that we can make it until it is time to step into eternity! Pour out Your strength inside of us that we will not faint and we will not be weary in well doing for the harvest is great, God, Hallelujah!

We want to partake in the harvest, Hallelujah. We will bless the Lord, oh, our souls, and all that is within us, bless His Holy Name! Will You bless His Holy Name on tonight? Thank You, Jesus. Thank You, Jesus. Thank You, Jesus. Thank You, Jesus!

Help us to focus our minds on Thee and the CALL You have made for us to come higher in our thoughts. Higher in our desires. Higher in our intentions to serve. You purify us, cleanse us with Thy Blood. Sanctify us the more, sanctify our lives, sanctify our thoughts, sanctify us in the Name of Jesus from the crown of our heads to the souls of our feet and then, God, pour out Your Spirit as You said in the last days You would pour of Your Spirit upon all flesh. Pour it out now in the Name of Jesus upon every Soul in this building! Upon every home represented, upon every member of this church, pour it out now, God, this we ask. We want to partake of Thy anointing on tonight, yea, God, Hallelujah! Pour it out in our Souls. Let the anointing destroy every yoke!

We come against the enemy, Satan, the Lord rebuke you. Satan, the Lord rebuke you. Satan, the Lord rebukes you in the Name of Jesus! Take your hands off our homes. Take your hands off our children. Take your hands off our loved ones. Take your hands off our stuff! Get your hands off now in the Name of Jesus, Hallelujah! We have consecrated ourselves. We are sacred and holy before God. We are God's sacrifice. You cannot defile the sacrifice of God. Take your hands off us! Take your hands off our minds, and thoughts. Take your hands off our mouths and lips! Get off our tongues. We will speak only good things! We will think only good things; we will do only good things in the Name of Jesus. The work we are doing is great!

We are not coming off the wall, we are going to pray!!! We are going to pray until the break through manifest! We are going to pray, we are going to pray until every demon leaves! We are going to pray until God's Will be done everywhere in this church, in every department, in every ministry! We are going to pray until this city knows this church is a praying church and the glory of God rests upon us!

Give God some praise in here, Hallelujah!!! Hallelujah, Hallelujah, Hallelujah! Now, God, I pray for super-natural strength. This prayer, God, as we give our Souls to Thee, it depletes us, wears us down, and the Devil might feel like he can attack while we are weak, but oh no, I call for the strength of Zion to come and flood our Souls! I call for the strength of the Holy Ghost to come now and anoint us to stand, Hallelujah! I call for the anointing of God to strengthen us in our prayer and in our praise, in our service, in our understanding, in our commitment, in our lives, in our homes, on our jobs, in school everywhere we go. Let us be strong in the power of His might.

Hallelujah, bless God, bless, You, my God! Bless You my Savior. We lift You up, Hallelujah! We give You the glory, all the glory belongs to the King of Kings! He is worthy, worthy is the Lamb of God. Give Him some glory in this place! If He is worthy, somebody cry out, "Hallelujah, Hallelujah, Hallelujah, Hallelujah!" Now, God, it is just that serious. We need Your help and instructions for this year as we now have entered into the second week for this year. We thank You for bringing us through the first week. You have kept us alive. You have allowed us to make it back to the house of prayer. Now, God, we pray even during this service You will still bring strong deliverance, oh, by the faith, the people of God would put their trust in You. We are not trusting in Potentates, Princes, Kings or Queens. Presidents, Senators or Governors, we are trusting in Thee.

Make a way for the people, God, for we are Your people, for Your Name sake. Even though, God, You gave a sentence of wonderment, they had to wander for 40 years. You still fed them, You still provided for them, You still kept them alive and healed their bodies and You did not allow any other Nation to make them slaves. You let them be rich and prosperous in the wilderness. We pray now, God, we don't want to be in the wilderness. We want Your prosperity to be upon us because of Your mercy and our willingness to be obedient to the call to come up higher. If anyone is in the wilderness, God, I pray for Your mercy that You would sustain them, give them a mind to ask for forgiveness, restore them, and they would hear the call and obey the call to come up higher to see You.

The King has called and we are going to see the King, in Jesus Name. We have prayed these prayers for this seventh day thanking You for allowing us to come to call upon Thee. Now, as we transition, we ask, God, You would move in this place. Saturate this place with Your **PRESENCE** as this Earth has been saturated with the rain. Let an abundance of deliverance, healing, joy, regeneration, restoration take place in this physical building. Let it be so powerful and strong, that people's lives would forever change and be strengthened as our God visited us on this seventh day. We have prayed these prayers by faith. We have offered up the sacrifices of prayer and praise. Bless everything, which takes place. Let it be done to Thy glory, You might receive the praise and honor that Your people would be strengthened and encouraged to know their God, the God of the Bible, Abraham, Isaac and Jacob still lives. Hallelujah, in Jesus Name, we have prayed this prayer. Be it done now. Amen and Amen.

Closing Scripture: Psalms 145 (KJV)

"All thy works shall praise thee, O Lord; and thy saints shall bless thee. They shall speak of the glory of thy kingdom, and talk of thy power, to make known to the sons of men his mighty acts, and the glorious majesty of his kingdom. They kingdom is an everlasting kingdom, and thy dominion endureth throughout all generations. The Lord upholdeth all that fall, and raiseth up all those who are bowed down. The eyes of all wait upon thee; and thou givest them their [food] in due season. Thou openest thine hand, and satisfiest the desire of every living thing. The Lord is righteous in all his ways, and holy in all his works. The Lord is [near] unto all those who call

upon him, to all who call upon him in truth. He will fulfill the desire of those who fear him; he also will hear their cry, and will save them. The Lord preserveth all those who love him, but all the wicked will he destroy. My mouth shall speak the praise of the Lord; and let all flesh bless his holy name forever and ever."

END OF DAY 7 PRAYER SERVICE

Personal Note:
This concludes our first week of prayer. I will never forget this day where I was lost in God; lost in the praise! I went to a place in praise I have never been before! I love you Lord! I'm not going to stop praising you, never! Thank you, God, for fattening my soul!

Pastor stated "God has given us a better life; an upgrade." You did not sign up in God's army to be kicked out or for people to like you. You are here to do the Will of God. You will stay on the wall of prayer and faith. People want to do great things for God. However, are they willing to do what it takes to be great?

Lord, give us a mind to do some work! Give us a blessed mind, a healthy mind, a godly mind, a mind like Jesus! Can you imagine thinking like Jesus did, processing information or life situations as He would? Wow what a fruitful life you would have! What good choices and decisions you would make! Philippians 2:5 says, "Let this mind be in you, which was also in Christ Jesus." God, I want that mind!

Our scripture reading came from Psalms 7:1-17 and Nehemiah 4:6 – "So built we the wall; and all the wall was joined together unto the half thereof: for the people had a mind to work."

Have a mind to work. Work to build the wall of prayer. Just like the enemy in the scriptures, Satan is our enemy and he hates it when we pray. He knows there is power in prayer!

Sanballat in these scriptures represents every negative person. Do you have someone negative in your life who is trying to stop you from building your wall of life?

~ Evelyn

**LEARN TO FIGHT FOR WHAT YOU BELIEVE!
START TODAY BY BUILDING YOUR WALL
OF PRAYER & FAITH!**

STEP 8/DAY 8, MONDAY

"New Beginning & Resurrection"

Personal Note:

Today's prayer is an inclusive prayer not just for the Temple of Prayer in general, but for everyone. On this day, we included eight hours for eight days of fasting. Eight is the number for new beginnings. You should ask for a new beginning, a new mind, new direction and instructions. None of us wants to error; we want to please God in everything. We understand we will have an assured guarantee with successful results in life if we do it God's way and follow His instructions. It is just that serious.

    As we travel up this mountain, we do not need any extra weights. The flesh is heavy! Fasting crucifies the flesh! Fasting and praying is a great combination to spiritual success. Pastor teaches we can pray without fasting, but we cannot fast without praying. On this second day, we take our second step up the mountain and we want to reach heaven! As we take this journey, we ask God to give us the strength and fortitude to climb this mountain into the "Holy of Holies."

~ Evelyn

DAY 8 PRAYER SERVICE BEGINS

Opening Remarks:

    We first reflect on a young girl who was set on fire by her stepfather. She was found with no clothing. God has been kind to keep our

A Call Into His Presence

minds, to keep our children safe, and we will pray God continues to do so. People are being found dead. These things could be right at our doors, but God has been kind. We pray not only in these 40 days but we should always pray for God to keep our family and loved ones safe.

Another young lady was raped and car jacked by several young men and this happened in our city. The reason I placed these things before you, is because we travel these areas and we pray God would not just protect our young girls, but our older ladies also. We do things with wisdom. Ladies should not travel alone and out late in stores. Unless it is an emergency, wait until the morning because you can't trust people anymore like it use to be able to. It is better to wise than to be than sorry.

When God speaks to us, when we say, "Something told me," or something tells you don't go, then don't go. Something tells you don't park there, then don't park there. Maybe go to another store, but follow the Lord's leading because the ending result is a better one than the one of disobedience. With disobedience comes consequences and sometimes the consequences are extremely hurtful.

These are just a few things to remind us why we are praying. We are praying and asking God for His protection, praying God would have mercy on us. Praying for our children, our loved ones and that You would keep us alive and let us enjoy the year. Let this not be a year of sorrow and sadness, but let this be a year of joy and excitement. We are not old. We still have a long life ahead of us and we want to enjoy it. We want to try and prepare a way for our families that they could have a better life than we are having right now and that is kind of hard to do if we are dead. If we are alive, we can work toward making it easy for our children because we believe by faith, at some point in time, our children will wake up just like we did. We all spent a little time out in the wilderness, so to say, but God brought us back. He can do the same thing for our children, our loved ones and bring them back and then they

> There is truth in generational curses, but that does not have to be an ongoing thing when Jesus came and gave His life, shed His blood, got out of the grave which is a rebuke to every curse.

can have another chance to continue the establishment of success in the bloodline.

Yes, there is truth in generational curses, but that does not have to be an ongoing thing when Jesus came and gave His life, shed His blood, got out of the grave which is a rebuke to every curse. He took Himself and made Himself a curse for us. Therefore, our families don't have to suffer what we have suffered. We don't have to suffer what previous family members have suffered, if we go to God and ask God to help us and humble ourselves.

This is the eighth day which is a very symbolic day, a very significant day for this church because this is the eighth year of our Ministry. Eight is not only the number of new beginnings but a more important emphasis should be placed on eight as the number of resurrection. Resurrection means God has placed something in us that maybe has not been brought out yet. This is the year for those things to be brought out. Seven means not only completion but it means the completion of a cycle and we have gone through a progression of seven days of prayer. It was the same with the seven years of ministry—having gone through a process and the eighth year is now, the time for us to see some results. Eight days is a new beginning and resurrection. Therefore, our prayers should be more fervent than they were seven days ago. As we go into prayer tonight, we want to continue to believe God. This Scripture, Psalms 8, reminds us of God's love and of His glory.

Opening Scripture: Psalms 8 (KJV)
"O Lord, our Lord, how excellent is thy name In all the earth, who hast set thy glory above the heavens! Out of the mouth of babes and sucklings hast thou ordained strength because of thine enemies, that thou mightest still the enemy and the avenger. When I consider thy heavens, the work of thy fingers, the moon and the stars, which thou hast ordained, What is man, that thou art mindful of him? And the son of man, that thou visitest him? For thou hast made him a little lover than the angels, and hast crowned him with glory and honor. Thou madest him to have dominion over the works of thy hands; thou hast put all thins under his feet: All sheep and oxen, yea, and the beasts of the field, The fowl of the air, and the fish of the sea, and

whatsoever passeth through the paths of the seas. O Lord, our Lord, how excellent is thy name in all the earth!"

Insight As We Prepared For Prayer:
Who is man that thou are mindful of him? God did not have to create us but since He did, it shows not only that He loves us, but the fact He gave us dominion over everything in this earth. There is no way we should just allow the Devil to beat us up and take away what he wants to take away. We have a right to fight for what God has given us, and we fight for it through prayer. So when we pray, we are asking God for His help, His guidance and His wisdom and to let us know what to do in the real life situations we sometimes find ourselves facing. I just have to believe the Word of God and He is going to help us like He promised He would.

His Name is so excellent. His name is powerful; wonderful, it is better than any other Name. It is a Name which brings comfort; consolation. It's a Name, which brings about relief for any type of sorrowful situation. It is a Name that has power. Therefore, that encourages us anytime we pray, to use the Name of Jesus. As we use that Name, I don't care what is lying dormant, we can use that Name and bring it back to life, resurrecting it by using the Name of Jesus. We went into prayer believing God would answer us. He would resurrect some things the Devil has tried to kill and to destroy, but Jesus has come not only that we would experience the abundance of life but also that we would live!

Let Us Pray: Singing "O Sweet Wonder"
Oh, bless Your Name, God, Hallelujah, Jesus, Jesus, Hallelujah, Hallelujah, Hallelujah. Thank You, Lord, thank You, Lord, thank You, God and we bless Your Name on this eighth day of this year. We bless Your Name on the eighth day of life. Oh, God, we have so many things we are praying for, so many things we have asked You for, but, God, we want to tell You thank You for allowing us to pray. For giving us a mind to pray. We pray You strengthen us during this prayer, God, which we would continue to pray fervently, honestly, effectually, God, by being led by Your Spirit. We pray for

A Call Into His Presence

the strength, God, that after these 40 days we would continue with a praying Spirit for this year.

We are asked a question in the Scripture, "Who is man that thou are mindful of Him?" You have made us a little lower than the Angels and You have given us dominion over all the animals, and cattle, creeping and crawling things, things in the sea, the birds in the air, Your power, God, often times we do not use.

On tonight, we are here to use the authority You have given us in Jesus Name. God, Your Name is excellent; Your Name alone is worthy to be praised! Your Name alone has all power in it and we want to use that Name on tonight as we pray.

God, this year has been a short time, but we need Your help even on this eighth day, God, because many tragic things have happened as we just listed a few things. Many, many things have happened but during all of those things, You were kind enough to let those things pass by our homes, pass by our loved ones. You have spared our lives, You have kept us safe. You have provided shelter, food and clothes for us once again and we are grateful, God. Even as the weather begins to turn cold, God, we continue to pray for every family and every member of this church, Lord God. We ask that You would provide and let there be heat in our homes, Lord God, that no one would go cold or go without. We pray, Lord God, You would sustain every member of this church. All of the families, Lord God, that no one would be evicted or put out during these cold months, Lord God.

We pray for a mind, Lord God, a mind to give You praise and thanksgiving for what You bless us with every day and we would adhere to the scripture and not be concerned about tomorrow for today is the day You have given us life, tomorrow has not been promised to us. So, we pray, Lord God, a prayer of thanks for today and, God, we love You and we want to let You know we love You.

We need You, God; we need You more than we have ever needed You in the history of mankind. Not only are there rumors of wars, but there are wars already, which have taken place. This country is involved in so much and, God it is going to have an effect on our children and their children. Oh, God, we do not know what the future holds for us, but if the present is a dictator for how things will be, then, God, we are in trouble. Only, God, if You extend Your mercy toward this Nation and look down upon us and hear the prayers of the Saints all over the country who are praying and asking You, God, to spare this country from this disparaging times, God, from bad economic times, God. The rich are getting richer and the poor are getting poorer and there is no longer a middle class any more, God, it's called the working poor. We need Your help, God.

You provided for the children of Israel during famine times. You fed every family; You made provision during the hard times for them. God, we call on that same God of the Bible, the same God the scriptures say Your Name is so excellent because You are so excellent. We call upon Thy Excellency, Lord God, to smile down upon this church and spare us. Smile down upon the body of Christ everywhere and spare every Christian, God, who prays, cries and calls out to You for help, for mercy for their families, for their loved ones.

We need You, God, we need, You, we need, You, we need, You, we need, You, we need, You, and we need You, Lord! Oh, God, we need You. God we pray now, You would infuse us with Thy Spirit. Not just fill us, God, but let it permeate throughout like fire and the leading of our souls, God, we would be more like You. We would take on the image of Christ in our actions, God, willing to sacrifice ourselves for the benefit and gain of others, we would be willing, God, to do whatever it takes to win souls, to let people know times are changing and they are not changing for the better. Sooner or later, Jesus, the Savior, the Son of God, He is going to return and the world will no longer be the same.

God, we are asking now, You let us take part in the great revival to take place throughout this country, God, we want to share Christ with any and everyone who would give us the opportunity to let them know there is a better way of life; Jesus is that way. God, we believe now in the miraculous power which comes through Your Son's Name according to Your Scripture, two or three gathered together in Your Son's Name, and whosoever calls upon the Name of the Lord would be saved, and if we pray in Your Name to Your Father, You would answer whatever we ask. On tonight, God, prayer requests have been made known and we are praying, God, You look on the church, the pastor who is in trouble, look on the congregation during these times of emotional distress.

Look on my mother-in-law down in Florida and the Saints in Florida. We are praying for my mother who is in the nursing home. Help everyone, God, who is sick and afflicted, whether they are in a nursing home, hospital, at home or a jail cell. Help them, God, and let them experience Your miraculous healing power. God, You have the power of life and death in Your hands and You have given us a reasonable amount of power according to Your Scripture Proverbs 18:21 "Death and life lies in the power of the tongue." God, we speak life into their situations now, in the Name of Jesus.

God, we are just crazy enough, we are just foolish enough, according to the wisdom of men they would call it foolishness, but according to Your Bible, we are wise to call upon You in the time of trouble. Therefore, we call upon You in the time of trouble for signs and wonders, miracles to be wrought as You have done before in this congregation. We ask now, Lord God, as the young man lies in the coma, Lord God, we know You have the power to call him back wherever his soul might be laying, God, even if it is dormant inside of him. This is the eighth day, the day of resurrection! On this day, by the power that is in the Name of Jesus, I call for his soul to come active again inside of his body, God, the same way, God, you blessed our son. The doctors said he would not live. They said he would not survive. God, they told us to take him off life support, but we said, "No!" We had faith to believe and pray and to call upon Your Name and to pray all night, Lord God. Father, we know death and life lie in the power of the tongue, so therefore we speak life! We call upon Thee. What a great testimony it would be to go throughout this city, God, that Saints came together, prayed, called upon Your Name and called for his soul to come back! Activate his body, Lord God, and let there be no brain damage, let there be no damage that he would be blind or a vegetable. They said our son would be that way but he is not, Lord God, therefore I believe! If You say so, it will happen. I believe! God, if You say, "Yes, it will happen," I don't care what the doctors are saying, if You say, "Yes." We want to hear from You, God, we want You to speak to this situation. We want You to speak in this matter. We just don't know but we are calling upon Your Name, Jesus, Jesus, Jesus!

Help us now, God, help us now, help us now if there is any unbelief in this room, bind it and cast it out. If there is any unbelief in his mother's life, bind it and cast it out, God. Speak to her soul, speak to her mind and let her know this is not a one-time thing. This has to be a dedication for life to serve You, to live for You. Not just to come begging, asking and not willing to give her life, but to give her soul unto Thee, regardless of what the outcome.

We have to be like the three Hebrew boys, if we burn up, we burn up, but it is not because our God is not able to deliver. They didn't have an attitude, God, they didn't try to fight, they didn't try to break away but they were thrown into the fiery furnace knowing, knowing some kind of way You would move and, yes, You did! You sent Your Son down there in that fire with them, Lord God. You conditioned them for what they were about to go through and the fire did them no harm.

We pray now, Lord God, as we go through the fiery trials and tribulations of this year, You would condition us and prepare us. We are not asking You put the fire, out we are asking You condition us for the fire and You be in the fire with us. We don't want to be in any situation during this year, nor the rest of our lives, by ourselves. We want You to be in the situations with us. If You are in it with us, we know everything will be alright! If You are involved in a situation, we know everything will be alright. If You speak, God, we know everything will be alright!

In the Name of Jesus, we ask You would speak to the minds and bring revelations, God, bring revelation, bring revelation and let Thy glory be revealed in the minds. God, we need Your instruction for every home. I pray for every parent in every home, God, every home, You give them instruction, God, to resurrect that love that seems to be dead between their relationships and their families. God, let peace abide. Bring the peace back. Bring greater peace than ever before. God, bring a family atmosphere of joy, kindness, self sacrificing. God, let people not be selfish, but people self sacrificing, God, for the good of the family. God, let every family live! Let us live, God, that we might train and teach our children in a way that they should go according to Your Word. That we might bring them to the house hold of faith where they can be taught and learn everything You need for them to have in order to make it in this life.

For as parents, we won't always be alive to be here with our children. There is going to be a time of separation. There is going to be a time when they are going to have to make decisions on their own, God, but we want You to resurrect every Godly thing we have planted inside of them, God, that they would make the best decisions for their lives. They will not make the same mistakes we have made and they would raise their children to be good godly adults, God we pray that, be up standing men and women in the community, God, we pray that they be great career minded and professional people, Lord God, to be people of prosperity and not a race of poverty. I bind the crab mentality that runs throughout generations from bloodline to bloodline! I bind the addictive spirits, God, that have been running rampant in our families. I bind it now in the Name of Jesus! I bind every spirit of addiction. I don't care if its alcohol, crystal meth, crack and whatever it might be God I bind it now in the Name of Jesus and cast it out by the root!

God, I loose, I loose the clarity that comes through the Spirit of God. You clear out their soul, God, clean it out in the Name of Jesus and fill them with Your Spirit from on high, God. Give them a mind for success. I bind the mind of failure. I bind the mind of excuses. I bind the mind of mediocrity. Take the blinds off their eyes, God. We bind the curse over this city, the Spirit of confusion where people cannot see the truth. The truth is always in their face and they are not realizing or seeing it, God. According to Your Scripture, God, of having a zeal for knowledge and a zeal for power but never coming into the truth, God, we ask now, God, the truth be made known and the truth will make them free according to Your Spirit, God, according to the Word of God be it done now in the Name of Jesus.

We pray now for every church, God, which has not fallen down. Every church standing in their commitment to save souls, God, that commitment to go out to the hedges and highways and compel men and women, that commitment to go and pray for people, God, that commitment to stand for what the Bible says. There are churches, which are standing against society, and they are standing alone.

They have been isolated and attacked, God. As a small church, we don't experience that too much, but these larger churches are taking a stand against wrong, God, against same sex marriages, God, Hallelujah, they are being attacked! As a smaller church, all we can do is pray for their strength, God, and pray You would strengthen them, lead and guide them, God. Protect them God from the attack of this world, from the cruel things that would be said about them. The lies that will be told on them, God, the people who will try to set them up for failure, but I speak strength, I speak strength, I speak strength, I speak strength, God, I speak strength, God, Hallelujah!

I pray for the people who have fallen by the wayside, God, in this the day of resurrection. God, did we pray for a resurrection spirit in them? Raise them up once again, God. Give them the joy of salvation. Give them a love for You, God. Let them ask for forgiveness and repent from their hearts. God, empower them again. God, fill them with the Spirit of God once again. God, let them go out and teach people according Psalms 51. God, David said, "Don't take Your Spirit away from me. Create in me a clean heart, renew in me a right Spirit" then we will teach transgressors Your ways, God. Help us now in the Name of Jesus, as the church of God to stand everywhere all over this world to proclaim the Gospel! To proclaim the good news! To proclaim the time of deliverance is now, in the Name of Jesus and we give You glory and we give You praise! We give You honor! We give You thanksgiving for You are worthy! You are worthy, You are worthy!

We bind the attack of the enemy, which comes against this church, Hallelujah, from me down to the youngest child. We bind every spiritual attack, which comes against us, God. We are endeavoring to persevere to make supplications and prayers for all Saints everywhere, God; we are doing our best to stay on the wall of prayer. We desire to stay on the wall of faith, to stay on the wall of praise, and to stay on the wall of service, God, Hallelujah! God we don't want to come down. The devil is pulling at our feet. He is trying to get us to give up, but we refuse, God, and we are going to praise You in the midst of a famine time! We are going to praise You, God, we are going to give You praise for life itself! We are going to thank You for salvation! We are going to thank You for our families! We are going to thank You for our jobs! We are going to thank You for our homes! We are going to thank You for the very clothes on our backs! We are going to thank You for letting us eat today! We are going to give You praise we can see; we are not blind! We are going to thank You for two legs which still work; it might be arthritis in them, but we give You praise we can feel the pain! The paraplegic can't feel anything. We thank You, God, we thank You, God, we thank You, God, for basic life!

We thank You, God, for what You have done on this eighth day! We thank You, God, that murder has gone by our homes! We thank You, God, fire has not consumed our homes! We thank You, God, the molester has not reached our children. Hallelujah, bless Your Name, God, bless Your Name, God.

Satan, the Lord rebukes you! Satan, the Lord rebukes you. We will give God the praise! He is worthy of the praise. He is the sustainer of our lives! He is the Bishop of our souls! He is the King of Kings! He is the Lord or Lords! He is great I am! He is the Great Counselor! He is the magnificent Doctor! He is the best Lawyer! He is our Defense, according to the scripture on last night; God is our defense, Hallelujah! He is a very present help in the time of trouble!

God, we are in trouble in this Nation! We are in trouble in this city! We are in trouble in our homes, but free us from trouble! Give us rest! Give us victory over troubled times, Hallelujah, Hallelujah, bless His Name! I will bless the Lord! I will lift Him up! I will exalt His Name, His Name alone is worthy! His Name alone is worthy! Jesus is His Name and the Bibles says "Whosoever calls upon the Name of Jesus shall be saved!" We want to be saved out of our calamities! Touch our finances. The devil has attacked us but he will not get the victory! Let the latter be better than the beginning. Let the end bring glory and honor to our situations, in other words, victory come! Victory come, let victory come now in our souls! In our souls, let victory come now! Everywhere, everywhere we walk, everywhere we go, let victory proceed us! Let victory follow us! Let victory be in us, Hallelujah!

Thank You, Jesus, thank You, Jesus, thank You, Jesus, thank You, Jesus. Wonderful is our God, mighty is He! Great is our God and greatly to be praised! He is excellent! He is our majesty! He is God and there is none other! We lift Him up higher, higher, higher above our problems! We lift Him up above our logic! We lift Him up above every attack of the enemy! We lift Him up over our flesh! We lift Him up over our trials and tribulations! We lift Him up over our failures! We lift Him up over the advice of men and women! We put God first! We put Him first, He is God, yes, Hallelujah, bless His Name! Let Your anointing destroy every yoke. Let Your anointing destroy every yoke, let the power of the Holy Ghost flood this place, Hallelujah!

As we give You glory and we give You the praise, as we lift Your Son's Name up out of our souls! Out of your belly, praise Him and let the rivers of living waters flow out of your soul. Will you give Him praise?! Will You reach down inside and step out of your comfort zone? You want God to do something out of the box but you won't step out of your own box! You got to step out of the box to get what you want out of the box. Oh, give Him the glory, give Him the glory!!! Hallelujah, Hallelujah, Hallelujah, halleluiah, Hallelujah.

Lord, we praise You and we thank You for this eighth day. Every day is a great day and we thank You for this great day. We thank You, God. By faith we've prayed these prayers according to Thy Spirit. According to the promises You have given to us in Your Bible and, God, we look to You to sustain us for the rest of this night and keep us safe in our homes, on our jobs and bring us back on tomorrow if it be Thy will for the ninth day of prayer. But, God, if You call us and our time is up, we will have no complaints for whatever You have for us, we know it is far better than this. However, if we are going to stay here on this earth and work, we ask You empower us and give us the strength to do Your Will and to be obedient to Thee. We ask God, when we call upon Thee that you deliver us, for David said, "If he called upon Thee, You heard Him, You answered Him and delivered Him." We are asking the same thing. We know You have heard us, we need Your answers and we need You to deliver us because that is the only way we can make it on this earth and do Your work. If You don't help us, God, we can't succeed, but if You help us according to the promises You have made, then we will make it. We will succeed.

We have prayed many prayers before this eighth day, and there is more to come if You bless us to live. But one thing remains consistent, we ask for the salvation of the souls in our families. Regardless of money, health, jobs, and materialistic things, nothing compares to the souls in our families. We will continue to pray for the unsaved loved ones that You would bring great harvest to each and every family of this church and save our entire family beginning with our immediately families. God, our children, husbands and wives, mothers and fathers, and let the fire be contagious and spread abroad in the family. Let cousins, uncles and aunts, nieces and nephews be saved. Stepfamilies be saved, best friends be saved, just save in our circle of family and friends because we know the Bible says, "Jesus is going to come back again and whoever is caught with their work undone, that is going to be the end for them. And if he calls someone through the process of death and they are not saved, it's the same judgment." So, we ask, God, before time runs out for the individuals in our families, You save them, God. You are a merciful, kind and loving God and Your Bible says, "You desire that no man should perish but that all would have life through Christ." Help us, God, to be like You; to love all men enough to give them Christ.

Let us invite seven souls. If we are faithful in that, let us try You and see if You are God. If we would just be obedient, God, we would know for ourselves, You have given those instructions or not. Help this church to be obedient that we might reap a great harvest of souls.

Now, God, I pray something some people might not even pray, that is the weather. Wintertime is about to set in, which means we are going to have flu's, colds, and sickness. I am asking now that You would remove sickness; the common colds, sore throat and flu's which normally take a toll on us as human beings. We are asking You would strengthen our immune system, and our children's, so these things won't attack us and keep us back. Strengthen us, God, and we will make it through this winter, strong physically and robust so we will be able to serve You in these cold months. Touch our transportation; our cars, our legs, bikes, buses whatever means we use which we will be able to make it to work and school with no accidents, no deaths. God, help us to have enough sense to not schedule You out of our schedules, but to put Your first and to come to the house of the Lord for prayer.

During these 40 days, God, to pray and after these 40 days, God, to work, because You are going to give us precise instructions on what to do and how to do it and it is up to us to do it. We make a declaration, a pledge, as a church and we will be obedient to do what You instruct us to do, even if it sounds silly or appears to be foolish to men. We will do what You have instructed; we will do what You've instructed. "Your ways are not our ways," the Bible says, "Your thoughts are not our thoughts as far as the heavens are separated from the earth, so far is our thoughts and ways separated from Yours." We submit our wills to You once again as Paul said, "We die daily and we continue to pray that self would be crucified and that You would be glorified in us and in this church." These prayers we have prayed on this eighth day believing You will bless and answer the prayers of Your people. The prayers, which have been placed in this prayer box, this oil, has been consecrated through this time, God, let it be returned to those owners. Let it be blessed, let it be used as You give to do according to the examples in the Bible. Be it done now, in Jesus Name and the people of God say Amen. **Will you give the Lord some praise!**

Closing Scripture: Psalms 108 (KJV)

"O God, my heart is fixed; I will sing and give praise, even with my glory. Awake, psaltery and harp; I myself will awake early. I will praise thee, O Lord, among the peoples, and I will sing praises unto thee among the nations. For thy mercy is great above the heavens, and thy truth reacheth unto the clouds. Be thou exalted, O God, above the heavens, and thy glory above all the earth. That thy beloved may be delivered, save with thy right hand, and answer me. God hath spoken in his holiness; I will rejoice, I will divide Shechem, and measure the valley of Succoth. Gilead is mine, Manasseh is mine; Ephraim also is the strength of mine head; Judah is my lawgiver; Moab is my wash pot; over Edom will I cast out my shoe; over Philistia will I triumph. Who will bring me into the strong city? Who will lead me into Edom? Wilt not thou, O God, who hast cast us off? And wilt not thou, O God, go forth with our hosts? Give us help

from trouble; for vain is the help of man. Through God we shall do valiantly; for he it is who shall tread down our enemies."

<u>END OF DAY 8 PRAYER SERVICE</u>

STEP 9/DAY 9, TUESDAY

"Wisdom"

Personal note:

Today was the ninth day of the year as well as the eighth day of fasting for me. I went before God denying all food for eight hours. Eight for a new beginning in me, oh, how I wanted to be like Jesus. As I wept before my Lord, asking Him to do a new thing in my mind, my soul, and my body, the total me, everything about me for He knows me because He made me. I fasted and prayed for a new thing to take place for our Pastor and my church family, the Temple of Prayer Church. Thank you, Lord. What a wonderful experience when God wakes you up and says, "I want to commune with you. I want to talk to you." Wow! Something happens to the flesh. It is like my flesh stayed in the bed as my Spirit got up and visited with God. Tiredness left, life situations left and nothing attached to this world came in, just me and my God. Bless His Name.

It was 5:30 a.m. and it seemed like the world was asleep. Everything was silent and nothing moved as God spoke into my being. Oh, how I love Him. I don't want to be a second without Him. As I read these Scriptures from Psalms 23, 1 Corinthians 2:9, and Revelations 21:1, I thanked Him for being my Shepherd. I waited to experience the things God has prepared which I have never seen or heard or ever entered into my heart, knowing one day this earth will pass away and we will be with our Lord and Savior forever. I love you, my Lord, I love you.

~ Evelyn

DAY 9 PRAYER SERVICE BEGINS

Opening Remarks:
God has been kind and has shown us mercy and we want to show Him how grateful we are as we continued to pray. It's not particularly easy to pray for an extended period of time, but if we would just pray for one hour a day. If it was as easy as it sounded, I think more people would pray. Not because it takes up your time, but it is a spiritually draining event and the things God talks to you about, and the questions He asks really makes your mind start to roll. Think, it's almost like your mind is like a boulder which is coming down a mountain and it starts to pick up so much speed it can't slow down, and now you start to think about one thing. Then God puts something else on your mind. You start thinking about the next thing and before you know it, all these things keep going, going and going and it adds to your prayer list.

God starts opening up your eyes to so many other things you need to pray about, and the next thing you know you have a long list of things to pray about. When you have a concern about those things, and see the importance of it, you now see the seriousness of your prayer life. So, now we don't just pray a prayer "Now I lay me down to sleep I pray the Lord my soul to keep." We don't pray one of those types of prayers, we start praying, "Lord, not just keep me safe," but now you start adding all these other people to your list as you start seeing their face and calling out their names. That takes up time and energy, and as it takes energy away from you, spiritually, we have to go to God and ask Him to give us more energy to continue those types of prayers on a consistent basis.

We are seeking God's wisdom for this year. We are praying, as the Lord gives it to us, we will apply it correctly and we would use it more than this year. Once we learn it, hopefully we would keep on using it. We don't want to be like the typical student, especially college students (and some of us have been guilty of this), who learn things just for that time period just to get a grade. If we had to take the class again a year from now, we might not get the same grade. We forget. It is the same way in life. We learn things and we use it for the moment. Then afterwards we just throw it in file 13, forget where we filed it at, and when we need to use it again, it's almost like starting all over for scratch.

How many of us remember how to deal with fractions? How many of us remember how to find the most common denominator? We had to learn how to do things like that it in order to be where we are today, but if we had to go back and do it, we would need help. If someone puts it in our face and says, "Figure this out," we would say, "Wait a minute. Do you have a reference book?" We don't want to be like that. Don't go through 40 days then afterwards forget to pray and forget the seriousness of prayer. Let this be something, which continues in your lives. The wisdom God gives during these prayers take them and file them spiritually were you can find them when you need them.

God can speak something today we might not need tomorrow. We might not need it until October 3rd, but because God spoke it to us on January 9th, the Bible says, "The Spirit will remind us of all things Christ has said." When we call on God to remind us He will bring it back to our remembrance.

Being open and receptive to the Spirit of God means that when He speaks, we want to make sure we take in the information and let it be useful, let it not be just a wasted time of prayer. These 40 days of prayers are very serious. We do not try to fit into our own thinking that we are being more holy or something of that nature. When we take our time of prayer seriously, God will do miraculous works. There is a testimony pertaining to someone who had been in a coma for over three weeks and the doctors said they believed they would be in a vegetative state for the rest of their lives. It is my understanding, while we were praying on the previous night, the Lord gave me to call for the soul to come back. I was told that the person began to move their head, move their arms and they became more responsive since they had been in that situation.

If you have the faith, whatever you place in this prayer box, whatever you place before God in the prayer box in your heart, ask God for it. Don't be scared. Ask Him for it. It doesn't matter how incredible it might sound. If it's in your heart, ask God for it. The worse He can tell you is no. If He tells you no, it's for your good because Romans 8:28 reads, "And we know that God causes everything to work together for the good of those who love God and are called according to this purpose for them." God is not going to tell us no when yes would be better for us. If yes is the better answer, He is going to tell us yes.

Opening Scripture: Proverbs 9:1-12 (KJV)
"Wisdom has built her spacious house with seven pillars. She has prepared a great banquet, mixed the wines, and set the table. She has sent her servant to invite everyone to come. She calls out from the heights overlooking the city. "Come home with me," she urges the simple. To those without good judgment, she says, Come, eat my food, and drink the wine I have mixed. Leave your foolish ways behind, and begin to live; learn how to be wise." Anyone who rebukes a mocker will get a smart retort. Anyone who rebukes the wicked will get hurt. So don't bother rebuking mockers; they will only hate you. But the wise, when rebuked, will love you all the more. Fear of the Lord is the beginning of wisdom. Knowledge of the Holy One results in understanding. Wisdom will multiply your days and add years to your life. If you become wise, you will be the one to benefit. If you scorn wisdom, you will be the one to suffer."

Insight As We Prepared For Prayer:

We thank God for the Word. We want to be as the wise person who builds our house upon wisdom and we seek after wisdom. We reverence God and I believe all of us in our lives can have wisdom, and more wisdom added to us. When the Scripture says, "Fear the Lord," it means to reverence God and we reverence God in our prayers and commitment. We started this year off correctly, building it upon prayers and asking God for wisdom. That is the beginning of understanding. We can have an understanding for our lives! Ask God to help so we will not to be like the people listening to others calling, wanting to do things in secret which seems to be exciting, but they are wrong in our minds.

We want to learn from this even how to deal with people. You can't correct someone who is a mocker. You can't really correct someone who is a scorner, someone who has a bad attitude; if you do, you are just wasting your breath. You try to correct the wicked and you will get hurt according to this Scripture. We might have

A Call Into His Presence

some wicked or scorners in our families. If we are going to win them to Christ, we must remember the Word that says he that wins souls must be wise. We are going to have to learn how to deal with them and how to invite souls to Christ. We can't go condemning people and correcting people if they don't have it in their mind to do right. You are going to turn them off. People, who have it in their mind to do right, even if they are not saved, make a mistake. If they sin, if they have it in their mind to do right, we correct them and tell them what God has said. They will receive it, think about it, and pray about it and you will see the change made in their lives.

We need wisdom according to this Scripture even with how to deal with people. We must start in our own homes. Charity begins at home. Let us be concerned about our loved ones. On this ninth night, let us ask God to give us wisdom, give us a completion. Nine is another number for completion. Ask God to give us completion and finality in wisdom and how to apply it to winning souls and convincing people Jesus is still the answer.

Let us go to God in prayer believing God is going to instruct us and He will give us wisdom if we ask for it. We need it because we really want to win souls for Christ.

Let Us Pray:

Thank You, Lord, thank You, God. Lord, this is our ninth night in prayer. You have blessed us with eight wonderful nights and eight wonderful days in this year. On tonight, God, just from reviewing these Scriptures, listening to the words the Proverbs said, we are extremely, extremely humbled more than any other night in this prayer because, God, wisdom is something we all can use an increase in our lives. We really do need Your wisdom. Life is just that serious, God, life is just that tough, it's just that hard. And those of us who are adults, even as we look back over our lives, we can see many instances, God, where the lack of wisdom has cost us so many precious things. We are grateful, God, You have opened up our understanding to see the importance of wisdom. But now, God, we need You and we need Your wisdom like never before. Now, we are not young and by ourselves like we were before we had children. We have families, we have loved ones who we are concerned about and we see the same bad mistakes we have made. They are going down those paths and we don't want them to suffer from a lack of wisdom like we did. So, we are praying on this night, that You would give us the wisdom to be wise in the winning of souls in our own homes, in our own families, God. We ask that You would help us to be able to talk and deal with our loved ones we know in our circle of family and friends. Help us now, God, on this night to be receptive as You speak to our hearts and minds to know by faith, God, You are going to teach us and give us wisdom in this year. We are praying You do it sooner than later. We are asking, God, we are saying just by our **PRESENCE**, just by this prayer, we know we need it now and we want it now. Wisdom.

We want Your wisdom. We want to be wise with the decisions we make for ourselves on every level of human existence. Whether it be career choices, whether it be something simple, Lord God, to buy an item or not, where to send our children to school, where to look for finances for college, to get a loan or not to get a loan, just the things of basic human needs, issues and concerns. We are praying for wisdom on how to be able to take the verbal abuse people give us, the mistreatment that is so often placed upon the Saints, how and when, God, to show anger or not show anger. Help us, Lord God, to be wise even with the tone of our voice we use in response to people. We are coming to You, God, asking, asking You boldly but yet asking You, God, in Jesus Name, to pour out Your wisdom tonight as You did for Solomon, because he asked for wisdom. He didn't ask for wealth, riches, fame or glory. God, You gave him all those other things because he just simply asked for wisdom because he wanted to rule his nation wisely. Well, God, we want to govern our homes wisely. There are other things we need, and we have prayed for those things up until this night, but on this night we are asking for wisdom. And that we retain it when You give it to us, and use it properly. We can use it when we need to do certain things, God, we will not be afraid to be wise, we will not be afraid to share wisdom with others, we will not be ashamed to walk away from people who we love but they are not in the mind to hear wise council. Help us to seek out wise council and when we are given the opportunity to be taught wisdom, help us, Lord God, to have a mind to be receptive, to hear what people will tell us, help us and give us information to better our lives. If we are rebuked by a wise person, God, let us be like the innocent person who says in the scripture, "God, let us not be a scorner, a mocker, a wicked person, let us be the righteous people." Let us be the people who will take the rebuke, carefully look over the information, look at the holes in our lives and apply wisdom to every hole which needs to be filled, because, God, what we desire is not to just to go to heaven, but we desire heaven on this earth. It is that serious to us. You created us in Your image which means You have given us the ability to love and we do love people, all people, God. We love souls.

We have young ones, God, who need to be taught more so than ever before in the existence of human begins. Things are wicked then they have ever been. Our children can't just go outside and be safe anymore. We can't just let them go two or three blocks and not worry about things happening to them now, God; we have to keep our eyes on our children all the time. Because of this wicked society we live in, God, kids are being snatched every day and a lot of this information is not being reported on the news, God. Our children can be a statistic, but we thank You they haven't been to this point. As we ask, God, You would impart wisdom into us that we would impart wisdom into our children that they would know, God, not to trust strangers, not to get caught up in the 'bling bling,' as they call it, in this life of people having nice things. Other youth might have nice things and they may have gotten it in an illegal fashion. Help us to teach them not to hang out with children who are breaking the law and to not be around the criminal element of the community. To stay away from people who would introduce them to drugs, or selling drugs or using drugs or breaking into homes, or cutting classes, drinking, stealing all kind of things, God, that when they become adults, they would be sorry for it and regret those actions. It could even kill them or cost them to kill someone else. This night we pray for that kind of wisdom because only You can impart that kind of wisdom into us for us to impart it into them, because it's a new breed these days. It's a greater challenge than our parents had, God, and we need wisdom on how to reach our youth. We need wisdom, God. We even need wisdom on how to reach other adults in this society. People are not the same anymore, God. So many people in this world just don't care about anybody else anymore. So many people just don't care about themselves. How, God, can we be wise in soul winning? We are asking on tonight for You to open up our understanding. How can we be wise in soul winning to encourage people to care about themselves again, to care about other human beings to care about society? Just because things are wicked, doesn't mean You have taken a nap and You are not aware of the things going on.

The Bible is being fulfilled. Prophecy is coming to pass. The stage is being set for the return of Christ the Savior and people are blind to this, God. Help us, God. The only way people eyes can be opened up, they must be converted and accept Christ as their Savior, then their eyes will become open and aware to the world and the changes going on which You have all ready ordained before the foundation of this World. You knew these things would take place. You said, "In the last days perilous times would come." Perilous times are here, Lord God. Perilous times are among us. We live in perilous times. We live among people who have become desperate, God. Not desperate to steal, and to kill for their families, God, but desperate to steal and to kill for their addictions, God, some are just evil angry people refusing to work to earn things but they rather steal it from other people who do work and earn things. God, we need wisdom in this society. We need wisdom in this society, God, even in the business world.

Oh, God, we are not praying a prayer saying it's an excuse why we haven't succeeded, but there are many obstacles we face and we need wisdom on how to be successful in a business aspect, God. There are so many things we are not aware of, information which would help our lives be better financially that we need to know about. There are so many things, God, which is not shared for our own benefit because we are so afraid. Many have been misused throughout the years, God, we don't know who we can trust. We don't know who is giving us information which will help us or who is just trying to rob us and keep us down.

We are praying now, for the wisdom You give us, will allow us to see through the schemes which people have laid out for us in life, God.

A Call Into His Presence

We ask now, You would give us the wisdom to be able to control our urges and things we want to buy sometimes not needed, God, that we will not go out and buy but save money. Help us. Give us wisdom even in our finances, God. This is the reason, or one of the reasons, why this night, God, is just as serious as or more serious than any other night we have prayed, because this night exposes us in our lack of wisdom.

We need help only You can provide. God, it's not like there are a lot people out there who are willing to teach us. People are hoarding money and making so many millions and billions of dollars, God, and won't even share, Lord God. One has to wonder about our government, who spends hundreds of billions of dollars rebuilding nations, who have torn up, and in our own nation, we have people in our country who need help! We need to go to school for free! If someone signs up and says they want to go to school to be a doctor, we need the government to say, "I will pay for you. Go." We need that in our country. How is it we can pay for other countries to send their children through medical school; to be lawyers and architects? Give us the same opportunity, God. We pay taxes, we vote, we support our government; we fight and die for our country. We need wisdom on how to get around those things and how to funnel our children and every other child into situations of success, God.

Bless every child who has the desire to learn and wants to go to college to be able to go. God, we are praying on this night for the betterment of Your people, for the betterment of our families. We want to be better in every area of our lives. Help us, God, we pray. You opened the eyes of the children of Israel. You opened the eyes of the Prophets. You opened the eyes of the people who prayed to You for wisdom, God, and You let them know things of the enemy in advance. You taught them and showed them how to be successful even in a famine time. We are praying for that for every church! We are praying that for every family in this church. We are praying for all of our families, God, Hallelujah, that You would do for us like You did in the Bible, God. You said, "Fear is the beginning of wisdom," God, we want to start on tonight. God, all the wisdom we think we have, we throw it aside.

A wise person even knows they are not the wisest person on earth. A wise person even knows they gain more wisdom and knowledge through listening; being slow to speak, God. Help us to be slow to respond. Help us to be slow to speak. Help us to be able to control our thoughts, God. Help us now, God, we would be silent and learn to be obedient to that which was taught us. Help us. God, we don't want to be making the same mistakes from generation to generation. The only way we can teach our children, God, is by example and not just by telling them but by showing them, God, that wisdom works! The first thing we can do, God, is be saved, committed and serve You and praise You. That is wisdom in doing that, God, and if we can show our children we can live saved, God is the way, it would help them in their lives, God. We can show other human beings, God, it is wise to say, "I don't know the answer." It is wise to say, "I don't know," but it is even wiser to say, "but I know how I can find out. Let me pray and ask God. God will show me or God will lead me in the direction to meet someone who will give me the information needed that my family will live and not die!"

Help us; help us in the body of Christ. We pray, God, I pray God. I placed not myself in this position. I did not choose to be in this position. I did not want to be in this position; God, I believe You called me, You chose me to be in this position, therefore I pray for this church that You would bless us. If You bless this church like You have blessed other mega ministries, God, I declare it before Your people, and I have declared it before You privately, and I declare it again openly, we will do kingdom work, kingdom ministry than just sit on the money, God. We will develop programs. We will have more than just an education school; maybe we can have a school or programs to offer people on how to balance their checks books. Maybe we need to go back to basic living skills. God, I don't know but we can take the money and do something good besides putting money in the bank and brag about how much money we have. Besides being on TV, besides buying church buses, besides buying jet planes, and another car or a mansion; we can do something else with the money, God, Hallelujah! Why can we not set up scholarship funds for our children of this church and other children who may need it to be able to go to school, God, not just having basic tutoring programs? Why can we not have world-renowned professors and pay them $10,000 instead of paying a Bishop, or preacher $10,000 to come in and preach one message. Why can't we pay

A Call Into His Presence

some world-renowned professor $10,000 to come in and give us a seminar on how to better our lives and how our children can be a success besides being an athlete or entertainer? Why can't we do things like that? We can, God, because You said we can do all things through Christ that strengthens us.

God, there are millionaires in the body of Christ who have much information which will help people, God. We need to tap into those sources, God! We are praying for the wisdom to be filled with the Spirit not just for speaking in tongues or shouting and dancing. Not just for saying Hallelujah but for living this life more abundantly the way You promised we could live this life, God. Help us, God, to see there is more to holiness than what we have been taught. There is more to holiness than what we think. There is more to holiness, than what we see on TV, God, everything concerning holiness is in the Bible. Wisdom is a part of it and we have lack, we have lack!

We ask for Your forgiveness as a church. We ask for Your forgiveness as heads of our families. We ask for forgiveness. We ask for forgiveness on this night for not seeking wisdom more diligently, for not seeking wisdom more earnestly or fervently. For not adding it to our daily prayer, God, we pray for so many things every day, but we have failed to ask for wisdom on a daily basis.

Here are our thoughts for this year. We turn toward wisdom, seeking wisdom, praying for wisdom, asking for wisdom, God, because we need wisdom. How can we do anything great without wisdom? How can we be great without wisdom? How can we win souls without wisdom, God, how? We need Your wisdom on tonight. We don't want any child, any child in this city to not have an opportunity for success. The government can't do everything, God. It is time for us, the citizens, to take up the call to put our minds together to use the wisdom of experience. We have experienced things good and bad. We might not have college knowledge, God; we might not be the economic geniuses of the world, but some things we know because we lived them. Some mistakes we can talk about and say won't work or the likelihood of that succeeding is not great or it's too much risk in that. Then they can say, "How do You know?" We can say, "Because we lived it!"

Help us not to be afraid to stand in the arenas where people will have more book knowledge than us with no life application. If we could stand and say what sounds good on paper, but the people I live with, the people who I am trying to reach, they are not going to read the paper. They are not going to read the latest edition of the Wall Street Journal. Hallelujah, we need to get this information to them in a way they will receive it, a way it can reach the masses! The quality of life can be improved, and even if it is not improved, at least the information can be given.

Somebody wants a better life! Somebody wants to live better! Somebody fits in the scripture "They will not hurt us. They will scorn us!" There is somebody, God, who is wise, and has a wise spirit and a desire for wisdom and if they get the information they will say, "Thank You." They will say, "I didn't know. I made mistakes. I was doing it the wrong way. Thank You for giving me this information. I will improve my life!" There are some people in this city; there are some people in this church, who want a better life! We don't want to keep spinning our wheels and burning up our energy in the same situations. Like a mouse on a Ferris wheel who doesn't have enough sense to know that they can jump off! Hallelujah, they are betrayed over and over again, not knowing there are bigger Farris wheels they can get on. They know nothing but what they know. What we are saying, God, we fall in that situation. We only know what we know and it takes faith to step outside the box.

On tonight, we pray we would apply our faith even in this prayer for wisdom and we will be honest from here on in and tell You, God. We don't have to share it with one another, but we do have to share it with You we don't know everything. We don't know everything, God, we don't know everything. I don't know everything, I don't even know a portion of what I need to know and I am saying, beginning with me in this church, flowing down to every department head, every preacher, every missionary, every deacon, every member, every baby, God, let wisdom permeate in our souls from heaven, and let us receive the wisdom You give us. Let us use it, God and, let us not be ashamed to use it. Let us not be ashamed. What I mean by saying that is let us not say "I was smart or I was this", no, let us say, "I really didn't know but God gave me the answer! God pointed me in the right direction. God sent someone my way who gave me the information I needed."

God, let us give You the glory! Give us wisdom and we will give You the glory, God, give us wisdom and we will praise You. Give us wisdom, God, and we will share it with others. We won't be selfish, God. Give wisdom, God, that our homes would flourish with love, with peace, with joy, with understanding all for one and one for all in the family and nobody is against each other, it is all for the benefit of the family. If one makes it, we all make it. If one falls, we all have to go down on our knees and pick them up. It cannot be separation. That is unwise. The devil wants to divide the family, so he can conquer. He wants to isolate us as a church family so he can conquer us. I rebuke that in the Name of Jesus! I speak unity in our homes. I speak unity in the body, in the minds, in the souls of every individual in this church. Every member on the membership roll, I speak unity! In every department, I speak unity in everyone in this church, God, unity in the spirit. Bind us closer together, God, with Your love. Bind us closer together, God, with wisdom, Hallelujah. God, we don't want to be like the children of Israel who did not practice wisdom, God, they spoke against Your Word. They spoke against You and Your prophet and we will not speak against what You have said. We will not speak against You or Your prophet, God. We are saying yes in our souls, God.

There is room for all of us, Hallelujah. Let us be wise and be different in our situation. We are being squeezed. For we are not going to burst, we are not going to break. We are being compressed so we can be fitly joined together according to the scripture, God, Hallelujah, so we can be built up in Thy most holy faith, God, and we are praying now even in the spirit, God. Because we are being lead by the spirit in this prayer, oh, bless Your Name, oh, bless Your Name, oh, bless Your Name. We pray the words we are saying, God, we know they are not idle words. The same God who has heard us all of our lives, all of us have prayed prayers before and if You would not have answered those prayers before, we would not be here. Somebody else prayed for us, and You answered those prayers. That's why we are here, God. We've prayed for others and You have spared their lives. You moved on the boy last night, God, who is in a coma.

We pray now in the Name of Jesus, the same God of the Bible, the same God of Abraham, Isaac and Jacob. The same God of Moses, Aaron, Hur, Joshua and Caleb! The same God of Ruth, the same God of Naomi, the same God of Debra, the same God of Isaiah, Ezekiel, Jeremiah, Micah! The same God of Zechariah, the same God of the Disciples, Paul! The same God of Timothy, Hallelujah, we call on the God of the Bible on tonight! We have asked throughout, for You to pour out joy, and the spirit of praise, but on tonight, we ask You pour out wisdom! We want an over pour, an out pouring! We want excess, we want the over flow, we want wisdom! We seek it, we pursuit it, we pursuit it, we want it, God, we need it, we can't make it without Your wisdom. Not man's wisdom but God's wisdom. We need Your wisdom. How can we make it, God, without Your wisdom in this world? We need Your wisdom! We need Your wisdom, God, help us, help us! Help us, God, help us! Give us wisdom, give us wisdom, give us wisdom, give us wisdom.

Oh, God, we pray for the owner of the business behind us. Her body is racking with pain, God. We add her to our prayer list. Touch her body, heal her now, heal her now in the Name of Jesus. She is the glue that is holding her family together, God, she is the glue. She is the hope of salvation in her family for her unsaved loved ones. Give her the wisdom to win those unsaved loved ones over to You.

God, we pray for ourselves, for the older people in our families, God. We know they might be tired and they might want to leave here. We cannot stop them from being tired and wanting to be in Your **PRESENCE**, but we need them to be around here a little bit longer because we need their wisdom. We need their wisdom. We are not as wise as our parents were; we are not as wise as our grandparents. We have dropped the ball, God, but we thank You, we thank You for a new beginning. Help us to take on their spirit. Help us to take on their wisdom, Hallelujah. Resurrect the spirit of wisdom in each and every one of our families so we can take it, we can take a little and make a lot. Stretch it, stretch it, stretch it, and stretch it, God, they prayed, they prayed over those meals and it stretched!

They were grateful for those sacks of potatoes and onions. They made meals out of those things, God, and took the leftovers from the animals, the things people didn't want, ham hocks and ox tails, now they are in our stores at high prices. These same scraps are now a delicacy. In other words, God, You taught them to use what they had and to be successful and make great things out of it.

Teach this church how to use what You have given us and to make it great! The little You have given us, teach this church God, teach us and our families to take the gifts You have placed in each and every family member how to make it great. Teach us how to make millions off it, teach us how to make money off it. Teach us how to bless and help others off it. Teach us how to send children to college, not just our children but how to sponsor others off it. God, teach us how to be a light in this community, Hallelujah! Teach us God, this we pray in Jesus Name. We believe by faith that it is done and we ask now, Lord God, as David said in the 23rd division of Psalms, that goodness and mercy would follow Him, let goodness and mercy follow us. Let wisdom be in us, this we pray because we are just that desperate. We are desperate for wisdom. We are desperate for You and all You have promised we can have. We believe the Bible, we just don't know how to get those things You have said. We are admitting it; we know it takes faith. We have faith, but You said, "Faith without works is dead." So that means we have to apply what You have given us and that is what we are asking. You give us the wisdom to know how to apply it to our faith so we can have some works.

Next week we won't have to pray this prayer. Next year, if we live to see it, we won't have to pray this prayer but we will ask for a different kind of increase in wisdom. We will be praying a prayer, "God, how do we handle the abundance? How do we handle the overflow? How do we handle the influx of souls? How do we handle two services instead of one? How can we expand?" God, those are the kind of things we want to pray for, wisdom for more than how just to make it. How can we start from scratch?

We are grateful You touched our minds to pray that prayer and we are starting from scratch believing the scripture, God, from Ecclesiastes 9:4 "That A living dog is better than a dead lion." It is better to start now than never to have started seeking and pursuing

Your wisdom. We love You, we do love You, God, we do love You, and we thank You for allowing us to come to You on this serious matter in prayer asking for something more valuable than riches. We believe by faith even now, God, even now, even this night from this moment forward, wisdom is ours and You are pouring it out, and You will continue to pour it out in each of our souls and in our homes and we thank You now in Jesus Name. We pray and the people of God say Amen.

Closing Scripture: Ecclesiastes 9 (NLT)

"This too, I carefully explored: Even though the actions of godly wise people are in God's hands, no one knows whether or not God will show them favor in this life. The same destiny ultimately awaits everyone, whether they are righteous or wicked, good or bad, ceremonially clean or unclean, religious or irreligious. Good people receive the same treatment as sinners, and people who take oaths are treated like people we don't. It seems so tragic that one fate comes to all. That is why people are not more careful to be good. Instead, they choose their own mad course, for they have no hope. There is nothing ahead but death anyway. There is hope only for the living. For as they say, "It is better to be a living dog than a dead lion!" The living at least know they will die, but the dead know nothing. They have no further reward, nor are they remembered. Whatever they did in their lifetime —— loving, hating, envying —— is all long gone. They no longer have a part in anything here on earth. So go ahead. Eat your food and drink your wine with a happy heart, for God approves of this! Wear fine clothes, with a dash of cologne! Live happily with the woman you love through all the meaningless days of life that God has given you in this world. The wife God gives you is your reward for all your earthy toil. Whatever you do, do well. For when you go to the grave, there will be no work or planning or knowledge or wisdom. I have observed something else in this world of ours. The fastest runner doesn't always win the race, and the strongest warrior doesn't always win the battle. The wise are often poor, and the skillful are not necessarily wealthy. And those who are educated don't always lead successful lives. It is all decided by chance, by being at the right place at the right time. People can

never predict when hard times might come. Like fish in a net or birds in a trap, people are caught by sudden tragedy. Here is another bit of wisdom that has impressed me as I have watched the way our world works. There was a small town with only a few people, and a great king came with his army and besieged it. A poor, wise man knew how to save the town, and so it was rescued. But afterward no one thought to thank him. So even though wisdom is better than strength, those who are wise will be despised if they are poor. What they say will not be appreciated for long. Better to hear the quiet words of a wise person than the shouts of a foolish king. Better to have wisdom than weapons of war, but one sinner can destroy much that is good."

Closing Remarks:

Prayer is a very must weapon. What is the purpose of having a divine power if you don't know what to do with it? You have authority and power. You want to use all the power God has given you. When you use faith in conjunction with what God has given, then you will have a good outcome.

God, help us to use the weapons you have given us. We need the people of God who will be bold and courageous to ask God for the impossible! Remember the weapons you are fighting with are not the weapons of this world. Go in the authority of God!

<u>END OF DAY 9 PRAYER SERVICE</u>

STEP 10/DAY 10, WEDNESDAY

"We are Disciples of Christ"

The tenth night was unusual and you will see why. The call for disciples was made. We are to do the work Jesus' Disciples did. The Word of God came from Matthew 10:1-22 and it reads at thus:

DAY 10 PRAYER SERVICE BEGINS

Opening Scripture: Matthew 10:1-22 (KJV)
"And when he had called unto him his twelve disciples, he gave them power against unclean spirits, to cast them out, and to heal all manner of sickness and all manner of disease. Now the names of the twelve apostles are these; The first, Simon, who is called Peter, and Andrew his brother; James the son of Zebedee, and John his brother; Philip, and Bartholomew; Thomas, and Matthew the publican; James the son of Alphaeus, and Lebbaeus, whose surname was Thaddaeus; Simon the Canaanite, and Judas Iscariot, who also betrayed him. These twelve Jesus sent forth, and commanded them, saying, Go not into the way of the Gentiles, and into any city of the Samaritans enter ye not: But go rather to the lost sheep of the house of Israel. And as ye go, preach, saying, The kingdom of heaven is at hand. Heal the sick, cleanse the lepers, raise the dead, cast out devils: freely ye have received, freely give. Provide neither gold, nor silver, nor brass in your purses, Nor scrip for your journey, neither

two coats, neither shoes, nor yet staves: for the workman is worthy of his meat. And into whatsoever city or town ye shall enter, enquire who in it is worthy; and there abide till ye go thence. And when ye come into an house, salute it. And if the house be worthy, let your peace come upon it: but if it be not worthy, let your peace return to you. And whosoever shall not receive you, nor hear your words, when ye depart out of that house or city, shake off the dust of your feet. Verily I say unto you, It shall be more tolerable for the land of Sodom and Gomorrha in the day of judgment, than for that city. Behold, I send you forth as sheep in the midst of wolves: be ye therefore wise as serpents, and harmless as doves. But beware of men: for they will deliver you up to the councils, and they will scourge you in their synagogues; And ye shall be brought before governors and kings for my sake, for a testimony against them and the Gentiles. But when they deliver you up, take no thought how or what ye shall speak: for it shall be given you in that same hour what ye shall speak. For it is not ye that speak, but the Spirit of your Father which speaketh in you. And the brother shall deliver up the brother to death, and the father the child: and the children shall rise up against their parents, and cause them to be put to death. And ye shall be hated of all men for my name's sake: but he that endureth to the end shall be saved."

Insight As We Prepared For Prayer:

We believe the whole Bible to be the only infallible written Word of God. Our desire is to do as the Word says we can do in 7-8 *"And as ye go, preach, saying The kingdom of Heaven is at hand. Heal the sick, cleanse the lepers, raise the dead, cast out devils: freely ye have received, freely give."*

Oh, how sad it is that some don't believe in the power of prayer and miracles. Jesus commissioned us to GO! Go and do what? Preach! Preach what? The kingdom of Heaven is at hand! Then He gave instructions to heal the sick, cleanse the lepers, raise the dead, cast out devils, freely ye have received, now freely we need to give back!

We must continue we are ¼ of the way there. Thirty more days to go through and see what the Lord has to say to us and what He has for us as, our family, our loved ones and children. We saw on the evening news that a young boy ten years old was snatched from his bus stop in another state. As we went to prayer they hadn't found him; we prayed against these things every day. Someone had a baby out in the state of Oregon in 38 degree weather and left the baby, the placenta, and the umbilical cord on the steps of a Nursing Home. The baby was wet, freezing and suffering from hyperthermia. The baby could have died. These are the types of things happening in our society every day. When we pray, let us include the innocent children because it is important. We want them to live. Some people don't believe this 10th chapter was Jesus just not referring to the twelve disciples, but to all of us who are Disciples of Christ. We are not the original twelve, but we are followers of Christ. We are His disciples now.

We thank God for the Word coming from Matthew 10:1-22. We pray it helps us to be strong enough to endure to the end that we would be saved. These words Jesus spoke to the twelve are things happening in our time. Parents are killing their children and children are killing their parents. Brothers are against brothers, family against family members. Those who stand for the truth are being persecuted for Christ's sake, but if we endure, we shall be saved. All along with what Jesus said in those first few verses, He gives us the power against unclean spirits, to cast them out, and to heal all manner of sickness and all manner of disease. If the Bible says it, then we believe it. Therefore, we pray in God's strength we will be obedient to the instructions God gave us through the Gospel of Matthew, we will go out and witness to people. In inviting seven souls a week, we know we have the power through Christ Jesus to come against unclean spirits and to cast them out. To pray for healing, when it says all manner of sickness and disease, that covers everything even HIV. There is no illness God cannot heal. It is up to us to believe those things when we pray, people will be healed from all manner of sickness and disease.

Personal Note: An Altar Call Was Made

The anointing poured into my soul like a volcano and I cried to the people saying: "Please don't come if you don't believe!" Spiritually it was like God took my hand and poured oil in them, anointing them with fire! Souls began to come to the altar and the yokes were destroyed! We will call on the only Name, which has power, and that Name is JESUS! Get ready for God to burn up everything inside of your heart, mind and soul! The fire of God is going to purify and burn everything not like Him. We cannot go forward and do greater works for God if we are in constant battle with the same things inside of us over and over and over! As we yielded to God, we could feel the heat! I cried out from the "cross" of my soul asking "God to burn me up!" Burn the carnal thoughts, everything in me not like Chris, burn it!

As I stood in the fire, the fire was flaming in my soul. I begged God to burn any sin, anything that wasn't like Him! "God, please let your Holy Ghost take over me, take over my life, take control of me and that it would be Christ inside of me! No longer 'I' but Christ lives inside of me!" God we believe! We believe everyone who received would come out changed. We believe everyone we encounter, everyone we witness to will know there is a difference in us and it's not us, but it's the Christ inside of us! Thank you Jesus!
~ *Evelyn*

Let Us Pray: Singing "My soul loves Jesus"
Let us go into prayer on tonight, as we go into spiritual warfare, binding every unclean spirit, casting them out of our homes, our loved ones, believing God, praying for the sick, praying for strength that God will help us stand. Also, praying for peace in our homes; it will not be brother against brother, sister against sister, fathers against the families, and mothers giving up their babies.

Oh, God, thank You once again for allowing us to come on this tenth day of prayer. On this night, God, according to Your scripture, we believe, we make a profession of our faith, we believe the Bible. We believe the scriptures and the instructions Jesus left the disciples, which includes us. God, we are praying and binding every unclean spirit, casting them out of our homes, and out of every unsaved loved one in our homes regardless of who they are. We bind every unclean spirit in this church and every unclean spirit that has come against this church that comes against us as individuals.

We cast them out now according to the instructions and the power in the Name of Jesus.

We pray, Lord God, we adhere, listen to the instructions and obey the instructions which has been given on this night as You have lead us to this 10th chapter of Matthew, Lord God. Jesus told them to take the Gospel to the lost sheep of Israel first, Lord God. He cared about his own bloodline, family, and people. Lord God, we are commissioned, on this night, to take salvation to our homes, our loved ones, to those who are the lost sheep of our households, God, our blood line and share with them the Gospel. God, we first want to take the Gospel to our communities, the circle which we move and operate in. We are not trying to take the Gospel abroad yet, God, but we want to reach this society. This is the country we live in. We have our various neighborhoods and we have our various circles of operation in which we live. God, we are praying, if our minds and our boxes are small fitting in this community, You would take us out of our boxes and take us beyond the logic of our minds and give us the boldness to invite seven souls a week. Give us the boldness, God, to share with people the Gospel. Give us the boldness, Lord God, to live it before them. Without even saying a word, God, we can witness to people and draw them to a closer perspective of Christ, a better perspective, a better viewpoint as they see the light shining in our lives as we show kindness, as we show compassion, as we show strength in the time of calamities in tragedies, Lord God.

We can stand firm and profess our faith at the appointed time verbally that nothing can move us or move our faith away from the fact Christ died for everyone and God loves everybody, Hallelujah. Help us, Lord God, because in our world, in the society we live in, there are people who are hopeless. We know this, Lord God, because of what we see and hear on the news. Every week, every day there is some tragedy. Somewhere along the line, God, some parent has murdered their child or abused their children, God, or some family member has done this or some child has killed their parents, killed their brother or sister. Lord God, it's the family situations, which are not looking so good in this country any more. But we pray for the strength of our families. We pray for the strength of the family structure everywhere.

Within the churches, God, give the churches, members, the pastors and the leaders of the church the strength to stand up and proclaim the truth. If they are not receptive, then let us follow the instructions, shake the dust off our feet and move on to the next person, move on to the next family, move on to the next situation. Help us now, God, to not be compassionate to the point our compassion means disobedience. You said shake the dust of our feet and move on God, we want to shake the dust off our feet and move on. Somebody wants to hear the truth. Somebody wants a better life, God, everybody in this world is not satisfied with misery, God, everybody in this world is not satisfied with the drama which comes through sin, the shame and degradation that comes because of failure to listen and be obedient to You.

Somebody in this world, God, wants to go to heaven. Somebody in this world wants a better life here on this earth. Somebody in this world wants peace in their home and to be able to tell one another within the family 'I love you' and to hear it and know those words are meaningful and heartfelt. Somebody in this country is tired of thinking horrific thoughts of hurting someone in their family, hurting themselves, God, somebody wants a better way, and they want a solution an answer to their situation, God.

You have shared with us and told us according to Your Bible Jesus is the answer, therefore it is incumbent upon us to take prayer serious, Lord God, serious enough to pray without ceasing. You have given us instruction according to Your Word to pray for strength, obedience we will follow to the letter, to the tee, God. We would do as You have instructed these Disciples and every other Disciple who has read these scriptures or was taught by those Disciples while they were alive to do the same thing, God, and don't worry about provision. Don't worry about what the people would like, don't worry about what the people would receive. Don't worry about when they take us before councils of men. There might come a time we are taken before other people who will have greater knowledge, power or authority, God, who will try to ask us questions, or trip us up or say what we believe is not true. We don't have to sit down and plan our defense, according to Your Word in that same hour You will give us what to say.

Therefore, we pray now, Lord God, for the importance of the knowledge of knowing we must be filled with Your Spirit. We must be filled so You can speak to us and remind us and bring these things we have read and heard throughout our lives according to the Gospel, God, which is in our spirits. Sometimes we cannot recall as fast as we need to, but the Spirit itself, Lord God, will bring all things, whatever You have said, to our remembrances which is according to Your Gospel of St. John, Lord.

Help us now, Lord God, we pray the Word back to You. We pray Your Word back to You, we pray Your Scriptures to You, God, We know that Your Word, it is not our words, it is not our prayers that impress You, God, it's Your Name sake. It's Your glory, it's Your might, Your power; it's Your love, Your mercy. We have nothing outside whatever You have given us. And whatever You have given us is because of Your kindness and Your favor. We prayed for Your favor on last night, God, for everyone who is not smart, not rich. According to Your Word in Ecclesiastes, not everyone who is strong has finished the race first, God, some have not finished the race at all, God. Some people who are the fastest don't finish the race. God, You determined these things for the one who endureth to the end, God, is the one. We want to endure to the end. According to the Scripture in Matthew, if we endure we shall be saved. We want to endure, God, the hardships that are placed upon this society which affect us.

After all these years, God, these four or five years this war has been going on, we now hear they didn't send enough troops, setting the stage for more troops to be sent. Setting the stage, God, for the draft to be started back up again; setting the stage for our loved ones, children and teenagers who are going to be adults. For those who are all ready in that age group who don't have a choice but to sign up for the selective services and if their number gets called, they have to go to war and put their lives on the line, Lord God. We cannot go to our Senators, Congressman our Mayors and Governors. We have to call upon You to make a way, Lord God, for this Nation! Make a way for our children; it's not only our children when we say "our children." We are talking about the children of every parent in this Country, Lord God! We are talking about all the children whose parents are Saints, God, who are praying these same prayers, shaking their heads, God, saying, "What have we gotten ourselves into?" We need Your help. We need Your help for strength. Some of our children will have to go. Some of our children will die. Some of us will be in funerals, God, and we pray for the strength of those families, God, who is going to have to look at their child, the child they brought into this world. See that child die before the parent. We pray now, God. We pray for the strength of those families, God. We pray for the strength of every family who has already experienced that; whether it is through the war of Iraq or whether it be the war of crime and drugs within our own communities. Innocent children are being shot by stray bullets. Children who had wonderful futures have been caught up in the society of materialistic things and gaining these things by doing illegal and illicit acts to gain money and possessions, God. For the family who has been for years, the last 40 years throughout the bloodline; great granddaddy was a drug dealer, granddaddy was a drug dealer, Hallelujah, my daddy was a drug dealer, now I am a drug dealer, God. We bind that generational, unclean spirit now in the Name of Jesus! Hallelujah,

Your Word says "If the living is joined to life there is hope a living dog is better than a dead lion." We are not praying for the dead, we are praying for the living. Even those who are caught up in sin, they are alive. There is hope and we pray You use this church; You use every church in this country, God, to bring the message of Hope. Christ is the Hope of Glory. Lord, let this be the pivotal year, as this is the year of resurrection, for the eighth year for this ministry. This is a time of resurrection. Resurrect us, God, bring us to a different dimension in our thinking, in our acts, God, that this will be the year of turn-a-round. We will not talk about it, we will go out and do it, God, as we have talked about unsaved loved ones but nobody will witness to them. Nobody will tell them the life they are living is going to bring death. We talk about these things and they are dying, God, because we are talking and there is no action.

During these 40 days of prayer, God, we thank You as we are ¼ of the way there, God, only by Your power, Your might, Your Spirit, Your glory and by Your grace You have brought us to this point. We have not been able to pray these nights in our own strength! We have not been able to make it this far in our own strength, therefore we are asking now for the power of God to take us as You took Elijah! You took him on a trip, God, faster than the horse, faster than the chariots. You took him to a town to bring forth a message, which You had given him, God. We pray now spiritually, You take us, Lord, strengthen us physically and give us the power, the speed, the endurance and the might, whatever we need, the wisdom, God, we prayed for on last night. Help us to be wise in the winning of souls in our homes, our schools, on our jobs in our communities, God. We pray for the people in New York, Alabama, California, Georgia but we don't live there, we live here in this city! We need wisdom on how to go in and out in this city! In the communities in this region, we need wisdom on how to get finances to help the dream become a reality, God, that we can be a church who can help people!

We are praying for this time, this place for these people, these members, this church, God. Help the members to understand, let them see, God, I am only responsible for the souls in this church. As this church grows, the responsibility, the covering grows. It is important the covering grows, God. There are not many who are praying and staying on the wall in this time, in this society, God, it has been reported throughout the land of Christendom, prayer is an oddity. Forty days of prayer is not a normal thing, God. Coming to a church for 40 days in a row is not a normal thing. People make the assumption we mean pray at home and we just half hazily go through this, but what we desire is just that serious. Our loved ones are just that serious!

We bind every spirit of hopelessness in this church! Any mother or any father who felt like the lady who left her baby out in the cold, God, at the nursing home freezing who could have died. We pray against those types of spirits, which attacks us, and say it's hopeless and I can't raise my child or I don't want my kids anymore. We bind it in the Name of Jesus! We bind the same spirit that will sexually molest a daughter or step-daughter or set them on fire and try to cover up the crime, we bind that! We bind that suicide spirit that will overdose on pills, take a gun and blow out their brains, get in a car drive recklessly under the influence, trying to die; we bind that according to Matthew the 10th chapter! You said You gave us the power against any unclean spirit to cast them out! We come against every unclean spirit! We come against every unclean spirit, which attacks these families in this ministry! I come against them now! I plead the Blood of Jesus! Our children's lives, our children's lives, God, we pray for all children but we don't know every child in this world, we know our own. Our children live in this church, it's just that important whether they be 25, 45 or 100 or whether they are one month or one day old. They are our children, God, we want them to live. We want them to live! We want them to have a chance at life, we want them to have a chance at making a mistake. We want them to have the chance rather it is to go to heaven or to hell, but if their life is cut short, they don't have a chance! Somebody kills them; somebody rapes them. If a child is kidnapped, 75% of the time, they are murdered within the first three hours of being kidnapped. We pray about these things and we hear about these things happening all the time, God, we are not so special that it cannot happen to us, but because of Your goodness, because of Your mercy, You have spared our children. Our children often go through their daily activities never thinking somebody is watching them, never thinking somebody has been spying them out for a month. Never thinking somebody knows all of their habits as they get off the bus, when they get on the bus, who they are hanging with; never thinking, looking for a weakness when to snatch them, God! But because we pray, because these parents pray, because somebody is on the wall and is not coming down off of prayer, binding the unclean spirit, binding the bad minds, sending out Your Angels, Your ministering protecting Angels, God, to keep them safe even in this unsafe society. God, keep them safe.

You have been kind to this church. You have been kind to this church. You have been kind to this church, God, Hallelujah! Hallelujah, You have kept our children alive. You have kept them alive, God, and we thank You, and we thank You! You have kept the parents from killing them. You have kept the children from killing the parents, God, thank You, God, thank You, thank You, Lord, thank You, Lord! If our children will just realize their parents, love them and want the best for them. It is important they obey their parents. We pray for a great spirit of obedience in these children, God, we pray that they won't question their parents and buck up against their parents and come against their parents for the parents are doing all that they know to keep the house going. All that they know to keep the lights on, all that they know to keep some food in their stomach. All they know to keep some hope in their hearts! All they know to keep them before Christ! We might not be perfect as human beings but our love is perfect because we desire the best through Christ! Give the parents the strength to drag these kids to church if that is what they have to do to keep them before God, to keep them continually in prayer! To keep them reminded not to lose themselves in so call friends or they will let You down!

The Bible tells us to put no trust, no confidence in no man. Not in Kings, not Princes, not in Potentates but only put our trust in the Lord. With all thy heart, trust in the Lord, with all thy ways and lean not to our own understanding. Our children need to realize that. People want to see them dead, God. My heart is saddened when we live in a society where people are sick and they want to see kids dead. They torture them; they sacrifice them and offer them up in satanic rituals. There are hundreds and thousands of missing kids every year who are never found and nobody talks about it. God, help us, Lord, help us that it won't be ours. Continue to protect them, God, touch their minds they won't be sick individuals themselves, God, don't let the sickness in this society spill over into their lives, God. Don't let the sadness and hopelessness spill over into their lives when they feel the only way they can get relief from the pain, inside of their minds and their emotions, is to turn to drugs and alcohol or some illicit or bad behavior of promiscuity. Lord God, don't let them give themselves over to the lust of the flesh and ungodly manners, unnatural manners, Lord God, this brings about a temporary relief. A temporary pleasure, which brings about long lasting heartaches and suffering, oh, God, help our children to realize You are the only guarantee for success.

God, help this church. Help us to realize, God, we really do need You this year and we cannot afford to take one day off and say "I don't need God today." We cannot even afford to take one minute off and say "Lord, I don't like You anymore, I don't want You anymore, I'm mad at You. God, just leave me alone." We cannot afford to think that way not one minute nor not one second of our existences! God, You mean just that much to our existence. We are no longer the 'old man' but we are the 'new man' for we are new creatures in Christ. The old man thought that way. The new man does not receive those thoughts. The old man thought they could make it on his own, the new man knows there is no way we can make it without Christ. The old man said "Oh, what is the use. Nothing is going my way, I might as well." The new man says "There is hope, hope in Christ, and hope in God. If I endure the hardness in this life as a good soldier, Hallelujah, there is a reward for me. Not just heaven but here on this earth."

David said, "I had fainted, unless I had believed to see the goodness of the Lord in the land of the living." He said that in the 27th division of Psalms and the 13th verse when he was about to give up! But he believed, God, while there was blood in his veins, You were going to bless him.

We believe now, God, as the weather is getting cold, spiritually it is cold in this city. As the weather is turning towards below freezing, spiritually there is a chill in some churches, God. There is a chill in society, in Lexington, God, but we ask now, God, we don't faint as the chill has even come this way. We will endure, Hallelujah, if we wait and not faint because there is a blessing here in this life! On this side of this life there is a blessing for us, God, and if we give up we will never get it. If we quit, we will never receive, if we don't believe it, we will never have the experience of the increase. 'Faith without works is dead.' God, give us the strength to have some works behind this faith, God, we proclaim and profess in Your Son, Jesus.

We pray these prayers in the powerful Name of Jesus! We bombard heaven with these prayers in the Name of Jesus! We pour out of our hearts concerning our children, God, in the Name of Jesus. We pray for strength on how to win souls and wisdom on how to win souls in the Name of Jesus! We need Your help and we are calling for Your help in the Name of Jesus. We need for Your glory to be poured out in the revelation of our minds in the Name of Jesus! We bind the devil in the Name of Jesus. We come against all the principalities and wickedness over this region, God, in the Name of Jesus! I bind the spirit of inconsistency! I bind the spirit of disobedience in the Name of Jesus! I bind the spirit of murmuring and complaining! I bind the spirit of discord

A Call Into His Presence

and disunity! I bind the spirit of lackadaisicalness and laziness! I bind the spirit of mediocrity! I bind the spirit of poverty! I bind the spirit of envy and jealously! I bind the spirit of sickness. There is a spirit of sickness, not a natural occurrence, but a spirit of sickness, which attacks the spirit that brings about natural manifestation. I bind that spirit! I bind the spirit of hatred! I bind the spirit of low self-esteem! I bind the spirit of depression! I bind the spirit of anger and frustration! I bind every unclean spirit, sexual immorality, unnatural affections, and effeminate spirit! I bind the greedy and money hungry spirit! I bind, God, the spirit of anything that is ungodly! I bind the kingdom work of the Devil! I bind every high place and pull it down! I bind every strong hold in the Name of Jesus! In the Name of Jesus, I bind doubt, I bind doubt. I bind the spirit of doubt and complacency. I bind it now in the Name of Jesus! You said 'whatsoever we bind on earth You would bind in heaven!' Whatsoever we would loose, You would loose. I loose the spirit of obedience in the Name of Jesus! I loose the spirit of hope! I loose the spirit of peace! I loose the spirit of strength and power! I loose the spirit of faith! Not ordinary faith, but reliable and consistent faith! I loose the spirit of faithfulness and consistency and new commitment! I loose the spirit of a willingness to yield our minds, our wills, and our ways to Thee! I loose an outpouring, a seven-fold manifestation of the Holy Ghost and the anointing of God! I loose the spirit of an unusual spirit of praise! I loose strength in our spirits for prayer, supplication before Thy throne! I loose spiritual eyesight that people would see the glory of our Lord in their lives! I loose salvation in the homes, Hallelujah, Hallelujah! I loose God's love, real love in every family, every parent and every child. Every brother and every sister, every individual, God's love be loosed in thy soul Hallelujah! I loose the chains which bind, that keep people from stepping out of the box! I loose! You said You have given us the keys to the Kingdom, Hallelujah, whatsoever we loose, You would loose in heaven! I loose finances, not just to pay a bill, but something to put in the bank, Hallelujah! I loose an overflow for this church financial situation, yea, God, Hallelujah!

I loose the spiritual prayer warriors to go forth into battle, Hallelujah! Casting out evil spirits in their homes, Hallelujah, thank You! We are praying against sickness in their homes, in their own

A Call Into His Presence

bodies! Loose the prayer warriors to use the weapons that are not carnal but they are mighty through God unto the pulling down of every strong hold. Pull the strong hold down, every strong hold that is going against us and against this church, and against the Saints. I loose the power of God, the Word, Hallelujah!!!

Let His glory be revealed, let Your glory be revealed, let Your glory revealed in this city! In this city, in this church, in our homes, let Your glory be revealed in us as we say "yes" to God yesssssssss all day! Yesssssssss all night, Hallelujah!

Satan, the Lord rebuke you! Satan, the Lord rebuke you, Jesus is Lord! He is Lord! He is Lord! Lord, over suffering, Lord, over our children, Lord, over our finances, Lord, over our homes and our jobs! Lord, over everything; our emotions, our bodies, our ministries, our gifts!

I loose the gifts of the spirit to begin to operate in this church. I loose the gifts of the spirit, yea, anoint them for Kingdom warfare, Hallelujah! Now, will you help me magnify the Lord?! Will you exalt his Name together, Hallelujah! Will you help me exalt Him, will you help me lift Him up in the praise! On this tenth night, the number of divine order, yeaaaaaaaaa, Hallelujah! Ring it out of your soul! Ring it out of your soul! Don't let the devil get the victory. Give God the praise! Praise Him! Step out of your Soul! Step out of your body! Step into the spirit realm and praise Him beyond your flesh! Praise Him beyond your situation! Praise Him beyond your tribulation! Praise Him beyond your tiredness! Praise Him beyond your lack of money! Praise Him beyond your lack of health! Praise Him in the abundance because He's worthy! He is worthy, worthy, Jesus is worthy! Worthy of all of the glory and honor! He is worthy!!! Thank You, Lord! Thank You, Lord! Thank You, Lord! Wonderful Savior!

Now, God, we have offered You everything on this prayer night. Tomorrow is not promised so we give You praise every day. Help us, help us, help us, this church, God, our families, God, we lift up our families. We love our families, God, we love this city, we love this community, and we love this country. Help every church and their communities as they pray for strength. Help every family wherever they might be when they call on You through Your Son's

Name, Jesus who is praying for deliverance, but whatever You do, don't look away from us. Oh, God, don't leave us now, don't leave us, God, whatever You do, don't take Your spirit or Your anointing away from us, but give us an increase in the Holy Ghost. Give us an increase in Thine anointing. There are many yokes, which must be destroyed, and we cannot do it without the anointing. The anointing of God destroys every yoke! Make a way, make a way, make a way for Your people we pray, the strength of God even now in a time of storm to take the Gospel out to this city! We pray these prayers in Jesus Name. Amen and Amen.

Closing Scripture Matthew 10:22-42 (KJV)
"And ye shall be hated of all men for my name' sake, but he that endureth to the end shall be saved. But when they persecute you in this city, flee into another; for verily I say unto you, Ye shall not have gone over the cities of Israel, till the Son of man be come. The disciple is not above his [teacher], nor the servant above his lord. It is enough for the disciples that he be like his [teacher], and the servant like his lord. If they have called the master of the house Beelzebub, how much more shall they call them of his household? Fear them not, therefore; for there is nothing covered that shall not be revealed; and hidden, that shall not be known. What I tell you in darkness, that speak in light; and what ye hear in the ear, that [proclaim] upon the housetops. And fear not them who kill the body, but are not able to kill the soul; but rather fear him who is able to destroy both soul and body in hell. Are not two sparrows sold for a farthing? And one of them shall not fall on the ground without your Father. But the very hairs of you heard are all numbered. Fear not, therefore; ye are of more value than many sparrows. Whosoever, therefore, shall confess me before men, him will I confess also before my Father, who is I heaven. But whosoever shall deny me before men, him will I also deny before my Father, who is in heaven. Think not that I am come to send peace o earth; I came not to send peace, but a sword. For I am come to set a man at variance against his father, and the daughter against her mother, and the daughter-in-law against her mother-in-law. And a man's foes shall be they of his own household. He that loveth father or mother more than me,

is not worthy of men; and he that loveth son or daughter more than me, is not worthy of me. He that findeth his life shall lose it; and he that loseth his life for my sake shall find it. He that receiveth you receiveth me, and he that receiveth me receiveth him that sent me. He that receiveth a prophet in the name of a prophet shall receive a prophet's reward; and he that receiveth a righteous man in the name of a righteous man shall receive a righteous man's reward. And whosoever shall give to drink unto one of these little ones a cup of cold water only in the name of a disciple, verily I say unto you, he shall in no [way] lose his reward."

Closing Remarks:

Thank God for the reading of the Scriptures. Let us be encouraged to be bold but yet wise in our pursuit of winning souls and sharing the Gospel. Jesus gave a very realistic view to the Disciples. They are not greater than the teacher and certainly they are not greater than the Master. If the Master had to suffer, we should expect to suffer. If people don't receive you, it's not you they are not receiving, it is God, so don't take it personally. Don't take these things personal which happen in your lives, expect for them to happen if you are doing the right thing. If they are not happening, then that should tell you either you are doing nothing or you are doing the wrong thing. Things happen to those who are doing God's Will and His work. Those are the people who are being attacked. Satan doesn't need to attack anyone who is not doing anything or the attack is not against his work. If you are not doing kingdom work for God, then you are already subdued. When he doesn't have you, he is trying to subdue you. So we are attacked because he is trying to subdue us. He is trying to overcome us and overtake us because we have made up our minds to do what God has instructed and assigned us His disciples to do. With the strength of the Lord helping us we can do these things, for we can do all things through Christ.

Matthew 10:28 says, "**And fear not them who kill the body, but are not able to kill the soul; but rather fear him who is able to destroy both soul and body in hell**."

People can kill you, they can take your natural life, but they cannot take your soul. They cannot take what God has for you. That is so encouraging because for those of us who are trying to do God's work, really trying to do God's work, we can tell because the devil comes against us in a mighty way. He doesn't want us to succeed because souls are at stake. It's not just your soul, it's all the people you can reach. He doesn't want you to reach anyone, and if you can reach people in your own home, in your own families, your own circle of existence, don't you know that encourages you and strengthens you? If 'I' can do this, then the world will be a whole lot easier than trying to witness to someone in your family. It's always easier to talk to a stranger when you don't know anything about them and they don't know anything about you. When we try to talk to someone in our families, whether we grew up with them or we know them, you already know the first thing. If you push them to hard, they will start saying, "Oh, who do you think you are?" "Like you never did any wrong" "Oh, you are high and mighty now or you have forgotten where you came from?" They start throwing those things at you to get you off target and for you to leave them alone. We have to be reminded, if any man be in Christ he is a new creature. So those old things, they can't bring them up because we are new, and that gives us the strength to do what God says for us to do.

The first 21 verses of this chapter says if people don't receive you then you are to shake the dust off of your feet and keep on going. Compassion. God did not say put no emotion over obeying him. Is that clear? We don't put any emotions over what God says to do. We cannot force people to receive salvation. If you go to someone and they don't want to do what is right, you have exhausted all of your means trying to deal with them and they have made it known they are not hearing anything you have to say. If they tell you "I don't want to hear what you have to say and leave me alone," then you have done your job. The only thing we can do is pray for them. It is so hard to shake the dust off our feet, but we must allow the Spirit of God to lead and guide us. We must remember there is a soul waiting just for you!

END OF DAY 10 PRAYER SERVICE

Personal Note: The Fire of God!

Our purpose is only to do the Will of God. On tonight, my soul cried out for Jesus to take me, use me and do as He did with the disciples. My mind, my soul, and my body were on one accord as I cried out like a raging sea. And then it happened. God spoke to me and said "Get the anointed oil and anoint everyone" because the fire of God was going to burn up everything in us not like Him! God said there are some people in His **PRESENCE** who have things inside of them that need to be burnt.

Have you ever seen a plant or weed wither to find out later it began to grow again? There are some things inside of us where the root needs to be plucked out and burned so it will never grow again! We have things in us, in our minds that keep occurring and we thought were dead, but it keeps coming back alive and we pray but we still keep facing the same challenges and doing the same sinful things over and over. It's not dead, it's just laying there but when you burn something, it's no more. It turns into ashes.

The fire of God represents two types of fires. First, God is going to burn up everything in us not like Him; everything in our minds, everything we are doing, everything we are saying which is contrary to Him. God is going to burn it up! But there is one condition: this call was only for the BELIVER. Only for those who will not doubt Him and receive what He was going to do. The second fire, is the fire of the Holy Ghost! There are people who have not been filled and baptized with the Holy Ghost with that FIRE! The Bible says in Luke 3:16, "John answered, saying unto them all, I indeed baptize you with water; but one mightier than I cometh, the latchet of whose shoes I am not worthy to unloose: he shall baptize you with the Holy Ghost and with fire." Why do we need the fire of God? Because it is the fire of God, which burns up and purifies things in us that come to stop us from doing what God has called for us to do.

~ Evelyn

STEP 11/DAY 11, THURSDAY

"The Number 11 Means Disruption & Disorder"

DAY 11 PRAYER SERVICE BEGINS

Opening Remarks:

Only God can help us. The number eleven stands for disruption and disorder. Wherever there is disorder, we ask God to flip it around and send disruption and disorder to the attacks of the enemy. The attacks of Satan upon us; all of his plans would be disrupted and they won't have any order so they won't have any success against us.

Opening Scripture: Psalms 11 (NLT)
"I trust in the Lord for protection. So why do you say to me, "Fly to the mountain for safety! The wicked are stringing their bows and setting their arrows in the bowstrings. They shoot for the shadows at those who do right. The foundations of law and order have collapsed. What can the righteous do? But the Lord is in his holy Temple; the Lord still rules from heaven. He watches everything closely; examining everyone on earth. The Lord examines both the righteous and the wicked. He hates everyone who loves violence. He rains down blazing coals on the wicked, punishing them with burning sulfur and

scorching winds. For the Lord is righteous, and he loves justice. Those who do what is right will see his face."

Let Us Pray:
    Lord, we thank You. We have come into this place on this eleventh day of this year, the eleventh day of prayer for this season for this time for our lives. As the scripture says in Psalms Lord that wicked people, those who are unrighteous that You would bring trouble in their lives, You would reward them, God, for the evil works that they are doing. We are grateful, God, You have touched us and delivered us in our minds, saved us and You have given us a mind not to do evil things, but a mind to serve You and pray and ask for Your strength that You would change our lives from a life of unrighteousness to a life of righteousness. All the things that are happening in this society, we don't have a complaint, we just pray for Your continued protection, Your help and to keep our eyes open, God. Lord, keep our ears attentive to the things going on around us that we would not become victims because of our lack of paying attention and focusing on our surroundings in the very real fact that people are doing very bad things these days.
    God, even with the situation concerning this nation, we can speculate and come up with many conspiracy theories, but we really don't know why people could have made better decisions but they didn't make better decisions and try for a more peaceful resolution verses the war. We have an inclination or idea, God, money is involved in this, but, God, we ask now, as it is being admitted this country has made a mistake in the tactics, we have chosen, the very reason for going into battle can be questioned, but there are souls at stake; people's lives. You told us to render unto Caesar what is due unto Caesar. If we sign up for the Armed Services, we have to do what they tell us to do as American citizens; we have to do what our government tells us to do as long as it is not contrary to what You instruct us. Therefore, God, we pray for their lives, the Soldiers men and women. We pray for their lives and we ask You would disrupt the plans of the enemy overseas, the enemy within our own nation, that You would stop their plans, God, from bringing this country to its knees. If this country falls, every family will suffer; whether the

families are good families or bad families is not important. Innocent lives would be lost, children... God, what will happen to the children? The people who are paralyzed or mentally challenged, who will take care of them? The People who can't live without electricity, their oxygen tanks have to be on. The people who need dialysis. The people who need all these types of treatments which only a modern society can provide that extension of life.

If this country is brought to its knees, God, then these people are going to die. We pray now, God, You would move and bring about destruction to all of the evil works of the enemies of this nation. Just like the children of Israel, God, there were many things they did which was sinful that made You angry, but You never ever let the nation be wiped out because they were Your people. This Nation is a Christian Nation, God. There are saved people in this country who are praying for the divine intervention of help, for mercy, for Your grace, and for salvation. We pray along with them that You would move, God, and we ask You would send strength to this church, to these people. Send strength to every church, members of the churches and their families, God, who have called upon Thee; cried to Thee as they walk into churches, funeral homes and hospitals as their loved ones have been maimed and crippled and murdered. Whether it is though the war in Iraq, Afghanistan or wherever overseas they are fighting or even in this country. The war of crime on innocent victims, the parents who receive phone calls their children have been found after they have been murdered. None of us wants to live to experience that, because we can empathize. We pray, God, You strengthen every family who has already gone through that, and strengthen the families who will have to go through these types of horrific times of sorrow this year.

God, with great boldness, as You have instructed us on yesterday, You have given us power against every unclean spirit and to cast them out and to pray against all manner of sickness and disease. There is a sickness and disease of sin and evilness in this country and we come against it now. The evilness in this city, we come against it now. We come against the wicked which will kill or hurt innocent people because they need fast money because of some addiction. Oh, God, help this city, help this city. Strengthen, God, Your people in this city. We pray for spiritual disruption of all the plans the principalities, the high places, Satan and his army have unleashed on this city. We pray for blindness, God, not naturally but spiritually and that You would remove the scales off the people eyes in this city for us to see, God. If there was ever a time for us to pray, the time is now, not tomorrow but today. Let today be the day of salvation. Let today be the day of deliverance. Help Your people, God, in this city; help us, God, to be an example to others that prayer still works. Help us to be examples to others, God, that there is no shame in calling upon Your Son's Name. Help us, God, to be an example to others, that we can look at life with a positive attitude. Help us to show that we can go to You and pray for blessing and pray for increase and not just pray, God, You would just help us to hang on, for You are more than a God for people just to hang on. You are a God who said the Earth is Yours and the fullness thereof and everything, and everyone that dwells inside Your Earth. This city is in Your earth, we Your people are in Your earth. We need Your help, God, we lift this city up to You, God; the Mayor, City Councilmen, Policemen, Firemen, Emergency response unit, Doctors, Hospitals workers, Lawyers, private industry, School Teachers, Hallelujah. Garbage Men, people who are working in factories, people who are working in Corporate America. We lift every company, organization, every church up, every family up, help us to bind together as a city, God, remove the hatred, which separates us. Bind racism that continues to grow and fester, God, remove prejudices, remove the hurt and pain from people who are holding on to things from 50 years ago, 100 years ago, 10 days ago 10 hours ago. Help us to realize regardless of how much money we have, education or whatever our color, background or where we were born has no effect on the fact all of us are Human Beings and we need each other to stand up and make a chain of Believers, a chain of Prayer Warriors. You have given us something no one else can duplicate. You have given us something in our heart, a concern, a burden in prayer, we must go to You; for this city will be successful.

    Help us, God, to realize, even though this nation has voted to raise minimum wages, it is still a joke. Nobody can live off $7.00 and some change an hour. That is not a living wage, God. Help us to be fair with one another in this city. Help this city to be an example to other cities throughout the nation. This state is supposed to be a part of the Bible-Belt, but yet, God, we have dropped the ball. But we are grateful, Lord, there is a remnant in this city and we are a part of that remnant. We are not the only ones, as Elijah was told, You had thousands of Prophets who had not bowed down to Baal. There are thousands of people in this city, who have not given over to the devil and they have not given in, they have not lost their hope and their resolve, God, to fight on spiritually and to pray. They are not popular, God, they don't gain media recognition but they are here in this city and they are praying, God, and they are asking for help. Help this city, God. Help this city, Lord. How can we pray for 40 days and pray for the membership of this church, pray for our families and exclude this city? It cannot be, God. We live in this city, our families live in this city. We live here, Lord God. How can You help us and not help this city? If You help us, You will help this city. If You help the city, You will help us.

Make things more pleasant for this year. Open up doors of opportunity from a professional career stand point, academic stand point, for us in this city. Open up this city, God, to bring more money into the city that people can get better jobs. Bring business here, bring cooperations here. Let them find favor with this city, God, that more jobs would be given to people. Respectable jobs where they can support their families, God, not these jobs which don't have benefits, no health insurance and split schedules, working people to death and wanting to place them on a temporary status that they won't have to pay more money for benefits, misusing people, God. We pray against that. We pray against that and for every dollar, which is earned, crooked, for every dollar, which is earned for the misuse of human beings, God, bring about a curse. Don't let it bring any joy or happiness to those people lives who are collecting that money and spending off of the backs of people and stepping on people and misusing people, God.

Everybody can see easy crime on the streets is wrong and selling drugs is bad and robbing stores is not good, but there is a robbery going on right in these corporations, how they are robbing the workers and mistreating them, God. Somebody has to stand up and pray against those things and we are saying we will. We will stand up and pray, we will stand up and say it is not right, God. It is easy to stand up and talk about the drug addict, the drug dealers but what about those who are embezzling money and never get caught. What about those who devise schemes to keep us under their feet and to keep us poor? To keep us struggling, to keep us stressed out! To keep us worried about how we are going to pay for this and pay for that. To keep us always trying to acquire something but never really obtaining it, and charging us ridiculous interest rates and making a ton of money so we can never pay anything off. Help us, God, help us, Lord. If the very foundations of the world were to fall according to Your scriptures, what could we do about it? Nothing, nothing but we pray to the God who has control and power over everything. You can do something about it; You can do something about these companies here. You can do something about these businesses here. You can do something, God, about the mentality of Corporate America verses those of us who are not in corporate America, God. You can help, God, and You can give us a voice! You can give us a platform; You can unify all of the working class people. All of the poor and indigent; all the sick people. You can unify us where we can put things which separate us aside and work for a common cause call of unity in this city, Lord God, where everybody can have a piece of the American dream.

We didn't write the Constitution; somebody else wrote it and this country is supposed to be governed by it. But everybody doesn't experience the freedom and liberty this country is supposed to bring in every area of existence. You created all human being equal in Your sight. No one is better than anybody else, God. We see these injustices but yet we are encouraged, God, that a better day is coming. You promised us, God, here on this earth not just in heaven. We said it on just last night and we are saying it again. David said he would have fainted unless he believed he would see Your goodness on this earth in the land of the living. Well, God, we are not telling You how to do it. We don't even have an idea on what to suggest as remedies to any of these problems, God, but we just know You are the problem solver. We ask You do something about it for Christ sake! For the sake of Your Body, the Body of Christ, Your Church. Help us, God, help us, God, help us, God, help us, God.

Look down upon us through the eyes of mercy and have compassion upon this church! Have compassion upon the members. Have compassion upon our families. Have compassion upon this city. Have compassion upon this state. Have compassion upon this region and this country. Look down even on this world and have compassion. God, let the Gospel be spread from east to west, north to south. Let every territory on this planet be covered! Where there is a human being, let the Gospel be brought to everybody. God, that they would have an opportunity to accept Your Son, the Savior, for Jesus is the only Hope. He is the way! He is the door; He is the open door! He is the life! He is our bread! He is our water! He is our everything! He is our only hope! We want to be a part of the spreading of the Gospel. God, let us not be like water but let us be like peanut butter; it spreads thickly, Lord God, and it can hold a torn piece of bread together. Let us have that type of anointing, God, where as we spread throughout this city. This small church can play a part like a small band aid to be able to hold pieces of this city together, to bind us together with love through the power of the Holy Ghost.

Bind this city together through prayer with the power of Your Word! We can speak a word to these members to bring hope into people's lives who they come across on a daily basis. People who feel like giving up because of how they have been mistreated on their jobs. Some are down about how they are being mistreated in their different work places and in school. And opportunities are being shut down on them at the banks, and finance companies and they cannot get a decent car loan and have to pay a ridiculous amount for decent lending, God! You can give us the strength to be renewed to keep people from going over the edge for worrying and just saying it's hopeless. Killing their families because they don't feel this world has anything good for their families to live in, so they kill their kids and then kill themselves. We pray against that spirit now in the Name of Jesus. People who have turned to alcoholism and other drugs and things have clouded their thinking and thoughts in their minds because they feel hopeless and helpless; they have been hurt, they have been bruised and the inner most part of their spirit, their hearts, have been torn and ripped apart! They say what is the use, they have tried over and over again to do it the right way, but there was no help. Let us be the one who brings the Gospel of hope to say, "There is help. Jesus is Your help." Hallelujah. "He can do a new thing in you; He can change your life. He can bring you up out of the pit and set your feet upon a rock and that rock is the Word of God. He can turn your life around from misery and make it one of joy and gladness. He can take you from poverty and take you to a place of overflow, Hallelujah! You can be struggling and not being able to support your family and Christ can lift you up where you can support your family and somebody else's, Hallelujah." That is the God, we pray to and Who is the God we believe in. That is the God, Who has power over evil.

People don't realize You created evil. You created everything. Evil didn't create itself; You created Lucifer before he decided to make a wrong decision! People need to understand there is no power, there is no force You are not greater than! Nobody created You; there was nothing before You, Hallelujah! We don't know Your beginning because You said, "You are Alpha and Omega; the beginning and the end!" You are our God, there is no other God and we believe You, Lord! We believe You, Lord, we believe You! We will not doubt You, we will not doubt You! We will hold fast to the profession of our faith. There is only one God, one Lord and there is only one faith.

People talk about people of faith, Hallelujah. We are not praying, Hallelujah, we are not praying for the increase of faith throughout this world in all these other gods. Even in this city, we are praying for the increase of faith in You, the True and Living God. We pray that people would turn to You and say, "Lord, help me, Lord, have mercy on me" and if they do, You are faithful and just not only to forgive them of their sins, and to help them out but make their lives better!

We pray for a better life, on tonight, for this city. We pray for a better life for the citizens in this city, which means us. We live here. We pray for a better life for every home, God. Help us as we are walking in mud right now and it is hard. Every step we take is one of labor. It's one that is draining us, but we are praying now, for

You to give us the strength to walk through this mud. To place our feet on dry ground, God, Hallelujah that we will be able to run for a while, we will be able to walk in ease, God. Things cannot always be hard. Things cannot always be tough. Just like the four seasons, it cannot be summer all the time. It cannot be spring all the time, or fall or winter. There has to come a time, God, when the changing of each season. Let this be a change, God, as the winds are blowing in our lives to bring about a change a transition point. Not one to take us down but one to take us higher in Thee. David said, "The soul can be like a bird and flee to Your mountain."

God, we have come to Your mountain for eleven days. We have been climbing this mountain of prayer. For eleven days, God, we have been climbing the mountain of hope. For eleven days, we have been climbing the mountain of praise. We want to get into Thy **PRESENCE**; we see the cloud! We see the glory You have allowed us to get a taste but, oh, God, we want to be **CALLED INTO YOUR PRESENCE**, Hallelujah. Thank You, Jesus, not for the rest of these 40 days, but we want to be **CALLED INTO THY PRESENCE** for the rest of this year! God, if we could be in Your **PRESENCE** for a year, what a difference it would make for the rest of our lives, oh, bless Your Name! Oh, bless Your Name! Oh, bless Your Name! If we could just come into Thy **PRESENCE**, God! Oh, God, if You would accept our sacrifices of prayer and praise! If You would accept us as we have been washed under the Blood of thy Son, if You would just accept us, God, as we have come in with worship! Come in with hope our hope which is in Thee, God. If You would accept us **INTO THY PRESENCE**. We cannot come in unless You call us, God! We cannot come in on our own, our own righteousness, our own thoughts, our own goodness; nothing. We have no righteousness! We have no goodness without Your Son Jesus. We need Him, God, to help us be ushered into Thy **PRESENCE**! Fill us with Thy Spirit, God. Open up our eyes that we can see that Your glory is here even now, God! Our ears need to be opened up. We want to hear the call to come into Thy **PRESENCE**! We need the strength to climb this mountain for the rest of these 40 days, God. We have twenty-nine more days to go, God. Take us higher every day! Take us higher until we get to the pinnacle, until we get to the top, God, where we hear and see Your glory!

Where we will experience the fire of Your **PRESENCE** in the Name of Jesus!

God, we believe, we believe, we believe, we just believe the Bible. We believe You called Moses up the mountain. David knew something about the mountain because why would he say his soul flees to Your mountain, God? Why would he say that unless he knew something about a mountain experience? About being in Your **PRESENCE**? Elijah was in the mountain in Your **PRESENCE**. You called Abraham up to the top of the mountain to bring a sacrifice. He saw You move, God, on behalf of his son, to send a ram God. We are asking now, Lord God, You move on our behalf. Our sacrifices fall short but oh, God, if You would anoint them! If You would empower them, if You would accept them, God, we would be able to come into Thy sight! You said present our bodies as a living sacrifice, holy acceptable unto Thee which is our reasonable service, God. That is what we are doing, that is what we are doing. Presenting our bodies during this hour of prayer, we present our time to Thee God, we present our souls to Thee God, we present everything to Thee. We present our children! We give You our brothers and sisters. We give You our husbands and wives, we give our mothers and fathers, we give You our jobs, we give You our money, our dreams, our hopes, our thoughts, our aspirations, our anger, our frustrations, our downsides, our upsides. We give You all that makes us who we are; we give You everything! Our failures, our successes, we give them all to Thee. We have no pride before Thee; we are abased. We are humbled, we have prostrated ourselves physically in this building that people, God, on their knees, on this concrete floor, on their knees, God, because they believe in You. There are people, God, sitting here; circulations stopping in their legs because their knees are bent up, God, there are people here who don't feel well. There are people here who could be doing other things, God, but we believe You are so worthy! We believe You are God. We believe You are the only one who can change things!

Therefore, God, whatever it takes we will do it, because it's just that serious. God, as I have stated, there are some things we could never take off our prayer list as long as we are alive here on this earth. You are the sustainer of life. You are the giver of life. You are the protector of life. If You don't protect our children, they won't live. If You don't protect us, we won't live. If You don't keep our homes safe, God, people will rob us, come in and bump us over our heads for prescription medications, or for some money they think we have, God. You are the one who has kept us alive. Therefore, God, we can't take that off our prayer list. Help us now in Jesus Name we pray.

Lord, we love You and we need You. We need You, God, we need You, God, we need You, God, we need You, God, we need You, Lord and we thank You for allowing us to come to You in prayer. This country needs You, the churches need You and we are the church, God. The people make up the church not the buildings. Not the organizations or denominations, it's the people. The people need You, God; the people need You in this city and in this world. We thank You for letting us pray. We thank You for disrupting the works and plans of the enemy, and we have the victory in Jesus Name, Hallelujah Amen and Amen.

Closing Scripture: Ecclesiastes 11 (KJV)
"Cast they bread upon the waters; for thou shalt find it after many days. Give a portion to seven, and also to eight; for thou knowest not what evil shall be upon the earth. If the clouds be full of rain, they empty themselves upon the earth; and if the tree fall toward the south, or toward the north, in the place where the tree falleth, there it shall be. He that observeth the wind shall not sow, and he that regardeth the clouds shall not reap. As thou knoweth not what is the way of the [wind], nor how the bones grow in the womb of her who is with child, even so thou knowest not the works of God, who maketh all. In the morning sow thy seed, and in the evening withhold not thine hand; for thou knowest not [which] shall prosper, either this or that, or whether they both shall be alike good. Truly the light is sweet, and a pleasant thing it is for the eyes to behold the sun; But if a man live many years and rejoice in them all, yet let him remember the days of darkness; for they shall be many. All that cometh is vanity. Rejoice, O young man, in thy youth, and let thy

heart cheer thee in the days of thy youth, and walk in the ways of thine heart, and in the sight of thine eyes; but know thou, that for all these things God will bring thee into judgment. Therefore, remove sorrow from thy heart, and put away evil from thy flesh; for childhood and youth are vanity."

Closing Remarks:

The battles of life are not yours; it's the Lord. God, help me to stand and to hold on. I will not fold! Let us praise God for His mercy that endureth forever.

END OF DAY 11 PRAYER SERVICE

STEP 12/DAY 12, FRIDAY

"The Words of the Lord are Pure"

DAY 12 PRAYER SERVICE BEGINS

Opening Remarks:

On this twelfth day, we thank God He has blessed us and He has kept us alive and He has sent us a guarantee that His Word is pure, tried in the furnace of the earth, purified seven times like silver. God is going to make sure His Word last forever. It is going to stand. The same book of Psalms, we read a few more chapters down: we know about the "Lord is my Shepherd I shall not want. He maketh me to lie down in green pastures." We know that by heart. We know Psalms 27 is an encouraging Scripture "The Lord is my light and my salvation; whom shall I fear." These Scriptures are part of when he says "His Word will stand forever as being pure," it's true.

God identifies and lets us know when we are safe, we are not just walking around like we are in Disney World and there are not evil things happening in this world. There are evil people and evil things are happening, but we are not to become fearful and act like we don't have any hope. We do have hope! We pray and offer a service to God. Our prayers of honesty to God. Yes, we need help, yes, we need God to lead and guide us. Yes, we need God to heal our bodies. Yes, we need God to do many things for us, but we are not praying a prayer of hopelessness. We are praying a prayer that is full of hope, for Christ is the Hope of Glory.

Opening Scripture: Psalms 12 (KJV)
"Help, Lord for the godly man ceaseth; for the faithful fail from among the children of men. They speak vanity every one with his neighbor, with flattering lips and with a double heart do they speak. The Lord shall cut off all flattering lips and with a double heart do they speak. The Lord shall cut off all flattering lips, and the tongue that speaketh proud things. Who have said, With our tongue will we prevail; our lips are our own; who is lord over us? For the oppression of the poor, for the sighing of the needy, now will I arise, saith the Lord; I will set him in safety from his who puffeth at him. The words of the Lord are pure words, like silver [tested] in a furnace of earth, purified seven times. Thou shalt keep them, O Lord, thou shalt preserve them from this generation forever. The wicked walk on every side, when the vilest men are exalted."

Let Us Pray: Singing "Oh Sweet Wonder"

Let us go to God in prayer on this night thanking Him for another day, thanking God for keeping us in the land in this evil time; asking God to let His Word be pure in our hearts and minds.

Oh, God, we thank You for this night. We thank You for what You have done in our lives and how You have kept us. God, as we prepare to enter into our Friday night service, oh, God, we cannot go into this worship service without praying and keeping our covenant on this twelfth day of these 40 days of prayer. We are so grateful You have kept us alive! These twelve days of this year, You have kept our families safe from all hurt, harm and danger. As we are living in the last days and perilous times are upon us, we are grateful, God, You are keeping us. We pray, Lord God, that even in the 12th division of Psalms, You said "[Your] Word is pure just like silver it is tried in the furnace of the earth: Seven times," God "[Your] Word is true and it is going to stand forever; generation throughout generation throughout generations." God, we come standing on the truth, pure Word. We don't want to be guilty. The scripture warns us don't add, don't subtract. If we added it would be added unto us, subtract it would be taken from our very lives, God, and we don't want anything added or subtracted that You have not ordained to be so.

A Call Into His Presence

God during this time, the culture we live in this country, current events and things are happening in the news. Soldiers and people in the Armed Forces are not happy. They are upset about the new plans to send more troops. People are going back to Iraq for their third tour of duty, or another duty. It has an effect on our country. Unhappy people, God, how can they protect us and fight for what is supposed to be liberty and freedom when they are not happy and their families are sad? We pray for their strength and we will continue to pray for their strength and protection, but we also added on this night, a personal prayer for our homes and our little children. God, if You bless them to live there is a realistic possibility they will be drafted in the Army and Armed Services. It is becoming more of a reality every day we live. God, we are not anti-patriots or against patriotism; we are not against this country, God, but we are just praying for justice to be done in this nation.

We ask now, God, for Your mercy to be extended; for You said Your mercy endureth forever from generation to generation Your mercy endures. We are asking for Your mercy to be applied, not just on our generation, but on the generation which is alive and is following us in life, God. Not to follow us in death but to precede us in death that is, but to follow us in life and have the opportunity, God, to enjoy the things You have given this nation to enjoy; freedom and liberties. We say that is a right every American citizen, or it should be understood that is a right for every Human Being.

We pray now for strength of every Preacher, every Teacher, anyone who is carrying the Word of God that they would stand in the pureness and the power of Your Word. Not just on healing of the minds and the heart, and the homes. There are situations, God, where the hearts are hurt from the many horrific things being experienced in this World. We pray now, Lord God, for the boldness of every church that they would stand in Your strength and not give up, and not give in. We pray that love will conquer anything; the love of God will conquer any type of hatred, any type of prejudice, any type of racism, any type of classism where people are separated because they don't make as much money as somebody else. Anything that separates this nation, God, we pray against it. Anything that separates the churches, we pray against it.

We ask for unification on tonight, as the number twelve is symbolic of God's Government, perfect unity, operation, and flow within the government of God. We ask that perfectness in government, operations and systems that an anointing not only be only poured out on this church, but upon our homes. God, this year, we flow, we will operate, and we will move and have our being like never before. Not only praying to enjoy the fruit of our labor but we praying we can set up something aside for our prosperity that they, our children, would have something in life they can look forward to. We pray, Lord God, everyone throughout the history of this nation who has laid down their lives as a stepping stone, for the next generation who can have a better life, that we also can fall in the pattern of history. We pray that we would lay something down, sacrifice something: our time, our prayers, our service, our feelings, our emotions. We pray that we would lay those things aside for the betterment of our families, our races, our people, for our country, this we pray in the Name of Jesus.

God, we ask now for the same God who raised people up from the grave, the same God who restored the eyesight of those who were blind, that the same God would move in our minds and help us. God, help us in this city, help us, God. Help this church, God, to be able to manage, to be able to operate, to be able to use our gifts in a spirit of excellence in a manner which would be more than pleasing to You. Using our gifts, bringing about results of lives being changed from the bad, to the good, for better, Lord God, than worst, from evil to salvation. We pray now, Lord God, for people in this church that their heads would be lifted up. That they would renew their commitment and sacrifice themselves and whatever else it takes for the success of the building of the Kingdom of God, in our souls, in our homes, in this city, in this state and in this nation and even in the world.

God, You know what our future holds. You know, Lord God, who will travel overseas. You know who will travel within the States; You know, God, who is going where and even in this state. You know, God, our very existences and what lies ahead of us. Therefore, God, we pray for the unknown in our lives; we don't know but You know. You know who in this church, You know who is a part of this membership, those who are in our families, God, who will be doctors, and those who will go before great people, who will have a TV audience, a radio audience, news media, print media, **PRESENCE** on the internet, school teachers, fireman and policeman. People who will work factory jobs, God, those who will be inventors, and those who will be entrepreneurs. You know these things. Those who will be parents, God. You know how many children our children will have. We are simply praying, God, whatever avenue of life they take and are walking down, Lord God, that You would lead and guide them and let them stand on the pureness of Your Word. The power of the Word, the conviction of the Word in their hearts; the trials they will face, that they would not be fearful; whatever evilness they face, they would not be fearful. Whatever sorrow they must face, they will not let the sorrow overcome them, and stop them from the pursuit of excellence in their lives.

We pray now, Lord God, for strength in their souls; even as the babies in this church, the toddlers, those who are eight, nine and ten, seventeen through twenty-five, whatever the age range might be, we pray for their strength and their guidance, God. We ask for supernatural increase even for some of us. God, we are somebody's child even if we are 80 years old, we are somebody's child. We still have life in our bodies. We are praying for guidance ourselves, strength and courage, God. We pray for wisdom to teach those who are younger than us the correct things to do in life so their lives would be successful and that they won't make the same mistakes we have made in our lives, God.

Help us to be a pattern and an example of good works according to what the scriptures teach us. Help us to be a people of prayer. God, we used to be a people of prayer but we have turned away our concerns and our thoughts to other things in this world and we have spent very little time praying as our forefathers once did. We are asking for that same anointing, even with a seven-fold increase, that we would pray more than our parents, grandparents ever prayed. We are praying that times do not have to be desperate to pray. They had it hard. God, things were very desperate in their times. They had no other choice but to pray. We have it so easy compared to our parents, grandparents, God, great-grandparents. We are praying now, God, that the ease of life, the victories which have been won and people have shed their blood for us to enjoy in this nation that it has not soften our resolve for battle or for war. The war is not over with, God. There is a fight even in this county. The war is not over with, Hallelujah. Help us, God, to stand up and tell the truth, help us as we pray against black on black crime, Lord God. Young men killing other young men. Just killing for no reason, God. We cannot replace a life, we cannot give life, only You can. Help us, Lord God, as a nation to value the importance of life, for no man can replace it. It can only be given by You, our God.

Now, God, there is a hope which lies in our souls. That's the reason why we are here praying, the reason why we are here in the middle of these 40 days of prayer. There is something You have placed in us: FAITH. God, our faith is in You. Your Bible tells us You have given everyone the measure of faith. We have enough faith in us to do whatever You have placed us on this earth to do, each and every one of us in this building, God. So, therefore, we pray, Lord God, You would reach deep down within our souls and we offer You everything we think belongs to us but really it belongs to You, because You gave us the gifts and talents that we have. We are not just giving You our sicknesses and complaints and our needs and all the other things on the list that we want You to do. God, we are giving You the best we have to offer: our very Being, our very Soul, our best efforts, our best gifts, our best talents, our best thoughts and our best wishes and ideas! Plans and goals, God, we are giving You our very best right now in the Name of Jesus, even our best praise! For even by faith, You heal us when we pray, the King hears us when we call. He will save us with His right hand. He will deliver us in the time of adversity! He will help us in this evil society and continue to protect our children from Pedophiles and weirdoes. He will help us and protect every woman in this church, Lord God, from being attacked by a rapist or being carjacked or being robbed. He will protect the senior citizens, Lord God, and keep them safe from people who have no heart, no compassion and no respect for the elderly. You will keep the men in this church, God, for it is hard for a black man to make it in this society. God, will You keep our minds that we will not become frustrated and want to commit homicide or suicide or just give up on life and not support our families and be there emotionally for our loved ones, God. You will keep us in perfect peace! Keep our minds in perfect peace, keep our minds stayed on Thee.

God, we are not here to impress anybody, we are not here to please anybody else, we are here because we have a desperate need for Your help in this year. Oh, God, help us now, help us now. We ask for wisdom and we receive the wisdom. We ask for management over those things, God, that we would be wise in all of our business. We ask we would be wise in our emotional relationship, we can be wise in our business relationship, every relationship; we can be wise, God, in soul winning. We can do what You have called us here to do to be the head and not the tail, God. We do not have to exist with a poverty mentality. We do not have to live on this earth in a sea of failure, God, surrounded around people who keep sinking to the bottom of the ocean of life, for You have given us formability, God. You have given us the ability to rise above every circumstance and situation because we have Christ in our heart. We have the Hope of Glory in our souls! We have the power of God flowing through our spiritual bodies. Thank You, Jesus, we have the Deity of Christ, the resurrected Spirit of the Holy Ghost inside of us that nothing or no one can bury us and keep us down. No problem, no situation, God, for we will rise above the natural positive thinking and positive affirmation because the Word of God said it: You will quicken our mortal bodies. You have quickened our thoughts and ideas, You have sharpened us, iron sharpening iron, God, You have kept us going, God. If it wasn't for us to be successful in our lives, then You would have not allowed us to be born. You would have killed us at birth, or You would have let us die.

We have been in some situations where we could have died but You let us live. You let us live for a reason; there is work to be done! We are saying we are here, God, we are here. We have punched the time clock and we don't know when the time clock is going to be punched and say our time is up. Lord, while we have breath in our bodies we are going to love You. We are going to serve You! We are going to love one another. We are going to pray for our enemies, we are going to bless them who despitefully use us. We are going to share the Word of God; we are going to give them the Gospel, the good news! We want to let them know it is hope and that hope is Christ! We are going to rebuke every demon and every unclean spirit through the power, which is in the Name of Jesus.

Jesus has given us the keys to the Kingdom to bind and loose when necessary. We will pray until a breakthrough happens! We climb the stairs of prayer until we reach the top! We will not give up in life, we will succeed! We are not failures because our Father God has never birthed any failure. We are success! We are successful. Success lies inside of our souls and we give You the glory now in Jesus Name! We give You the praise, Hallelujah! We magnify You because You are God and there is no other! Glory to Your Name, our King! Glory to Your Name, our Savior! We love God, we love You! We thank You for every life in this church! We thank You for every life in our families! We thank You for keeping our children safe while in school. We give You the glory for letting us come now for twelve days of prayer as we count down to 40, thank You, God, thank You, God, Hallelujah! Bless Him, bless Him in this place, bless Him in this place, He is worthy, He is worthy! He worthy, He's worthy of the praise, Hallelujah!

Death has not come by our way this week and we thank You for that, God, we thank You for that, God, we thank You for that, God, we are glad to be alive. A living dog is better than a dead lion. We are glad to be alive. We thank You for our lives, we thank You for our lives, God! Twelve days has already taken place, people have already died here in this nation, this country, in this World, God. They did not live to see the twelfth day of this year, but we are grateful, God, You let us live. We did not come in this place, God, to mourn, to cry and beg You and complain, but we came to make our prayer request known. You said come boldly before Your Throne, so we come boldly, God, Hallelujah! Hallelujah, Hallelujah to give You praise to lift up the Name of Jesus! To exalt Your Name on high! To magnify the King of Glory! The Prince of Peace, the Lord of Lords. Jesus is Lord, there is no other Savior! There is no other Messiah! There is no other Son of God, He is the Son of God, He is the King! He is the Bishop of our souls! He is the Counselor! He is a way maker.

You have never failed us, God, all of our lives, You have never failed us. You have never failed this church, God, and we give You praise even in the midst of suffering times, we give You praise, Hallelujah! If we don't have a dime in our pockets, we give You glory because we have life inside of these bodies and when these bodies die, God, it is going to return to the dust, but while we have breath inside of these bodies, God, we are going to give You praise! We are going to give You glory, we are going to give Your honor. We are practicing, God. We are practicing for Heaven; one day when we will stand before Your **PRESENCE** and give You all the glory! We will give You the praise with the rest of the Heavenly Host and cry out HOLY, HOLY, HOLY, HOLY is the Lamb of God! We want to make it to that point. Thank You, Jesus, thank You, Jesus, thank You, Jesus, thank You, Jesus, thank You, Jesus, Hallelujah, bless Him, bless Him, bless Him, bless Him in this place! He is worthy of the praise! Jesus is worthy of the praise! Will you give Him some glory in here? Will you give Him some honor? There is no one like Him, He is God and He alone! He is worthy of all honor, He is worthy of all the praise, Hallelujah! And we bless Your Name on this night, we bless Your Name on this night.

Now God bless the continuation of this service as we transition into a wonderful praise & worship service. We want to praise You on tonight; we want to give You the praise on tonight. We want to give You the glory for twelve days. Twelve days of this year, God, we give You the glory, we give You the glory, You are worthy! Do something special in this place. Do something extraordinary in the souls of these people. Visit us with Thy Cloud of Glory, let the devouring fire come and rest upon this church. Do something supernatural, destroy yokes because of Your anointing. Everything that is done in this place we offer to Thee. Be it done in Jesus Name and we thank You for the victory over the Devil, our enemy and adversary. Christ reigns supreme and the people of God say Amen.

Closing Scripture: Psalms 112 (KJV)
"Praise ye the Lord. Blessed is the man who feareth the Lord, who delighteth greatly in his commandments. His seed shall be mighty upon earth; the generation of the upright shall be blessed. Wealth

and riches shall be in his house; and his righteousness endureth forever. Unto the upright there ariseth light in the darkness; he is gracious, and full of compassion, and righteous. A good man showeth favor, and lendeth; he will guide his affairs with discretion. Surely he shall not be moved forever; the righteous shall be in everlasting remembrance. He shall not be afraid of evil tidings; his heart is fixed, trusting in the Lord. His heart is established; he shall not be afraid, until he see his desire upon his enemies. He hath [distributed], he hath given to the poor; his righteousness endureth forever; his horn shall be exalted with honor. The wicked shall see it, and be grieved; he shall gnash with his teeth, and melt away. The desire of wicked shall perish."

Closing Remarks:

This is an encouragement to every believer, who receives this Word. This Word gives us a good idea of what is going to happen to the wicked. We don't have to worry about what people are doing in this nation or in this world that is wrong against other human beings, against our innocent children. We don't have to worry about that. God has a place for them. He has something that He is going to allow to happen in their lives and we give God the praise as Psalms 12 says His Word is pure. If God said it, it shall come to pass!

<u>END OF DAY 12 PRAYER SERVICE</u>

STEP 13/DAY 13, SATURDAY

"The Spirit of Disbelief & Doubt"

DAY 13 PRAYER SERVICE BEGINS

Opening Remarks:

On the thirteenth night, we pray against hypocrisy, which is turning away, giving up and disbelief in what God has said and instructed. Pray for strength and continue to believe what God has said in these twelve days of prayer that your faith would increase. Believe what He says and that whenever He speaks to you know that it will be. We too have confidence to know first His voice, secondly when He tells us something, even if it sounds ridiculous, we will take steps to make it happen. If we do that, I believe God will make it happen. In II Corinthians, Paul encouraged them to be strong, not to turn away from that which they had accepted and obviously testified that they believed. We teach the same thing, not to crutch off me or anybody else. Examine your own self and prove your own thing.

If you believe God is God, God will talk to you just like He would to anybody else. Anyone who comes to Him first must believe that He is God and that He is a rewarder to them that diligently seeks Him. If you continue to do what you have done these twelve days for the rest of your lives the Lord will speak to you. When the Lord speaks to you don't doubt God is talking to you and don't let anybody else make you have doubt. Examine yourselves. He says prove all things. Do you have faith? Do you believe God will speak to you? Sometimes we can fade a little bit, of course and think we have to prove to somebody else that God has told us something. We don't have to prove to them, the Lord will prove Himself. All we have to do is do what God has asked us to do, and believe whatever instructions He still instructs us through the reading of the Word. It is very important we read our Bibles because God will lead and guide us through the Word. He will encourage us, strengthen us, and build up our faith because we are not reprobates. We are not people who will turn our backs on God. God has not rejected us and if that is the case, then God will hear us when we talk to Him and we should hear Him when He talks to us.

On this night, as we said thirteen scripturally, biblically deals with hypocrisy—doing things out of order, turning away from that which we believe, the Bible and God. A double-minded man is unstable in all his ways: so it can be like for two days we believe God, and then two days we don't believe God, two more days we believe Him again. That falls in the line of what Paul is encouraging us not to do. We want to believe God. It is better to start down here and work your way up, than to start way up here on the mountain. If you are going to stay up here in your beliefs then you really need to stay up here in your beliefs, because if not, it is going to be an obvious sign showing you are on the rollercoaster of faith. Faith is not a rollercoaster ride, and this goes for all of us.

Whenever we doubt God, that is a lack of faith. Doubt brings on disbelief; disbelief will bring on disobedience because our doubt and disbelief will tell us not to do or we cannot do what God says to do. What has God done for you, what has He done for you in your life? Has God done anything for you in your personal life? Has God done anything for you? We have faith in the Bible. One of our favorite Scriptures is Philippians 1:6 **"Being confident of this very thing, that he who hath begun a good work in you will perform it until the day of Jesus Christ shall perform it, shall complete it until whenever Christ return."** If God has done something for you, if he has started something, He is not going to leave it incomplete. There is no way we can look at our trials and tribulations as being permanent; we cannot look at them as having a permanent effect neither. It is not going to have a permanent effect, not negative, it cannot be, because once God starts something, once He answered that first prayer, He started something. He has to keep answering. Once God saved you, He started something. Once He blessed you, He started something. Once He got the Devil off you, healed your body, whatever your prayer request was and He answered, He has started something!

Opening Scripture: 2 Corinthians 13:1-14 (KJV)
"This is the third time I am coming to you. In the mouth of two or three witnesses shall every word be established. I told you before, and [tell you beforehand], as if I were present, the second time; and being absent now I write to them who heretofore have sinned, and to all others, that, if I come again, I will not spare, since ye seek a proof of Christ speaking in me, who toward you is not weak, but in mighty in you. For though he was crucified through weakness, yet he liveth by the power of God. For we also are weak in him, but we shall live with him by the power of God toward you. Examine yourselves, whether you are in the faith; prove yourselves. Know ye not yourselves how Jesus Christ is in you, [unless you are discredited]? But I trust that ye shall know that we are not [discredited]. Now I pray to God that ye do no evil; not that we should appear approved, but that ye should do that which is honest, though we [appear as discredited]. For we can do nothing against the truth, but for the truth. For we are glad, when we are weak and ye are strong; and this is also we wish, even your perfection. Therefore, I write these things being absent, lest being present I should use sharpness, according to the power which the Lord hath given me to edification, and not to destruction. Finally, brethren, farewell. Be perfect, be of good comfort, be of one mind, live in peace; and the God of love and peace shall be with you. Greet one another with an holy kiss. All the saints [greet] you. The grace of the Lord Jesus Christ, and the love of God, and the communion of the Holy [Spirit] be with you all. Amen."

Insight as We Prepared for Prayer:
Let us go to God in prayer rebuking that spirit of disbelief and doubt, praying for encouragement and strength: that we will examine our own lives and look and see what the Lord has done for

us. Standing strong in the fact that God loves us, He hears us each and every one of us and He is here to help us make it another day, make it throughout the year and the rest of our lives and throughout eternity.

Let Us Pray:
Now we thank You on tonight You have given us an opportunity, Lord God, to make it out to the thirteenth day of prayer. We have taken thirteen steps, Lord, closer to Thee. Some steps smaller than others, some steps larger or significant, but each step very important, as we go in the pace, the Holy Ghost leads each and every one of us in this place. Each and every one of those who could not make it who are praying every night as we have received word, God, that the Saints who are not able to come out every night are praying during this hour, praying and taking time out to join in with us as a church family to pray.

We pray against the spirit of hypocrisy, God, turning back on that we know as our faith or our beliefs, not as the definition that is given about religion, God, because serving You is more than just a religious act, but it is an act that encompasses our very life. Decision we make, people we are involved with, the people we chose not to be involved with, even our jobs, every details of our life, God, we are facing on a daily bases. We come, Lord God, because the significances of praying on this thirteenth day, we pray, God, binding the spirit of turn back, the drawback spirit. It is extremely crucial, because if we really do believe You have spoken to us, You are speaking to us, encouraging us telling us we can do great things. the prayer request that we are asking, some of the prayer request, Lord, are huge. More than hundreds of millions of dollars, we ask You to save a Soul, a loved one. That is huge for us, God. That is more than any amount of money we could ever receive. We would gladly trade these possessions for those Souls, our loved ones to be saved, even healed, God, and delivered from whatever binds them. Those are the kind of prayers we believe You have spoken and said victory is ours. Therefore, God, as a period of time goes by, the spirit of hypocrisy and disbelief begins to rise or raise its ugly head. God, the seeds planted somewhere in us when somebody drops a word of doubt or the Devil or one of his emissary comes with discouraging words or a trial of tribulation which knocks us back down. And now time seems to be our enemy and not our friend, but God, we know You control time. You created time and time has no meaning of boundary for You and what You say. If You say it, shall come to pass, it shall come to pass.

Therefore, God, we pray for the strength of this church, every family which is represented, everyone in this place on tonight. Lord God, we pray for our resolve to be a strong one that we will not come off the wall of faith in belief in You and hope. We will be encouraged, even when we are discouraged, we will be encouraged. We know You have not forsaken us, and what You have promised, what You said being confident of this very thing He that has began a good work, when You saved us it was a good work. When You healed us, delivered us, it was a good work. When You accepted our praise, God, and You allowed us to pray and then You answered prayers, it's a good work, Lord, and we are standing firm on that even going to the point of being like a Prophet speaking to our enemies; not only is it a good work, it is a great work, and it is not great for us to go back to same way of thinking and doubting and having questions in our minds.

We pray now in this place, Lord God, even as I am speaking on behalf of this church, God, that each and every individual on tonight would do as Paul has encouraged the Corinthians, to examine their own faith. Look and see what have You done for them in their lives, God, the things that are important to them, every one of us have something which is different, but yet just as valuable because it is important to us as individuals. God, we are not trying to mimic one another, we are not trying to copy or be like anybody else's church. We are trying to be like the church You are calling us to be. We are not putting on fronts and maybe we will never become a great this or a great that, but one thing we do consistently ask, God, You have given us a call for prayer. You have given us a call to be Prayer Warriors and from that, God, You have shown and shared with us by having great faith in Thee signs & wonders do take place, will take place for any believer, any believer and any Saint!

Anybody, God, who prays not doubting but believing whatsoever they ask, You said You would do it for them. So, God, we are praying and believing whatsoever we ask in Your Son's Name, You will do it, God. You have the power to do anything. God, we need many things, yes, Lord God, we are so appreciative for things developing in this church, Music Ministry, Fine Arts, God, teaching, working with the Youth. We have so many plans, so many ideas, God, but we set all of those things aside. We want the gifts of the Spirit to be in operation, God, that souls might be saved, somebody would be delivered from being bound and depressed, possessed by demons. We want that kind of power, God, that power might not ever gain us fame or fortune in this world, but it would sure gain us respectability within the Body of Christ and more importantly, God, it would help us to be an arrow which lights, and points towards You. People would be directed toward You, God, because those are the kind of areas in ministry, healing and deliverance, souls being saved, miracles being wrought, those are the areas that human beings can't take any credit. Not one ounce or one iota of the glory can be taken from You. People can be talented to sing, God, but people's talent has nothing to do with the gift of faith. Talent has nothing to do with the gift of prophecy. Talent has nothing to do with the gifts of helps. Talent has nothing to do with the gifts of teaching, the gift of knowledge. Talent has nothing to do with miracles being wrought, God, people being saved, God, talent has nothing to do with gifts. It has nothing to do with Your anointing and faith combined, and taking faith and doing some works with it. God, the gift of healing, we believe, God, in divine healing. We believe in the prophetic word. You can speak a word of knowledge and revelation, and discernment and anyone of us in this church to let us know what is coming down the line ahead of us, the plans of the enemy, where he is trying to ambush us. What he is trying to do to bring us down, the tactics that he is using to attack our families, and we can pray against that binding every strong hold and every principality.

We won't win an Academy Award; we won't get anything for recognition, God, but our children's lives will be saved! Our loved ones would be healed; salvation will be wrought in our very lives. God, the Spirit of Addiction will not come back within our lives ever again. God, lying and envy, jealously, hiding iniquities will be forever held that day not being able to possess us or oppress us.

Depression will be conquered; God, schizophrenia, and paranoia will be conquered. God, peace will be given, Lord God, because of the prayers of the righteous, the effectual fervent prayers of the righteous availeth much. God, we examine our lives and see what You have done for us. We will not turn away and say the things You have done for us were not done or man was reasonable. The things You have done for us only a God can do! Only the true and Living God could do. Only You could do, God, therefore we come here on tonight even while it is raining outside, God, You blessed us to make it here. You blessed more than one person to make it here so we meet the criteria for supernatural work to be done; two or three gathered in Your Name, You said whatsoever they ask of the Father in Jesus Name, the Father would do it. You said, God.

How can these great things come to pass? How can these great things be possible? Only because You give the power that one can put a thousand to flight! Two can put ten thousand to flight. What can three, four, five, six, seven, eight, nine, ten spiritual warrior's, prayer warriors do God?! We come and we have laid aside our pains and our own personal heart aches and our problems. We bind together in a spirit of love and unity in this place and we come against everything that brings doubt and fear against our church, against the minds of the people, God, who take away our hope! You have done so many wonderful things as we look over our lives which encourage us and it tells us You are able to do exceedingly abundantly above all we can ask or think according to the power that works in each and every one of us, God. It is important we stand together as a church united in prayer, because if somebody is weak along the way, God, somebody else's faith can scoop them up and help carry them until they are strong enough to be back on the front lines of prayer and get back into combat. It's just that serious, it's just that important, God!

We pray for love in every home. We bind the spirit of hatred. Spirit of argument, be bound. We bind the spirit of discord. We bind the spirit of jealousy and envy. We bind the spirit, God, of disunity. We bind the spirit of separation; bring together and unite every home. Every home through love, God's love through Your power! Let the Holy Ghost come now, as we often pray, we want signs & wonders. We want all of the glamorous or fascinating things we think the

Holy Ghost means, but You said He was a Paraclete. You first made mention that the Holy Ghost would be a Comforter. We ask now, the Comforter come and bring peace to those who need comfort in this church, that the Comforter would come and bring encouragement, God, to let people know they really can do all things through Christ. He will strengthen them, they can make it, God, and they will make it because Christ is the way. Let the Comforter come in the minds, God, and kick every contrary violent spirit out! Not violence that lies solely within the person, but the violence attacks us these demons, God, are not trying to lullaby us out of the Body of Christ or lullaby us, or long us away from You. They are violently attacking our minds, our homes, our bodies, and our works. We have planted seeds; they are violently trying to dig up the seeds we have planted to keep us from getting a harvest. We come against that now in the Name of Jesus!

Let the Comforter come and reign in our Souls for where there is peace, God, where there is peace, it is easy to have faith. So if You give us peace, our faith will increase and grow. Where there is peace, God, it is easy to think clear and we can have clarity in our thoughts. Where there is peace, God, there is not a lot of rumblings and a lot of noise being made and the Devil is trying to make a ruckus, but the Holy Ghost the Comforter will bring peace! Bring the peace of mind that is needed, God, that our ears will hear You clearly when You speak. Our eyes would see You and the move of the Glory of God being revealed God! Our very senses of touch would be able to feel the anointing of God when You come into the room, God! I am not asking for the anointing to just come into this church, this building, God, Hallelujah, because the Bible says "The Lord is in his Holy Temple, let all the Earth be silent!" We know You reside in Your Temple, but we ask according to what Paul taught: we are the Temple of the Holy Ghost, let the anointing come inside of our Temples! Let the anointing come, the anointing come inside every room in our Temples! Let the anointing come inside every home and destroy every yoke now! Let a testimony be given, God, from this moment forward starting on this day, after this day or when people have had this experience before, today would testify they felt the anointing in their homes. They felt the anointing of God while driving in their cars, not just here in the church. The anointing of God is supposed to be with us and follow us wherever we go! The anointing of God has been given to us that we can use it to destroy every yoke. We are the Anointed of God every Christian, Christ – like, because Christ is the Anointed one of Israel! We walk in the very image and footsteps of our Lord and our Savior! We ought to be anointed that whatever we bind should be bound! Whatsoever we loose should be loosed! And we are anointed to have the faith to use the Keys to the Kingdom! You have given us the power over life and death, death and life lies in the power of the tongue. You have given us power over every demon! You have given us power over very trial and tribulation! And we refuse to give that power over to the Devil; he is not going to rule in our lives! He is not going to be the king over our lives! He is not going to govern our homes and our children, or our loved ones, or our jobs, or finances or our health or anything which is tied to us. Satan, the LORD REBUKE YOU! We are not going to argue with you, we have no power to argue with you, but there is POWER in the Name of JESUS! Satan, the LORD REBUKE YOU! Satan, the LORD REBUKE YOU!

Thank You, God, for the realization. Open up the understanding spiritually in this place even on tonight, God, that people would see, God, that this is not a one time prayer, and binding something one time is not a one time prayer, and just coming against the things which come against our minds. The Devil is too crafty. He is cunning the Bibles says, Hallelujah; he is not just trying to attack us and leave us alone. He is going to attack and come back and attack again, take a break and come back and attack in the same area. He is trying to hit us in our weak spots and our sore spots. The spots that are vulnerable, but I speak strength to every area of weakness; let the weak say that I am strong! I speak strength to every area that the Devil is attacking; victory no longer, no longer, no longer, no longer. I speak strength to the mind that we would lose the mind of self. We would lose the mind of 'I', my way, my will and we will gain the mind of Christ! Not my will but Thy Will be done. We will gain the mind of Christ that we would submit our wills and ourselves to You. We would gain the mind of Christ and humble ourselves and be a servant of the Most High and Living God even if it means the very death of our lives, as our reputations might be placed upon a cross, as character assignation takes place. As we are betrayed by people who say they love us, they put us on a cross but that's alright, they put the Savior on a cross! We are not worthy to be placed on any type of cross rather it be symbolically or rather it be real. We are not worthy but we thank You, God, we have been placed on the Cross of Suffering for Thy Name sake! We give You glory! We give You praise!

The Scripture said we ought to be glad we ought to rejoice when men revile us for Your Name sake. When they say all manner of evil against us for Your Name sake, because we are not worthy, God, but we thank You that we can suffer! We thank You that we can be talked about. We thank You that people can tell us what we can't do. We are thankful, God, the Devil attacks us, God; he wouldn't attack us if he didn't think we had something of importance, something great inside of us! Something You planned for our lives, something that we have not walked into fulfillment yet, but the manifestation of the plans of God be made known this year! Bring it to pass! Open up, God, every open door spiritually! Open up the Red Seas in our lives that keeps us separated from the other shore. Take us over; take us over, Hallelujah, in the Name of Jesus! Hallelujah, God, the spiritual increase as we fight against the spirit of hypocrisy; we are not giving up! We are not turning back, we are holding on! We will obey, we are holding on! We will serve You, we are holding on! We will praise You, oh, Jesus, help us, help us to praise You! Help us to love You! Help us to worship You! Help us to sacrifice and give You everything; the sacrifice of praise with the fruit of our lips!

On tonight we put on the garment of praise for the spirit of heaviness, Hallelujah! We Lift up our voices like a trump in Zion! We declare Your works before the people glory, glory; gloooory is to be given to our God for He is glorious! He is glorious! He is wonderful, magnificent is He! Thank You, Jesus, thank You, Lord, thank You, Lord, thank You, Lord, thank You, Lord, thank You, Lord, thank You, Lord, thank You, Lord, thank You, Lord, glory in our souls all honor to Thee. God, we lift You up above our problems. We lift You up above ourselves. We lift You up above the attacks of the enemy. We lift You up above our short coming. We lift You up above any human being. We lift You up above any relationship. We lift You up above those we love. We lift You up above those who hate us. We lift You up over the criticisms. We lift You up over the sicknesses. We lift You up over human conditions. We lift You up over our failures. We lift You up over our successes. We lift You up over ideologies and philosophies! We lift You up over our thoughts and our desires. We lift You up, oh, God higher, higher than any Angelic Beings, Hallelujah. We can give You a praise they can't give! We can give You a praise they don't know about! We can wash in the Blood of the Lamb! Let the redeemed of the Lord say so! We have been redeemed by our Savior; the Angels can't say that; the Cherubim, and Seraphims, they can't cry they were redeemed. There is a praise inside of us that no Angel can duplicate! There is praise inside this church.

Will you get out of the FLESH?! Will you step into the SPIRIT and give God praise?! Will you worship Him in Spirit and in truth! Hallelujah, Hallelujah, Hallelujah, Hallelujah will you step out of your pain whether it be physical or emotional?! Will you step out of your trial, I don't care what it is it. Will you go a little higher up your mountain and give God the glory?!!! Can you give Him the glory? Will you give Him the glory? Can you give Him the glory? Do you want to give Him the glory! The answer is yes! God is here! Let us, all that is in us magnify Him, He is worthy! Worthy is the Lamb! He is worthy! Lift Him up in your soul, don't be ashamed! Don't be afraid, get out of self, step into the cloud the Cloud of Glory! God is calling for You to go higher! Step into the Cloud! Step into His **PRESENCE**! Step into His glory, let God deal with your mind! Let Him deal with Your body! Let Him deal with Your life! Let Him deal with Your children! Let Him deal with Your home! Let Him have Your job. Give Him Your financial situation, give Him everything, let Him deal with it. Take it off and stand on Holy grounds and give Him a holy praise!!! Holy, holy, holy, holy is God Almighty! Hooooooly is our Lord and King! Hooooly is the Savior! Hoooly is the Lamb of God! Hooooly is the Messiah! Hooooooly is Jehovah! Hooooooly is HE, Hallelujah!

Thank You, Lord, thank You, Lord, bless Your Name God. Wonderful Savior, bless Your Name, God. Bless Your Name. Now,

God, You are kind and we love You, we thank You for strength that has come on this night. We are not turning back, we will not turn back and let go to what You have spoken to us in our lives. We have received it and we praise You for it. We believe it, God, not to give up on what You have spoken. We believe it, God, not to give in, we believe it, God, not to quit for You are God. You are God, there is no other. Now, Lord, we believe that it is done and we thank You, God, for hearing us when we pray and making a way for Your people now in Jesus Name and the people of God say Amen. **Give the Lord some praise!**

Closing Scripture: Psalms 136 (KJV)

"OH, give thanks unto the Lord, for he is good; for his mercy endureth forever. Oh, give thanks unto the God of gods; for his mercy endureth forever. Oh, give thanks to the Lord of lords; for his mercy endureth forever; To him who alone doeth great wonders; for his mercy endureth forever; To him who stretched out the earth above the water; for his mercy endureth forever; To him who made great lights; for his mercy endureth forever; The sun to rule by day; for his mercy endureth forever; The moon and stars to rule by night; for his mercy endureth forever; To him who smote Egypt in their first-born; for his mercy endureth forever; And brought out Israel from among them; for his mercy endureth forever; With a strong hand, and with [an outstretched] arm; for his mercy endureth forever; To him who divided the Red Sea into parts; for his mercy endureth forever; And made Israel to pass through the midst of it; for his mercy endureth forever; But overthrew Pharaoh and his host in the Red Sea; for his mercy endureth forever; To him who led his people through the wilderness; for his mercy endureth forever; To him who smote great kings; for his mercy endureth forever; and slew famous kings; for his mercy endureth forever: Sihon, king of the Amorites; for his mercy endureth forever; And Og, the king of Bashan; for his mercy endureth forever; Even an heritage unto Israel, his servant; for his mercy endureth forever; Who remembered us in our low estate; for his mercy endureth forever; And hath redeemed us from our enemies; for his mercy endureth forever!"

Closing Remarks:
There is not enough time in life to delight ourselves in God's Word. God's Word is awesome! We can't explain it. In this division of Psalms, David exhorts us to thank God for His mercy. God is such a merciful and fair God, He is not selfish and His order of things is great. He is so assured in who He is, that He is not threatened or worried about other things, so therefore, He is not afraid of fearful of things being great. If we try to understand His nature and who He is and how much love and mercy that He really does have, things He created has to be associated with greatness because it comes from Him. He doesn't create things for them not to be great, and for them to fail.

Some people are like this: they will see something fail and be torn up because they don't want it to be greater than their own stuff. The thing that fails oftentimes comes from them, but they will not push that thing to be greater than they are because they don't want to lose their own greatness from the sight of people. The sun is great, but so is the moon and stars. If God can have His creation exist in harmony then why can't we? He said he created the sun to rule by day, it has its time, but when night time comes, He created the moon and stars to rule by night. Sun your time is up for this area let your family members your relatives come forth. The sun illuminates a brighter light, the moon illuminates light and so do the stars, let them have some time for some glory and God allows them to have a time to shine. God is so great in His resources.

We should never have to be envious or jealous of anyone or the gifts God has given us because He will give you your time to shine. God is so great and we know science supports this: the Sun never stops shining and neither does the moon. It is the earth that rotates so the sun has a period of time to shine in California but it might be dark in China. When the moon is doing its job over there, the time comes for them to switch a platform which is to show, God had created them to do such. If churches all over the world would be unique and grab hold to this concept, not only would we all have great churches from a humanist standpoint, but we all would do something that every church faces, and that is working together. If we all do this that means that everybody would understand that we all shine all of the time! Greater is He that is inside of me then he that is that is in the world! Do you believe the greater is inside of you? **Nothing in creation will ever shine greater than JESUS THE CHRIST.**

END OF DAY 13 PRAYER SERVICE

STEP 14/DAY 14, SUNDAY

"I Must Cross Over"

DAY 14 PRAYER SERVICE BEGINS

Opening Remarks:

We want to come before the **PRESENCE** of the Lord with a pure mind and heart. We should not have any preconceived notions about what things should be in our lives which puts us in a position that if things don't work out on that scenario, we become disappointed or upset. We want to come to God with a pure heart, pure mind asking God to strengthen us for the journey which lies ahead of us. For is it a great one and we are yet trying our best to go in the direction God has given us, instruct us for our lives. We are not just in here for today, we are here for the rest of our lives. In other words we want God to help us not just today but for the rest of year. We should want Him to help us for the rest of our lives. God is everything to us; He should be everything to us.

On the fourteenth night we incorporate these Scriptures from Deuteronomy 32 in our prayer. God gave Moses a song in this chapter and in that song there are words of life. He explains to Joshua that the people should not take his words lightly. They should adhere to what He said and the instructions He gave in that song, because it would be words of life for them. And God instructed Moses to come up the mountain again. God had called Moses many times to come up to the mountain or climb a mountain to talk to Him. This is going to be Moses' last time.

In reference to ourselves, we need to climb up the mountain and we need to let self be crucified. We need to climb up the mountain and ask God to kill anything that is not like Him. Our thoughts, our ways, whatever we harbor in our hearts, plans we have made that have not been approved by God. We need to ask God to kill it and let it die. Anything in us that is not like God will stop us because anything ungodly cannot cross over to what God has promised us. We want to learn from the mistakes Moses made. The Scriptures said Moses broke faith with Him in the **PRESENCE** of the Israelites. What Moses did in his disobedience to God was an open sin; he didn't do it behind closed doors. He openly disobeyed God. God still allowed the water to come that the people might live and not perish because it wasn't their fault Moses had disobeyed God out of his anger toward the people. God honored his compassion and still let the people survive but it required Moses' life, for Moses openly disobeyed God.

The same thing for Moses is the same thing for each and every one of us who is a child of God. When God instructs us to do something we are supposed to do what God says the way He says, when He says, and not worry about why He said to do whatever He said to do. We really want the type of life that Moses had even in his death. He did the greatest thing out of any Prophet in the Old Testament. The Bible said there was no other Prophet like Moses. If we want to be used by God in a great way, then we have to obey God. God will raise you up, and it will be said there was no other person who did whatever your specific area of ministry is that God has called you to before your time was up.

We want our children, our homes, things which are very close and dear to our hearts, to mean something. If it means to bring a sacrifice, then we need to bring a sacrifice and do like Isaac. When Isaac and Abraham went up the mountain, Isaac was old enough to carry the firewood for the sacrifice: so evidently he wasn't a little boy. Isaac had spent plenty time with his dad in worship and Isaac knew they didn't bring anything else as a sacrifice. He was old enough to put two and two together figuratively; so that means "I" am the sacrifice. When his dad called for him, he was not hiding and he didn't run away or disappear; he freely climbed onto the altar to be tied up to be killed by his father to be offered to God. We need to be like Isaac and freely climb on the altar of prayer and sacrifice whatever we need. If it requires everything, give it all unto God.

God will be the same God in that situation and provide a lamb, for his life was not required. That same mountain Isaac was to be sacrificed on, is the same mountain Jesus gave his life and was sacrificed on. God has not required us to do anything He Himself is not willing to do. He asked Abraham to give his all, his only son. God gave His all, His only Son except He did not make provision for Jesus to be taken off the cross because He was the only way we would have a chance for eternal life. We wouldn't be here if God would have taken Him off the cross. God did let His Son die so we would live.

Why can't we be like Moses? We hear God calling us. Let us go to the top of the mountain and let any and everything else which is not like God, let it be killed. Moses didn't run from God. Moses just simply obeyed God and God buried him. And no man to this day knows where his grave lies. Don't you want God to bury your sins and bury all the junk which is in us, that makes us contrary and disobedient to God? Don't you know God can bury those things where no man can find them? That is the kind of God we serve; He can bury those things that no man can put their hands on it. NO MAN! Even in all the things people say about Moses, he took them to the Promised Land but didn't take them over; it didn't hurt his legacy because there was no other Prophet like Moses. We ought to want to be like Moses in this instance: be willing to be used by God that God would use us in a manner people would say nobody can do that like brother so and so or nobody can do that like sister so and so; wow they really had God in their lives. That would be a wonderful testimony. Give the Lord some praise!

Opening Scripture: Deuteronomy 32:47-52 (NIV)

"They are not just idle words for you—they are your life. By them you will live long in the land you are crossing the Jordan to possess. On that same day the Lord told Moses, Go up into the Abarim Range

to Mount Nebo in Moab, across from Jericho, and view Canaan, the land I am giving the Israelites as their own possession. There on the mountain that you have climbed you will die and be gathered to your people, just as your brother Aaron died on Mount Hor and was gathered to his people. This is because both of you broke faith with me in the PRESENCE of the Israelites at the waters of Meribah Kedesh in the Desert of Zin and because you did not uphold my holiness among the Israelites. Therefore, you will see the land only from a distance; you will not enter the land I am giving to the people of Israel."

Insight As We Prepared For Prayer:
Let us go to into prayer on tonight believing God for a supernatural move in our souls. Ask God to take us to this mountain on tonight, take us up that self dies, that God might reveal and let us see the land of promise. Let us see the land of plenty and blessings. Let us see the place where He intends for us to be in Christ.

Let Us Pray:
God, we believe in the very literal God of the Bible. We believe in the Word, we believe in Your Word that You have written through the hearts of men. Moses himself, God, is responsible for writing what we read. You recorded and kept a journal of the events, things that has transpired in the Children of Israel's life and instructions You gave him that You told him to write. You instructed him, God, to leave behind for anyone that followed after them who would believe what was written, Lord God, the Chronicles of the Children of Israel the history, the Books of the Law. Things, God, that would be a blessing to our lives to see the examples of Your power and how You are far superior and far above any other god who could raise their small self up against Thee.

God, we pray on this night, as we listen to Your words that You have given the Prophet Moses, the words You speak through this church. The words, God, You speak through every parent, and their children every household who would listen to what You have given them, Lord. God, it is for their Land of Promise that they would live by it because they are the words of life, not death. God, we ask now by the power that is in Your Word by Your glory, Your glorious power, God, which has been manifested through the ages. Even before it was chronicled, even before we were created, even before time was called into existences, God, everything You called into existence before this earth knew and still knows about Your power. You are God and You alone.

We ask now, Lord God, that on this night we pray, Lord God, that the mistake Moses made, we will not make that mistake. We will not, Lord God, defy You and deny the faith openly or privately. We will say yes to whatever You instruct us to do and do it the way You tell us to do it regardless of how ridiculous it might appear or sound to someone else. Our very lives are at stake in our obedience. Disobedience will bring about death, we will not try to lie and not be able to walk in our promise land living and enjoying the fruits of our labor. But, God, we pray now, we pray now, we would learn from Moses and we would be like Paul and we would pray that self die daily, in this we are crucified with Christ. God, we want the 'I' to be crucified. Christ was crucified on a mountain.

We pray now, Lord God, as we have gone up this mountain of prayer, it would also be a place of sacrifice where we could place ourselves on the altar as Isaac did out of obedience to his father. We want to place ourselves on the altar, Lord God, we don't want anything in us; no hidden agendas, we don't want any hurts feeling, we don't want any ill feelings, we don't want any over joyous or any overzealous feelings where we think of ourselves more than we ought and think we are such a wonder and we are so this and so that, that it hinders us from doing what You have said for us to do. We want to lay aside every weight and sin; anything that besets us, God, and stops us from running this race. You said, God, the race is not given to the fastest, the strongest, the wisest but to the one that people chose. But if we quit and never run the race then we won't have to worry about winning it. God, we ask You help to lay aside every weight and every sin, Lord God, that we can run the race because if we are running the race we will win because we can't lose with Your Son inside of our souls. Your way, Lord, Your way, we believe that.

We pray earnestly on tonight, God, for a supernatural manifestation, not only in this place but more importantly in our lives, in our souls. Every yoke be destroyed! God, anything that is connected to the selfness of 'I' which is 'Self', let it be crucified. God, let any anger and any frustration be crucified. Moses was upset and he was mad at the people for their murmuring and complaining which caused him to disobey You. You did not excuse him, God. Human beings would say he had a legitimate reason but You did not excuse him for being disobedient and following the instructions You gave. Help us now in this place, God, even myself, not to be frustrated and upset. Lord God, teach us how to live a stress-less life! Teach us how to survive and make it under pressure, and thrive. God, teach us and don't let the pressure squeeze or push us into decision making, God, which will not beneficial to us or loved ones because it would push us to disobedience. Help us, Lord God, to be patient and wait on Thee. Wait for Your instructions and have an ear to hear what You have to say. Help us to have a heart to receive what You say whether we like it or not. Help us to have a willingness to do whatever You say, whenever You say and however You say for any length of duration that You say to do it God until You tell us to do something else. We will do whatever You say to do, however long, God, You say do it. In whatever manner You say do it. If You say pray for forty-one days, we will pray for forty-one days. If You tell us to pray every day for the year, we ought to be at this church to pray. We will be at this church every day of that year, whatever You say God! We will do it. We have a desire to serve You, not just serve You on a surface level, God, where people can pat us on the back and where we can receive some glory.

We want to serve You, God, behind closed doors where nobody is watching and we are travailing in prayer. Our flesh and our minds have been troubled and beaten down by this very life we live. We want to serve You when nobody will tell us thank you. We want to serve You when things are not going our way. We want to serve You when there is nobody in the church. We want to serve You when there is no microphone to pray in! We want to serve You when there is no camera on us! We want to serve You, God, like Moses did so we can have a legacy and a testimony after our lives are over with the great signs and wonders which was wrought through our very lives because we yielded ourselves as servants to You, the true and Living God. It cannot happen without a sacrifice!

A Call Into His Presence

Moses had to give up the life. A life he once knew of wealth, a life of fame, a life of being a part of the royal family, a life of favor. He had to come back to the realization of who his real parents were. He had to come back to the realization of who his real people were. He had to go to Goshen, God, where the slaves were making bricks with straw and water. Not eating steaks but eating off old parts of the meat. Not being able to take perfume baths and people wait on him hand and foot, but he had to become a servant. The chief servant of a nation to be ostracized and talked about when he pronounced great judgments and people who laughed at him and Pharaoh, his heart was harden by You, God. So therefore, the Nation of Egypt would be behind Pharaoh and look down on a former Prince of Egypt. He put all of that aside to do Your work that his people would be set free!

God, if it takes that, whatever it takes, I make the declaration in this place for myself, and for everyone, Lord God, who has yielded themselves to fall under the covering of these prayers that I have prayed, that we would put all of that aside for the freedom of our people! Our blood family, God, the unsaved loved ones and friends we want them saved. The sick in our families who are not healed, we want them healed, Lord, whatever it takes! We will place all that other stuff aside, God, to come up this mountain and say here we are! You don't have to tell us we are standing on Holy ground. From the examples we have seen in the Bible, we know we are standing on Holy ground, therefore we humble ourselves before Thy **PRESENCE**. We are not even coming up wanting to stand in the PRESENCE, God. We fall out, we lay out before You. We prostrate ourselves, we fall on our faces before You, God! We got rid of anything that was in us, God, and if there is anything hidden or trying to stick to us, remove it now. We are praying on this night because we don't want to be like Moses and can't cross over. We want to cross over! We just don't want to see it, we want to cross over! The land You promised the descendents of Abraham, Isaac and Jacob; You have promised things to the descendents of our seeds, God. You said it would be mighty upon this earth. If we would seek ye first and heed to Your instructions and we the seeds of Abraham, also by faith You said, God, in Your Bible in the fourth chapter of Romans tells us so.

Therefore, God, the covenant covers us as well. God, bless us, bless us, in this country. Bless us in this city. Bless us in our homes. Bless us in our souls! Bless us in our bodies. Bless us in our lives. Bless us within our Spirits. Bless us in our mouths that we would no longer speak things or failure doom and gloom, but we would speak life! Speak victory through the authority which comes through the Name of Jesus. Bless us in our minds that our thoughts would no longer be thoughts of failure, hurt, pain, doom, dealing with the past and saying the past is going to predict our future, God. When You killed Moses You hid him where nobody could retrieve his body! We pray now, God, as we lay ourselves out before Thee on this night, You kill everything of flesh, God, You would take it and bury it and we won't be able to find it! There will be no Dracula experience; there will be no coming back to life experience for the flesh. Kill it now! In the Name of Jesus, kill it now, God! There is a higher place which we can't even imagine. There is a place You haven't fully revealed to us in our souls, God, where You desire to take us in worship in Your **PRESENCE** in service, God.

According to Your scriptures, 'eyes have not seen ears have not heard the things that You have prepared for them that love You'. There is some place, there is some place in eternity, there is even some place here in the time dispensation here on this earth, in our lives, God, a place You want to take us where we can't imagine, God. And we can't get there if 'self' dominates, rules, controls us, dictates to us and holds us back. God, we can only get there by walking by faith. Operating by Your Spirit, not being bound by things of the flesh, we give them to You on this night, Hallelujah! Hallelujah, God, just as You spoke to Moses on many occasions speak to us once again. You dealt with Moses in signs and wonders which was wrought that people would know You were the one speaking through him. You were the one who gave him the words to say, the things to write down, the Laws, God, that people must live by.

Help us now and You stand behind us, God! Stand before us, God! Stand up in us, God, and let people see the God of the Bible! The God of the Bible, the God of the Bible, the God of the Bible, let the people see the God of the Bible! In this church in us let the 'I' no longer be 'I' but let the 'I' be the Christ that stands inside of us and helps us to get up every time we are knocked down by life! We will get up, we will not complain, we understand we have a job, a work which must be done here on this Earth. You have called each and every one of us, God, to do something for You, to serve You in whatever capacity great or small. We are saying yes and we submit our wills to Thee that we would serve You with a spirit of joy, excitement and excellence! Enthused and empowered by the Holy Ghost, bless Him, bless Him, bless Him, bless our God for He is worthy! He is worthy, He is God, He is God, He alone, He alone is God, we make that declaration. When we make that declaration, we are making an open proclamation of faith!

We will not dishonor You, God, by denying the faith You have placed before us and inside us. We will not disobey You, God, openly or privately. We are praying for strength for every person in this church, for every member of this church, for all the homes which are represented, God. We will never turn our backs, Hallelujah, on whatever You tell us to do, whatever You instruct us to do. Even if it means walking to our death like Moses, God! Even though he was walking, taking his own funeral procession, he didn't run, he didn't plead. He didn't ask for another day. He yielded himself and, God, I pray for everyone who has faith to believe and join in with this prayer, as Moses lived 120 years, his strength never wavered. He was 120 years old with the strength of a man in his 30's, God, fullness of health! God, I pray, not only for myself but for everyone in this place. I pray for every member who grabs hold, God, to the prayer which has been offered up on these 40 days, for everyone who has the faith to believe the God of the Bible; You can do it for Moses and give him the strength to do what You have called him to do without his physical strength fading away or waning, God.

We pray now in the Name of Jesus You strengthen me, Lord God! Give me that same power, give me that same strength, that You would strengthen every Leader in this church, God. Give them that same anointing of Moses, that You strengthen every adult in this church, God, give us that same anointing, God. We pray that You strengthen these children as they go into their adulthood and serve You and live for You, God; that You would keep them strong that their strength would never fall, God, as our strength rests and lies only in You!

Oh, God, these are the words of life You have given to this church as Moses told Joshua and sung that song before the people; had it recorded letting them know this is not just a song just because he wrote music. God, this is not just a prayer just because I pray. This is a prayer I have already prayed before this prayer started. Before I even came to this church on this night, praying that prayer inside of my soul, God, that You would instruct me on what to say, give words of life, of encouragement, life and power for this church. That every home who grabs hold and believes and adheres as Moses advised Joshua to tell the people do what was already said, to be done and they would be successful in life and they would be successful with the land You had given them to possess. As we look at the Scripture, open up their understanding; somebody was already living on that land! That land already belonged to somebody else! But You said the land was already theirs, it belonged to them. You told them go \ possess their land! Move those people out by whatever means necessary, God, if it meant killing them! They had to obey You!

God, whatever it takes. Every demon, demonic force that comes against us and the people which is on the land with us, we come against them with a Spirit of Violence! Spiritual violence, spiritual warfare! We chop every demon's heads off! We cut every demon's tongue out! We strip every Principality of its power in the Name Jesus! We do whatever is necessary by violence, by force to take what God has given us in this Kingdom for the expansion of God, the Kingdom of Heaven in our homes, in our lives. God, we speak death to every curse, every demonic evil force Satan himself has unleashed on our homes, unleashed in our minds, unleashed in our body; we curse it now! By the Blood of Jesus we speak life!

To everyone on tonight who has entered into spiritual warfare. Everybody in this room is not where they need to be, God. Everybody is not with him on tonight, everybody is not behind me, God, but for everyone who has taken up their cross… For everyone who has heard the battle cry to cry out to, God, out of their souls! Strengthen them now in their Inner Man, strengthen them in their inner man, and strengthen them in their souls! No demon that comes against them will ever rule in their minds, in their lives, in their hearts, in their homes! We are taking back our homes. We take back the Land of Promise You have given us! For those who are thinking carnally, we are not talking about a natural land, we are talking about a spiritual place here on this earth where there is peace! Where there is love, where there is health, where there is wealth, there is prosperity in the spiritual realm! God has it all!

Through signs and wonders, You backed up Moses. You stood behind him, God, You never let Him down! Just as Moses called and the frogs came, Moses called and it rained hail. Moses spoke and even the Death Angel came as You gave him to speak, whatever plague You told him, if it was flies, they came. Well, God, I am speaking because of Christ. We don't have to worry about the plagues and the curses anymore, but I am calling now, God, according to the faith You have given me. According to what I believe I am hearing You say in my soul, God. I can call those things that are not as though they were because I am one of Your son's. I am Your Servant, God. I didn't choose this work. I didn't choose myself to be in this position, but oh, God, I call now in the spirit realm for a break in the finances and let the overflow come now, God! Demons are laughing at me as it is chronicled and we have testified and told people, they will laugh at me. I have no bank; I have no money, I have no wealth of the natural sense, God. But what do I need those things for if everything belongs to You? And all we have to do is call for it to come and it will manifest itself in the natural realm of existence. Therefore, I call now, God. 'I' is one of the biggest concerns of this church and for the people in this church, is the lack of money. God, if it wasn't that, they would give more! They would give all that is necessary, God, not holding back on the little which they think they have or what they must have to make it, God, but Isaac was willing to give his life!

Abraham loved Isaac so much he never considered idolatry, God. Isaac was his joy. Isaac was his everything. There is no way on earth he would ever let anything happened to his seed otherwise he wouldn't believe the promise You gave him would come to pass. But he didn't argue with You, God, he didn't try to bargain with You, God. You told him to sacrifice his son. He went up the mountain to do just that! Give his son's life to You not knowing if You would resurrect him, give him another son. He didn't know what would happen; he just obeyed and You provided!

God, I obey Your Word that You speak in my soul. I don't know what is going to happen! I don't know how You are going to provide but You say just to say 'it' because You're, God, You will have to back it up! You're, God, You are the only one who can back it up. You are, God, nobody can stop You! You are God and You alone! You have done signs and wonders in our lives, God. In this church we have living testimonies of Your power and Your glory; therefore I stand on that, the memorial You have given me in my own home. I can look at him every day and see there is a God when I see my son.

God, we pray now for one of the Pastor in Texas. Move now in that congestive heart failure he has been experiencing, God, Hallelujah. Arteries clogged, oxygen not getting to body like it needs to, God, causing problems. He has served You a long time, long time, long time. God, he has not been rewarded by man the way other people have who have done less work. He has not quit God, oh God, touch his body now in the Name of Jesus, in the Name of Jesus. Oh, God, I believe in my spirit, he is not telling You he is tired; he still wants to work a little bit longer. A little overtime, God, let him work a little overtime, Lord, Hallelujah; let him work a little overtime, please, Jesus, please in the Name of Jesus. Take these requests before Your Father and have compassion and mercy upon that family.

Now, God, we know we must live naturally in this world. We don't walk on clouds. Moses didn't float not one time; he had to physically climb every mountain You called him up to worship. You have called us up higher to isolate us from the people who have not been **CALLED INTO THY PRESENCE**. God, we must physically make it every day to the time of prayer, regardless of how tired our bodies, our minds are wounded. We must take this time out to pray every day during these 40 days, God, if we want to go up to Thy **PRESENCE**. If we want to go a little bit higher in our calling, if we want to be deeper rooted, God, in the Word and understand the Word because no commentary, no class, no Bible study, no professor, no theologian can break the Word down and give us revelation the way the Holy Ghost can. The way You can, God, and if we make the sacrifice to physically hold on to our belief, during the 40 days You have called us to pray, God, things are going to be broken up in these 40 days. But the conclusion of these 40 days is, there will be an explosion! There is going to be an eruption.

Not one, God, which would necessarily be seen on the outside, but because of the eruption and explosion taking place on the inside of our souls, seeing signs and wonders, there will be an outward showing, God, and it will not be because we are feeling good. Not because we are enthused, not because we feel the Spirit upon us, but more importantly because we know the Spirit is in us! We want the Spirit dwelling in us so the revelation power of God will come, will bring great clarity to the Word of God. We want the Spirit to give clarity to the instructions You will give each and everyone who believes who has laid out this year before You, God, saying, "You order our steps!" You order the calendar of events for the year, not just for our church, for but our lives God!

God, You said 'mark the perfect man behold the upright for the end of that man is peace'. You said that in Psalms 37:37, so it lets us know we can have mentors and examples of biblical proportions of people who served You; parents, uncles, people in ministry, people in the church but there is no greater example then those You have recorded in Your Word. Christ is the chief example, but Moses was a type of Christ. He was that person You described in the verse. You said mark (study) the perfect man for the end of that man is peace. Every person You have allowed to be recorded in the Bible, in their works, there was something fruitful, peaceful, something strong left behind. We can take examples.

God I want to be like Moses which is nothing new. I told You before I wanted to be like Moses, God. I want to be a leader You can be satisfied with, one that signs & wonders would be wrought. God, the things You have done, I am grateful, but, God, I am not satisfied. I want more of You. A much wiser older Saint once counseled me and said, "Your church, churches take on the spirit of the leader." God, I believe it is truth in that statement. Therefore, I pray this church takes on the spirit You have given me; one of hunger, one, God, of a great desire to please You. One, Lord God, they would not ever be satisfied in anything they do for You, they will always say

"Lord help me to do better." Let this church take that spirit on. Let us have the Spirit that we want to do better and we are willing, God, first identifying what do we need to cut away so we can go a little bit higher in Thee. And then let us have a mind as a church that we say "yes," not sing "Yes" but say it in our hearts, "Yes to God." That we would sacrifice and cut away anything, even if it's not sinful, God, we will cut away if it means a greater anointing. We will get rid of it, God, if it means more souls being saved, healed and aspire to do better! We will get rid of it, God, if You would use us. Somebody has to be used to do signs and wonders.

You are the same God of the Bible and Jesus said greater works we will do! Not only would we do the same, He said greater works! He did signs and wonders. Everybody is not going to believe the Word just because it is the Word. Everybody didn't believe Jesus just because He was the Son of God but He said, "If You don't believe that I am the Son of God believe me for the very works sake!" God let us have some works in this church. Let some signs and wonders take place in our lives, God. Let some signs and wonders take place in lives of people we come across that when we pray, something is going to happen in their lives, God. There is going to be a great change in their lives, God. When we pray and come against unclean spirits and bind the devils and cast them out, they will leave! Because we said it in Your authority.

God, for this year, for the rest of these 40 days as we are climbing up this mountain, we haven't made it to the top just yet, but we are praying, God, we have added this to our prayer; we want to be taken to a level of praise and worship that even our minds, as we are in this room, can't imagine. We want an out of this world experience in Your **PRESENCE**. We want an out of this world experience out of our minds, out of our self worship experience with Thee. God, any way would be fine. If it is here in this church, great. If it is at home among our families and Your Spirit falls upon us, the anointing of praise, and we stop during the dinner hour while we are supposed to be blessing the food and it turns to praise, great! If we are taking a shower, great! If we are in the middle of sleeping, God, and You wake us up, great! I don't care how You do it; I don't care where You do it. I don't care when or how long You do it for, I am just asking You do it, God. We want to be taken to a place where our bodies become meaningless and our tiredness, our feeling, even our excitement and enthusiasm become meaningless; where it is all about worshipping You in spirit and in truth praying to You from the very essence of our souls with every fiber of our being! We want to be taken to that place, God, where it is about the spiritual praise and worship. Take us there, God, take us there, God!

We want to go there. It is a consuming fire burning in our souls! We want to go there, where Your voice is sounding like the voice of many waters; we want to go there, God, Hallelujah! We won't be able to testify! We won't be able to describe it! We won't even be able to stop crying, we want to go there where the cloud of glory is at! Take us there, God, in Your **PRESENCE**! Take us there, God, take us there, take us there, Hallelujah, Hallelujah, Hallelujah, bless Your Name! I want to go there, take us there, take us there! Take us to a place, God, where when we say, "Thank You" We mean it, we really mean it. When we say, "All praises to Yahweh" which is Hallelujah translated "All praises to Yahweh," we will mean it the way the Heavenly Host are worshipping You even now.

There is no question about their praise. Their praise is not polluted. It is pure, God. Take us to that place of pure praise! We have been washed in the Blood of the Lamb. Our sins have been forgiven. Therefore, there is no reason, God, except what lies within our minds trying to fathom or think it out trying to imagine what is that place or how that experience would be, take us beyond our thoughts and imagination, God! Take us to a realm, God, that is solely on faith and trust in Thee that we would stretch out of our souls and bless Your Name! We want to exalt Your Name and lift You up! Take us now, God, take us now, God, oh, bless Your Name. We want to go there, God! Take us to a place of praise, God, where we would praise You for not what You have done, but just because You are God! Just because You are God, just because You are God!!!!!!! Take us to that place, take us to that place in our souls. Paul said to be absent out of the body is to be present with You; take us out of this body! Take us out of this world! Take us out of our trials and tribulations! Take us to that secret place in You! Hallelujah, Hallelujah, yes. God, this is on our prayer list on tonight, we want to go there. God, we want to go there. We can't go there on our own, but Your Holy Ghost, Your anointing, God, Your Word, usher us in the Holy of Holies and let us stay awhile, God. Ooooh, Jesus.

We thank You now for this time of prayer. We do love You, Lord. We thank You for the encouragement which comes in our souls from being able to feel Your **PRESENCE** and know that Your glory is in this place. You have not forsaken us, You stand on Your Word. Help the Word to stand in us that we would be pleasing in Thy sight and in all of our words and deeds in our actions, God, help us that love would abide everywhere within our lives, the love of Christ. We pray these prayers in Jesus Name.

Look on the prayer list and on everyone who has placed a prayer request in this prayer box. God, move and answer. We have been praying and we have laid this oil out before You that You would consecrate it and anoint it, God. We don't have the proper formula. correct measurement of oil that they had in the Old Testament but, God, through prayer, through our faith, we know You can send Your anointing inside these bottles, the unseen, and You can change the chemical formula and turn this olive oil into real anointed oil. That is the faith of the people and the obedience of Your Word; laying on of hands and the anointing that yokes would be destroyed and deliverance would take place, healing. Now, we offer these prayers to Thee. Once again, thank You for allowing us to come before Your **PRESENCE** with thanksgiving and praising You and praying by faith. Be it done in Jesus Name and the people of God say Amen.

Closing Scripture: Deuteronomy 34 (KJV)
"And Moses went up from the plains of Moab unto the mountain of Nebo, to the top of Pisgah that is over against Jericho. And the Lord showed him all the land of Gilead, unto Dan, And all Naphtali, and the land of Ephraim, and Manasseh, and all the land of Judah, unto the utmost sea, And the Negev, and the plain of the valley of Jericho, the city of palm trees, unto Zoar. And the Lord said unto him, This is the land which I swore unto Abraham, unto Isaac, and unto Jacob, saying, I will give it unto thy seed. I have caused thee to see it with thine eyes, but thou shalt not go over there. So Moses, the servant of the Lord, died there in the land of Moab, according to the word of the Lord. And

he buried him in a valley in the land of Moab, over against Bethpeor; but no man knoweth of his sepulcher unto this day. And Moses was an hundred and twenty years old when he died; his eyes was not dim, nor his natural force abated. And the children of Israel wept for Moses in the plains of Moab thirty days. So the days of weeping and mourning for Moses were ended. And Joshua, the son of Nun, was full of the Spirit of wisdom, for Moses had laid his hands upon him. And the children of Israel hearkened unto him, and did as the Lord commanded Moses. And there arose not a prophet since in Israel like unto Moses, whom the Lord knew face to face, In all the signs and the wonders which the Lord sent him to do in the land of Egypt to Pharaoh, and to all his servants, and to all his land, And in all that mighty hand, and in all the great terror which Moses showed in the sight of all Israel."

Closing Remarks:

My God! Can you imagine God knowing you face to face? I want to have such a prayer life that God knows me, my situations, my mind, body and soul face to face. I want to stay in the face of God with praise and worship! The more we pray and talk to God, the closer our relationship becomes. How close do you want to be? Have you ever wondered what God looks like? One day we all will see our Lord and Savior just as He is! Wow, what a day of rejoicing that will be!

<u>END OF DAY 14 PRAYER SERVICE</u>

STEP 15/DAY 15, MONDAY

"God Is In Communication With You"

DAY 15 PRAYER SERVICE BEGINS

Opening Remarks:

We believe what the Scripture says, "He that doeth these things shall never be moved." The Lord blessed us and gave us an increase in prayer for fifteen days. We want God to keep us with the mind and even give us a greater mind for prayer. We want to do as the Word tells us and then allow us not to be moved from our resolve, to continue to pray and not to be removed from the Holy Will of God. We pray not to be removed from that secret place in God, not be moved from the place where God is talking to us and we are hearing him, because a lot of people talk to God, but they don't hear what He has to say. When God talks, we want to be quiet and hear what He has to say, and if God allows us to enter into His **PRESENCE,** we don't want to be moved from there. We don't want anything to push us away from God.

We pray that God will bless us to never be moved from our desire to please Him. Some people are seeking things this year which they haven't experienced before or they haven't experienced it in a long period of time. God allows us to achieve those levels and we don't want it to push us away. It takes hard work to get to that point in life.

To do all of that and be pushed away is a very dramatic and hurtful experience. We know the devil is ultimately behind anything which comes against us. So, we pray and we bind things on a daily basis. We don't want anything to push us from the **PRESENCE** of God. We want God's **PRESENCE** in our lives every day and everywhere we go.

Some people may think that this is unrealistic. Read the Bible and you will find where it says "man should pray and not faint, man should pray without ceasing." You are in communication with God; God is in communication with you. God lives inside of you, His **PRESENCE** is inside of us. We should always be ready to follow the instructions of God, whatever it might be, even in our prayer life. We want to follow the instructions of God and do great and wonderful things. But what about following the instructions in our prayer life? We should pray to pray keep an open communication with God and allow Him to speak to us and instruct us in our daily living, events, and occurrences. According to the Scripture in Proverbs the third chapter, we "should always trust in the Lord, acknowledge him all our ways; lean not to our own understanding, our ways and our thoughts." There is a benefit in being in the **PRESENCE** of God; more than a feeling, more than requiring some material things, more than getting our prayers answered. Just to be with God and know He is with you, should bring comfort in our lives.

Opening Scripture: Psalms 15 (NLT)
*"Who may worship in your sanctuary, Lord? Who may enter your **PRESENCE** on your holy hill? Those who lead blameless lives and do what is right, speaking the truth from sincere hearts. Those who refuse to gossip or harm their neighbors or speak evil of their friends. Those who despise flagrant sinners, and honor the faithful followers of the Lord, and keep their promises even when it hurts. Those who lend money without charging interest, and who cannot be bribed to lie about the innocent. Such people will stand firm forever."*

Insight As We Prepared For Prayer:
Tonight we go into prayer with worship. For we are standing on Holy ground and I know the Angels of the Lord are around.

Let Us Pray:
Oh, Jesus, help us, help us on this night. God, we're grateful, we are grateful for all You have done for us, Lord. We are grateful for another day, we are grateful for this fifteenth day of prayer, we are grateful for this fifteenth day of this year; another day You have given us life. You have kept our families alive, our children, our loved ones and kept tragedy away from our homes and we are thankful. Lord, You have been so kind. You have heard the cries of Your people. You have heard the testimonies of the Saints. You have heard our profession of faith in Thee and only Thee. Our request we have brought boldly before Thy throne, following the instructions of Your Word; the words we have uttered out of our mouths under the guidance of the Holy Ghost.

Now on tonight as the Psalmist laid out so elegantly Lord God, those characteristics needed by the godly people to be in Your **PRESENCE**. To be in Your Tabernacle to bind things and be in the whole Will of God. God we have a pure heart and clean hands, we have done no one wrong. We have not put our money to usury; we have not preyed upon the innocent in this world, God, as so many evil people have done. We have prayed and we pray, God, everyone in this church, every member of this church, God, we ask for forgiveness. We come before Your **PRESENCE** asking You to crucify the flesh. And now, God, You have blessed us to be "**CALLED INTO THY PRESENCE**" as Moses was called into Thy **PRESENCE**.

We are praying God as David has said in Psalms 23 that he wanted to dwell in the House of the Lord forever. You said, God, "He that doeth these things shall never be moved that they would be able to stay in Your **PRESENCE**," God, stay on the Holy Hill of God. We pray now, Lord God, because in our hearts, in our minds, even in our souls, even in the secret place of our Spirits, God, the place we hide from everyone except You, the real us, our true feelings, God. We bring our desirers, secret aspirations and goals we want to see accomplished, but often times we fear to ask You for permission to achieve these things. We want the strength to live these things and make them a reality in our lives and not just in our minds; in the sub consciences of men and women. We pray now, Lord God, that we do not offend Thee with our confidence in Thee, that we are not foolish in our statements, God, of Testifying of Your power and Your glory before men and women here and men and women any and everywhere.

We pray, Lord God, for Elder now that he stands and continue to be in Your **PRESENCE** even in Africa. You keep him, God, in Your **PRESENCE** and keep Your Angels around him and protect his life. Jesus, we pray now, Lord God, for our young men who are traveling and doing ministry on this historic holiday in America, Martin L. King Jr., Day, that they have a positive effect on the youth, on someone. That they just not get caught up with the history in this world but more importantly, to look at the history You have laid out before us through Jesus! Touch someone at that event that they would give their life to You. If we serve You, God, and do what the Scriptures have said, then we would treat all men equal that You have created; everyone. If we do what You have said in the scriptures, God, we would never hurt anyone, offend anyone purposefully. We would never do anything race motivated, nor any social injustices, no class separation. It would never be who has or who doesn't have; it would be about what we can do to lead people to Christ.

We pray now, God, on this fifteenth day, if You bless us to live, God, if You bless us to live, God, we still have twenty-five more days to go. Climbing up this mountain of prayer every night, God, trying to go higher and higher, we pray for the Saints, God, who could not make it here due to their work schedules, or being sick or afflicted, God, or traveling out doing ministry work, but as they have stopped in their schedules, God, and turned toward this place to pray along with us. Reminded of what Solomon said, "If anyone turns toward the Temple remember them God as they remember You to be the true God." We pray as the church body has united as believers everywhere, not just here God, but the Saints all over the World, praying, Lord God, for the Kingdom of God to be expanded in the hearts of man to every Human Being who would say yes to Your Son Jesus. Yes to the love He presents before everyone who is looking for something which cannot fulfill their natural needs, their emotional quivers, shapes and sizes of this society or other human being or family relationship, professional relationships. Life beats so many to a place of hopelessness, God, where the shape of their souls, instead of being able to bond and to share love and to share Christ with every human being, they can't. We know and understand, God, if You had to send Your Son and He suffered, we are not greater than the Master; we must suffer also. We are here, God, the few, two or three meeting that requirement that whatsoever we ask the Father in Jesus Name, You said You would do it.

We still pray for the young man, Lord God, who has been in a coma since the seventh of December. Lord God, as we have prayed for him and You have blessed and touched, now he has movement and has moved and has turned toward recovery, but we pray for a full recovery, God, with no damage, no damage to his brain, God, for being in that vegetative state for such a long period of time, God.

We pray for the sick and afflicted in our families who might be ill even in this church right now that You would bring about healing and deliverance, God. When You said it shall never be moved in the fifteen division of Psalms, God, meaning no sickness, no pain, no trial nor tribulations can ever remove us from Your **PRESENCE**. Remove us away from Your love, Hallelujah; remove us from being in the manifestation of Your glory, God. We just don't want to be in the manifestation of Your glory but we want to be like Isaiah, God; we want to see Your Train fill the Temple. We want to experience the glory in our soul, God. We pray that You have Your way in each and every one of us in this place, for every member of this church. Oh, God, give us the strength not to give up in this society which is so negatively filled with failure, doom.

We pray for people who have given up and become hopeless and helpless, people who prey on others, Lord God, with things to fit themselves. We pray for every elderly member of this church. We pray for the elderly in our families, God. Keep them safe from evil people who prey and take advantage of these people, God, who have spent their lives here on this earth. Help them that our lives might be better. Give them strength, God, as Paul said "We have fought a good fight we have kept the faith." God, they are just waiting for You to move them closer to You. God, we pray now for their health, we pray for their minds. We come against Alzheimer's, God, dementia, arthritis, diabetes, congestive and congenital heart failure. We come against high blood pressure and low blood pressure, God. We come against kidney failure, God, aneurysm, anything which brings about pain, suffering, affliction. We come against it now in the Name of Jesus.

God, we wouldn't be here if it wasn't for our parents and grandparents and the sacrifices they have made. Every one of our families, God, we look back through the telescope of history and we will see everyone of us have a Martin L. King figure in our own homes, in our own family tree who fought for equity in the family, who fought for rights for the family and sacrificed so our parents and grandparents would be able to live. If they didn't live, we wouldn't be here. We pray for every living member of our family this day that they would not be moved out of Your **PRESENCE**. Be with them God even in the nursing homes, in the hospitals, the convalescent homes, those who are home right now who are praying and can't be here because of this wet weather; be with them as they call upon You! God, they have called upon You throughout the years. You never left them or forsook them! If it wasn't for the prayers of our righteous forefathers, we wouldn't be saved now! Somebody taught us how to call on You! Somebody taught us how to pray, God. Help us as people, as a nation to go back to family prayer. It kept our families together, it kept us from losing our minds. You gave our parents, grandparents and great grandparents' innovative ways to make ends meet. Innovative ways to come up with new recipes and how to take the garbage of leftovers and make delicate meals out of it and exquisite meals that people pay a lot of money for now. God, recipes our grandparents and great grandparents came up with that is now in our stores and books. We ask that the same God, who gave them something innovative, God, touch our minds in this place.

The now generations, the X generation, the Y generation, the Z generation, whatever name is placed on us, the Baby Boomers, we are alive and we need Your help, God. We have access to more things educationally, but yet we are not as smart as they were. It is an insult to our families what we don't do compared to what they did do. They had way less than we have now and they did much more. Help us, God. If we're really going to be a people who have been called up the mountain to do better in our lives, God, if we're really going to be a people who are going to be in Your **PRESENCE** and exhibit the characteristics of the Holy Ghost, God. No one is bucking, jumping, shouting, quickening and speaking in tongues, God, and looking and trying to act like we are religious. If we're really going to be filled with the Spirit of God, then move in our minds, God, as we enter into Thy **PRESENCE**. God, move in our minds and give us what is necessary to make it here on this earth.

We have children. Their lives depend on it, their lives depend on it, their children's lives will depend on it. We cannot look toward the government to make a way, God. They are sending our young people to war! Killing them, killing them by the thousands, God; we need help! Help every church who stands, God, for what the Bible says. Help every church who stands for right. Help every church who will not give in to society. Help every church, God, who will not become glamorized, hooked on material successes and the bling, bling of life. Help every church who will still come together as a family, whether its thousands or whether it's ten members, in that church who will pray and call upon the true and living God, the God of the Bible. Help every church who is not afraid to make a proclamation openly that Jesus is Lord! Help us, God, help the churches everywhere! To not be moved from the rock which is higher than 'I,' the Rock which is Christ! Without Christ there is no Christianity! Without Christ there is no Salvation, without Jesus there is no power for the church! How can families get better if the church is getting weaker? The church won't stand for holiness any more. The church is being moved out of Your **PRESENCE**!

David said in Psalms 51:10 "Create in me a clean heart, O God, and renew a right spirit within me." Help the churches everywhere, God. David also prayed for forgiveness for himself which includes the church to pray every where "have mercy upon me, O God, according to thy loving-kindness; according unto the multitude of thy tender mercies. Blot out my transgressions." Create in us a clean heart, Lord, purge me with hyssop, and I shall be clean. He also went on to say, God, "Whatever You do don't take Your Spirit." Don't take Your Holy Ghost, don't take Your anointing, and don't take You **PRESENCE** away! If You take Your **PRESENCE** away from the church, God, we would be isolated. We will be vulnerable to the attacks of the Devil. He will beat us up. We will be

A Call Into His Presence

beaten in our lives, in our homes, and jobs, our relationship will be beaten down everywhere. The line is getting long, God, and we are standing on the side of righteousness. Help everywhere in this place to stand. We pray and desire to get into Your **PRESENCE** and how You have allowed that to be a reality, God, we don't want to be in Your **PRESENCE** for twenty-five days or 40 days or one hundred days; we want to be in Your **PRESENCE** for the rest of our lives leading into eternity, God.

We want to get to know You more, God, we want You to have Your ways in our lives. We want You to remove all the junk out of our lives. We want You to remove the fear and frustration out of our minds, God. We want You to give us the boldness that we would stand and not be moved by what people have to say, negative statements, criticism, God, we won't be moved by the media, God, we won't be moved by the theological world who doesn't agree and they won't say Jesus Is Lord, but they would say they are People of Faith! Faith in what, God? Faith in what, God? We can have faith in a plant! We can worship a tree, we can worship a building, we can worship a car, we can worship anything but people don't want to worship the true and living God! God, we are not here to be religionist! We are here because we are desperate and we need You! Thank You, Lord God, for saving a Soul on last night, thank You for moving in the young girl's life, God.

God, I have already prayed for Brother X, but I call his name out as I promised every day I would. I pray for X now, God, bind the Devil in his mind and pull down every strong hold, set him free from the spirit of confusion that reigns over this region, God. I come against every principality now in the Name of Jesus that binds not only him, but so many people in this city, God, bound by confusion! I bind that confusion now, God, having a form of godliness but denying the power thereof, forever coming into knowledge and knowing all those things but never coming into the knowledge of truth, God.

Oh, God, help us now in this city. God for every believer who is believing and believing, and believing and has been believing and is still believing and has had unwavering faith in Your power and in Your Word that whatsoever we pray for when we ask, believing and not doubting and whatsoever we ask in Jesus Name, You would do it! You gave Your Disciples power over every unclean spirit, even to the point of casting them out and to heal all manner of sickness and disease; that is Your Word, God. We pray Your Word back to You. Jesus also said, "Whatsoever he saith the Holy Ghost the Paraclete the Comforter would bring to our remembrance all things that He had said in his Word," and He said we could cast the Devil out and these signs shall follow them that believe! So we pray against every demon that attacks this city. The spirit of violence, rape and robbery and pedophilia, murder, and all type of abomination and bestiality; we come against it now in the Name of Jesus!

God, somebody has to pray somebody, has to stay on the wall and not come down. We are saying, God, we are available, we are willing, we will do whatever You say to do, not to have church as usual, not to pray a prayer of silence, but to cry out! To lift our voices like a trumpet in Zion and declare to the people thus said the Lord God of Host! It is not all spiritual, God. There are natural reasons which are important to us as human being. Every innocent child has the right to stay innocent. They don't deserve, God, evil men and women who are taking advantage of our children, God, hurting them physically, emotionally, demeaning their lives, crippling them that they most likely will never have a normal relationship with another human being ever again, God, because of the abuse that is taking place; the unreported abuse. For every case which is reported, God, what about the thousands of cases which are not reported? Every child who is kidnapped and found alive; what about every child who has been kidnapped and murdered and disappeared and their bodies have never been found, God. Who is praying for them? What news reporter is doing a story on those stories, God? What cold case investigator is spending countless hours trying to solve that murder?

You see these things, God. You see all things You allow these things to be, but, God, even when the plagues was poured out upon Egypt, there was a place called Goshen. A garbage heap town, a place we would call the ghetto compared to Egypt, God where the slaves lived, but those slaves were Your people who believed a deliver was coming. And when the deliverer came and declared the plagues as You instructed him, not one of those plagues ever came to

A Call Into His Presence

that city of Goshen. Even in famine time, You had a hedge of protection around Your people, God. Even during this time of perilous time, the Bible tells us and is so perfectly prophetically promised that in the last days perilous times would come. Perilous times are here, God. Men would be lover of them own selves more than lovers of God, the Bible says that, God, lovers of pleasure, lovers of all ungodly things.

We pray, God, You let the Blood of Jesus, just like they took the blood of the lamb and put it upon the door post of every home and the death Angel went by and no one got killed! No firstborn died where the blood of the lamb was applied. We now spiritually ask You take the Blood of Jesus and apply it over every door post in every home in this place! Upon every door post of every home represented here, Lord God, every member of our church whether they are here or not. Every Christian in this city, God, every Saint in this region who believes in the power of the Blood of Jesus, and we pray it be applied now, God, that the Pedophile Demon pass over! That the Homosexual Demon pass over! That the Rape Demon pass over! That the Murder Demon, the Addiction Demon, the Lying Demon, the Demon of Anger and Hopelessness. The Suicide Demon, every unclean spirit unleashed from Hell would pass over the Saints homes in the Name of Jesus!

You said, God, those who that meet the requirement in Psalms 15 would never be moved. We have been praying for fourteen days climbing up to meet those requirements. God, on this fifteenth day, we declare we will not be moved! We will be like a tree planted by the rivers of water. We will not be moved in our faith. We will not be moved one iota to the left or to the right. We are going to stand on the Word of God, we are going to stand in the power God has given us! We are going to stand on the anointing which comes in Jesus Name! We are going to walk by faith and not by sight, we will be rewarded because we believe there is a God and we diligently seek Him! We are the Saints of God, the righteousness of Christ, the effectual fervent prayers of the righteous availeth much! We will be emotional which means fervent! We will be dedicated which means fervent! We will be consistent which means fervent! We will be authoritative in our prayer because Jesus has given us power!!!! And we use that authority now in the Name of Jesus!

Satan, the Lord rebuke you! Satan, the Lord rebuke you! The Lord rebuke you, Satan! The Lord rebuke you, every demon that is left in this place, the Lord rebuke you! Get out! God, we call for the warring Angels, Hallelujah, come down in this place, sanctify this place the more, God, every unclean spirit that walks through those doors, that comes through the ceiling, that comes from underneath the ground, that walks through the sides of the walls! I call for the warring Angels of God to come now and fortify this church. For this is the safe Haven for the prayer warriors and we will bind everything in the heavenly! We will bind everything on this earth! We will bind everything beneath this earth! Seen and unseen that comes against the Body of Christ in this city and in this place. We will speak power and life, authority in Jesus' Name!

We call for the dispensation of the anointing of God that the Holy Ghost be poured out like promised in the last days upon all flesh. Thy Will be done in this place as it is in Heaven. Thy Will be done in us as it is in Heaven. Thy Will be done in every home as it is in Heaven. Thy Will be done in every family member, in every home as it is in Heaven. Thy Will be done in this city as it is in Heaven. Thy Will be done in the United States of America as it is in Heaven!

No evil person, no King, no President, no government has more power than God Himself. He is Jehovah God all mighty! We don't live with a pessimistic attitude or outlook; it is a realistic one for we are in the fight for our very souls, the very souls of our children and love ones. It's about souls, it's not about us. As Nehemiah said, we are doing a great work, we are not coming off the wall. We are not coming off the wall.

Now, God, as we close this prayer, we close with praise. We are thankful, God, thankful, God, thankful for our natural lives. We are thankful, God, You have spoken to our spirits and we have heard the call to salvation. We are thankful for our very eternal life which has been promised through Jesus and it is already guaranteed, God. We thank You now, Lord God, we thank You now, we thank You now for giving us a spirit of willingness to pray. We thank You, God, we know we are doing the unglamorous work, the work people don't want to do, the behind the scenes work. The sacrificial work, God, the work that will get no glory, no praise here in the Body of Christ, God, everybody wants to be up front. Nobody wants to pray, nobody wants to be a pillar of the church. Nobody wants to be a foundation any more, everybody wants to be a light. Everybody wants to be the diamonds, the gold that shimmers and shines! But we thank You for a willingness, God, to do the behind the scenes work. To be people who work in the septic tanks of spiritual sludge, God, where there is dirt, there is grime, things and all kinds of yucky things we have to deal with, God. But, oooooh, God, we thank You for a spirit like Hannah that we will pray until the conception comes! We will pray until the birth comes! We will pray until the soooooulsssss come into this place! Hallelujah, and we will give You praise, we will give You glory! We will give You honor, we will give You honor, God! We thank You, God, for we are reminded what the Prophet in the Book of Joel says, "Let the Elders come and lay before the porch and the altar and cry out for mercy and pray!!! Let the woman that is breast feeding stop her feeding! Let the married couples come out of the marriage chambers! Let everyone that hears the call come to prayer" and we hear the call and we have come to pray until the Bride Groom comes! We are here to pray and pray until healing come and manifest Himself!

We pray, God, for the souls. Let them come and experience the experience! Salvation and deliverance, healing, encouragement, and power in the indwelling of the Holy Ghost, yea, God! Hoooooly, holy is Your Name, God! H o o o o o lllllyyyy, oh, God, I hear the Heavenly Host in my soul crying out Holy, Holy! Oh, God, You are Holy, Holy He is Holy, He is Holy, He is Holy, He is Holy and He worthy of the praise! Thank You, Jesus, Hallelujah, Hallelujah, Hallelujah, Hallelujah! He is Holy Saints and His Holiness is in this place. The **PRESENCE** of the Lord, His glory is here! Will you praise Him?! Majesty! Magnificent Savior! He is Lord! Hooooly, He is Holy! Hallelujah, glory, glory, glory, glory! Glory, Hallelujah, thank You, Jesus! Thank You. Jesus! My soul. my soul extols Thee! We lift You up, glory, glory, thank You, thank You, thank You!!!

Now, God, strengthen us in our vessels, bodies and give us a resolve not to be bound by the flesh, tiredness, sickness and worries and concerns. We have laid them on Your altar once again, sacrifice and burn them up in the Name of Jesus. God, we have to be holy in Thine **PRESENCE** for You are Holy, oh, thank You, Jesus, thank You, Jesus. Great and magnificent things \ we ask and believe because of our faith is in You and we give You the praise now for You have done it in Jesus Name. Give Him some glory in this place for He is worthy! Give Him some glory in this place Hallelujah, Hallelujah, Hallelujah, He is, He is God, oh, thank You, Jesus!

Closing Scripture: Psalms 115 (KJV)
Not unto us, O Lord, not unto us, but unto thy name give glory, for thy mercy, and for thy truth's sake. Wherefore should the heathen say where is now their God? But our God is in the heavens; he hath done whatsoever he hath pleased. Their idols are silver and gold, the work of men's hands. They have mouths, but they speak not; eyes have they, but they see not. They have ears, but they hear not; noses have they, but they smell not. They have hands, but they handle not; feet have they, but they walk not; neither speak they through their throat. They who make them are like unto them; so is every one who trusteth in them. O Israel, trust thou in the Lord; he is their help and their shield. O house of Aaron, trust in the Lord; he is their help and their shield. Ye that fear the Lord, trust in the Lord; he is their help and their shield. The Lord hath been mindful of us; he will bless us, he will bless the house of Aaron. He will bless those who fear the Lord, both small and great. The Lord shall INCREASE you more and more, you and your children. Ye are blessed by the Lord who made heaven and earth. The heaven, even the heavens, are the Lord's; but the earth hath he given to the children of men. The dead praise not the Lord, neither any that go down into silence. But we will bless the Lord from this time forth and for evermore. Praise the Lord.

Closing Remarks:
Will you praise the Lord? Do you believe the Word? It says we are blessed! We are blessed, we are blessed, we are blessed, we are

blessed, we are blessed, we are blessed because God has said so and He will increase us

God is worthy of the praise. Will you praise Him? Will you praise him out of your soul? Not unto anybody but unto God for we give Him glory! Bless His Name of the reading of these Scriptures unto the reception of the Scriptures into our souls. We are blessed, we are blessed. The Word has already pronounced that we are blessed! Hallelujah! If we get in the Word and read the Word, God will blow our minds. The Word alone is mind blowing. No devil can convince me that I'm not blessed when God has said I am blessed and that He would increase us and our children. God has spoken it so let it be. Amen.

We thank God for this fifteenth day of prayer for the Lord has been kind. He has strengthen us, and renewed us day by day, to keep us going, not wanting to be at the same level on yesterday or the previous day, but to go higher heights. That is what climbing the mountain is about. You can't stop until you get to the top, and we haven't made it to the top yet so we can't stop. Every day might get a little more pressing than it was a few days ago because now we are getting higher, but to get closer and closer and deeper and deeper into God's, **PRESENCE** and manifestation of His glory in our souls, it's worth the climb. When the Lord can begin to open up the revelations of His Scriptures, you can receive it in your soul. You receive, not the knowledge of your natural mind but receive it in your soul, so then it is planted inside of your spirit. Then the Devil, and other natural occurrences, cannot remove or pluck it away. Whatever you know or don't know, or if you can or can't remember verses or you can't quote Scripture word for word, that is not required. What is required, is it that we believe what has been read or spoken or preached to you or God has given it to you prophetically or in a dream or a vision. He is never going to do or say anything which is contrary to what He has written in His Word; he is always going to stay true to what He has already said. So you might not ever remember what it says in Psalms 115 that we are blessed but you will know it says somewhere in the Bible that I am blessed. When the Devil brings thoughts and it looks like your life and everything is going wrong and messed up and something says, "Remember the Bible says, 'You are blessed'" that is the Holy Spirit trying to talk to you and encourage you and let you know God has said you are blessed and He would increase you. Do you believe that you are part of the increase? My BELIEF has already transitioned into FAITH and my FAITH has transitioned into a KNOWING! I KNOW WE HAVE BEEN INCREASED HALLELUJAH!

<u>END OF DAY 15 PRAYER SERVICE</u>

STEP 16/DAY 16, TUESDAY

"Seven Times a Day Will I Praise Thee"

DAY 16 PRAYER SERVICE BEGINS

Opening Remarks:

On the sixteenth night we pray specifically for God to help and bless the members of the church. We pray each one name by name as the Lord led. We ask God to honor this Psalm as we pray it back to Him. These sixteen verses you will find everything we have prayed for fifteen days which we have accomplished in these sixteen verses. Our main focus, what we started out with, was asking God to give us instructions and directions for the year. As David said "let my soul live" we have asked God to let us live; we said if you do, I am going to praise you. We must continue to praise God. Some people don't get it or understand and we can't force anyone to receive the revelation, but there is no way or no where that you will find where praise is to be exempted when it comes down to being before God; praise is always included. When we say we want to be in God's **PRESENCE** and want to stay there, then there has to be a continuous praise as David said "I will bless the Lord at all times and his praise shall continually be in my mouth." We must have a continuous praise if we want to be in the **PRESENCE** of God on a continuous basis. God's Word is true and we are going to stick with what the Word instructs and encourages us to do. We are going to be diligent about doing it; for there is a reward for them that diligently seek Him.

Opening Scripture: Psalms 119:160-176 (KJV)
"Thy Word is true from the beginning; and everyone of thy righteous [ordinance] endureth forever. Princes have persecuted me without a cause, but my heart standeth in awe of thy word. I rejoice at thy word, as one that findeth great spoil. I hate and abhor lying, but thy law do I love. **Seven times a day do I praise thee**, *because of thy righteous [ordinances]. Great peace have they who love thy law, and nothing shall offend them. Lord, I have hoped for thy salvation, and done thy commandments. My soul hath kept thy testimonies, and I love them exceedingly. I have kept thy precepts and thy testimonies; for all my ways are before thee. Let me cry come near before thee, O Lord; give me understanding according to thy word. Let m supplication come before thee; deliver me, according to thy word. My lips shall utter praise, when thou hast taught me thy statutes. My tongue shall speak of thy word; for all thy commandments are righteousness. Let thine hand help me; for I have chosen thy precepts. I have longed for thy salvation, O Lord, and thy law is my delight. Let my soul live, and it shall praise thee; and let thine [ordinances] help me. I have gone astray like a lost sheep. Seek thy servant; for I do not forget thy commandments."*

Let Us Pray:
I pray for one of our sisters now if only she would hear the Word from Matthew 6:33 "Seek ye first the Kingdom of God and all of Your righteous then all of these other things will be added." God, open up her mind before her life is torn into complete shambles. God, there is no true happiness outside of Christ, everything else is temporal. It's temporary, it won't last forever; only eternal joy can come through the service of our Lord and Savior Jesus Christ. Protect her life, God, as a woman going throughout this society from wolves in sheep clothing as she is looking for love in all in the wrong places. Move, God, in her mind, move in her home, God, let her realize You have kept her from being a statistic all because

A Call Into His Presence

of Your love and mercy. Let her know that the Saints are praying for her, calling her name out in prayer saying "Help God!" We call for help from Zion! Help her, God, help her, God, help her, God, and help her, God. Set her free in her mind, God. Set her free in her mind, God. Satan, the Lord God rebuke you in her mind. Satan, the Lord God rebuke you in her mind, Satan, the Lord rebuke you in her mind. The Blood of Jesus come against you and every demon now. We pray for mercy on her soul, God, Hallelujah, mercy, Lord, mercy, Lord, mercy, Lord, mercy, Lord, oh, God, mercy, mercy, Lord, we pray for mercy, God.

Oh, Jesus, look on our sister now (23yrs) look on her daughter now. God, not our wills but Your Will, God. Let her know not her will, but Your Will God. Help her now before it is too late and tragedy comes back into her life once again. Oh, God, ooooh, God, Jesus, Jesus, Jesus! Oh, God, open up her eyes now, Lord God, as You had to do for Baalam to see that the Death Angel was right there waiting with his sword, God. I rebuke death now in the Name of Jesus! God, let Your mighty warring Angels, God, be around that home now. God, the Death Angel is soaring over that place! Oh, God I rebuke death in the Name of Jesus! Satan, the Lord rebuke you, Satan, the Lord rebuke you. God, look on her daughter's life now (6yrs). God, don't let her be another statistic of some child kidnapping, abused, God, molested by some friend or someone who has been let into the home, God. Protect her now in the Name of Jesus. Oh, God, oh, God, oh, God, oh, God, oh, God, oh, God, oh, God, protect that child now in the Name of Jesus! Satan, get your hands off! Satan get your hands off, the Lord rebuke You, the Lord rebuke You in the Name of Jesus! Have mercy, God, have mercy. Your Word is true. Your Word is true from the beginning. You said we could call upon Thee and You would answer us. If we pray, You would help us, we could intercede and You would move, God, for Your Son sake, for Jesus' sake. Oh, God, oh God, help us, God, lift up her head. God, I bind the spirit of low-self esteem in her life (the mother), lift up her head, God. She won't try to please other people, she won't try to please any young man, she won't try to please her friend, God, in the Name of Jesus. Lift up her self esteem, God. Give her some resolve, some hope. Take her out of the sea of sorrow, God, give her some spirit

A Call Into His Presence

inside, some life inside of her, God, do it now in the Name of Jesus. Let every obstacle which is placed in front her, God, will only point her toward You, where she would break inside of her soul and yield her life to Thee 100%. God, do it now in the Name of Jesus.

Lord, I pray for Sister X now. Help her Lord. Move now. The race is not given to the swift, it's not given to the one who talks the talk for we have to walk it, we have to walk it, God. Touch her now, God, oooh. You are holding her accountable for the words she has said, she knows the way, she knows what is right. God, everything that comes against her, every unclean spirit, every strong hold, we come against now. The strong hold of things in her past life, we come against now. Set her free, set her free, God. Everything that comes against her mind, depression, God, and sadness, Lord God, the feeling of failure and lost hope, and worthlessness, God. Brokenness, God, not brokenness in a sense that she's broken and has given her life to You, but brokenness in a sense, God, that it seems like everything she has tried to do has failed. Come tonight, we come against those failures and those thoughts of failures and everlasting perpetual failure. We bind that now in the Name of Jesus. God, bring her to her knees in her spirit! Bring her to a place, God, where she would turn to the wall and pray to Thee and ask for life! Ask for strength. Bring her to a place, God, where she would come back to the House of Worship broken, God, in a sense of being broken in her spirit, not her will and not her way, but Your Will Your way would be done in her life, where she would yield to Thee! Satan, the Lord rebuke you that come against her, Hallelujah. Every work of the enemy, we curse it now in the Name of Jesus by the Blood of the Lamb. We speak liberty; we speak liberty in her body. We speak liberty in her mind and her thoughts. We speak liberty the Spirit of God and the Word of God to her soul. Be thou set free woman wherever You might be on this night, be thou set free in the Name of Jesus! Jesus, Hallelujah, Hallelujah, Hallelujah! God, send Your Word into Sister X life for Your Word is sharper than any two edge sword. I see her in my mind trapped in a bubble God, which she can't break out. She wants to break out but she can't break out. She can't seem to break out of the bubble. She seems to have some type of elastic properties, God, where it is moving and stretching

A Call Into His Presence

with her instead of her being able to break through, God. But touch her in her mind and let her know it has to be total submission to Thee and she must have complete faith in what You have spoken in her life, God. Let her use the Word, God. You said salvation is nigh unto thee; deliverance is nigh unto thee even in thy mouth God. Let her began to use the spoken Word which You have placed down in her soul, God, that she would use that two edge sword to cut a loose the elastic chain which is binding her and keeping her from getting out of her box, getting out of her circle, God, let the bubble be burst now in the Name of Jesus!

Oh, God, help us on this night, help us on this night. God, we are fighting for the Saints, help us on this night. We are fighting for our loved ones help us on this night. We are fighting for our Souls. Help us on this night, God, to be like David, oh, God, to go into the camp of the enemy to take back what he has stolen from us, help us! To resurrect all of which has been buried in the Name of Jesus, in the Name of Jesus, in the Name of Jesus.

Look on one of our Mothers now, Lord God. Strengthen her body, remove the pain. Set her free. Give her a season, God, of peace from the pain in her body. God, even by her own statement, she said she wants to stretch out. She has a burning desire to do more for You, God, be more, to be more active to do more. To be more productive in the Body of Christ, to be used by You. God, anyway; she didn't put any stipulations, God, she just said she wants to be used! Move in her mind, move in her body. Let the fire of God burn up everything which is holding her back. The pain, God, disappointments and heartache, the concerns about her children and grandchildren & great grandchildren; let her give them all, all those things to Thee God. Word her mouth, let words of wisdom come forth, God, power and anointing to destroy things which come against her family. God, like any matriarch, God, who is concerned about the continuation of her family, God, she is concerned now, but lift the burden of her son, lift the burden of her daughter off of her heart! In the Name of Jesus, let her place them on the altar, God, and You have Your way in their lives. Oh, God, You said the truth would make us free, let every word that would come out of her mouth concerning her family, her children and her love ones, they would come to her

A Call Into His Presence

for advice, seek truth, God, and they would be made free! From guilt shame and sin, free from excuses that they didn't know better because she would have given them the truth. Oh, God, anoint her now in the Name of Jesus. Anoint her mind, Lord God, open up her understanding to the revelation of the Word like never before. God, we need the seniors in the church, God. We need their wisdom, we need their **PRESENCE**, we need their prayers, we need their experiences, God; we need them now in the Name of Jesus! Satan, take your hands off her body! Take your hands off her finances; take your hands off of her mind. Deliverance, everywhere, strengthen Mother now, in the Name of Jesus! Be it done, Hallelujah, bless You, God, and bless You, God, thank You, Lord.

Oh, God, look on Brother C now. Help him, God, help him, God. Lord, don't let him stop praying, keep a prayer in his heart. Don't let him become hopeless, cold and callous like many other men have after bitter experiences they have gone through in their lives. Help him, God, to remember what has been prophesied to him. Keep him and his soul praying, oh, God, keep his natural life safe, keep him safe, keep his soul safe. Keep his emotions and his heart filled with hope. This confusion and gigantic question mark from the pain he has experienced, great weight on his shoulders, lift the weight now, there is hope for him, God, there is hope for him. Lord, I pray for the hope that lies within him. Jesus is not buried and dead; He was resurrected and He is alive. Jesus in his heart is being buried, God, by the inconsistencies in his family life. Oh, God, You are the same God who resurrected the living Christ; resurrect the Jesus which is in him. Resurrect Him now, God, resurrect Him, God, resurrect Him now, God, help him Lord, help him, help him! Jesus, Jesus, oh, God, oh, God, oh, Lord, extend Your mercy to that young man, please Lord, please Lord in the Name of Jesus.

Look on our Sister now, God, oh, Lord, teach her how to lean on You. Teach her how to depend on You, solidly oh, God, she will need to learn to do that, it's the only way she will make it in this life to achieve the lofty dreams and desires which is in her mind. She needs to lean and depend on You every step of the way. Every door, God, which is closed, we have already prayed You will open, let it be true. Not only give her favor, God, but give her the courage, strength and the boldness for when it is time for her to do what she needs to do what is required of her, she would do it with the spirit of excellence. There are no obstacles, no test, no interview, no audition, nothing, God, which will be able to stop her from achieving those tough obstacles. They will only be stepping stones, God, which will only propel her toward greatness and success as she praises You and worships You. God, open up her creativeness to a new level in the Name of Jesus. As she opens up the Bible and begins to read, God, and study and search out the scriptures; and as she listens to music, God, which has great inspirations, heavenly meanings and messages of hope and inspiration and laying upon Jesus as the deliver, I ask that You would give her vision and thoughts. Interpret things people can't seem to see, the same things that she sees, God, but You would bring about these things, God, through the interpretation of arts, through the interpretation of writing, through the interpretation of dance, Lord God, that she would be able to express the experience she has had with her soul in worship and communion with Thee. We bind everything in her past, we bind her current situation. God, things she has seen love ones do that is ungodly. Things she has heard her friends say, things that have hurt her, things that have tried to push her down and things that have tried to keep her to a level of commonality, but there is nothing common about her brain. There is nothing common about her soul. What You have placed inside of her, God, You have already given at birth but we are asking for maturation. We are asking for maturity to these gifts, God, as she is now a young woman venturing out into the world and must make it on her own, God. She will not be able to rely on her mother or her grandparents, or her aunts or uncles, not even on this church. For she needs to rely on You for You are the Hope of Glory! You are the Hope of Glory, You are the Hope of Glory, she needs to rely on You, God, and she needs to put her trust solely in Thee. Give an increase now, God. Bring her before great men and women in this world! Take her to her to a place where we can only imagine to go to. Lift her now in the spirit. Help her now in her body; touch her mind in the Name of Jesus! Give her wisdom beyond years, let her learn how to love and treat people with respect, kindness regardless of who poisons her mind with their opinions and their thoughts. Let her learn to be independent in her thinking, God, that she would treat people how she would wants to be treated. Let her learn to be like Jesus, God, even though she is bruised, even though she is wounded, she will never rise up and afflict or strike anybody. She will never withhold any good thing, complements or praise. She will never withhold gifts or anything from anybody else, knowing she will never have to be envious or jealous of anybody. Not even her peers, not people who she looks up to, for greatness lies within her, God, greatness lies within her, Lord, in the Name of Jesus. We pray a prayer of protection over her life as she will now venture out. We cover her as she is, God, desiring to go to college, desiring to get into the work world, desiring to get into the professional career of arts and dancing and writing and things, God, where she will have to be by herself. Take her to cities; take her all over this country and all over this world, God, we pray that You would keep Your Angels around her as she will not be abused in any manner physically. Financially, people will not take advantage of her, God, and make millions of dollars off of her and she not get any type of payment out of these things. Keep her, Lord God, where Professors will not steal her ideas or try to squish her creativity, God, to the point where she gives in her will to their way, but let her will never be broken. Let her resolve never be hindered, God. Strengthen her now as she looks to You, You, God, as You give her inspirations from the Holy Ghost where there will be success, there will be success, there will be success! There will be success, lift her head up in her soul, God, to let her know she is a young woman now. Help her now, God, not to look for love in all the wrong places. Help her not to accept the first person who comes her way who says he loves her, Hallelujah, God! Give her discernment like never before that she will know who really loves her. Give her discernment of who her friends really are, who really cares for her what's good and what is bad. What is evil and what is godly. Help her now, God, for she will not be with us forever. She will not be with her mother forever. She is a young woman now, God. She is going to have to step out in society on her own. It's not so kind out there, it is fearful in the real world, but You can protect and keep her. We pray for a prayer of protection not just for the year but for the rest of her life! Keep her from the wolves,

God, keep her from the demons, God, keep her from the evilness in this society and don't let her get so drunk off success. Don't let her get the big head because she does a few things and people pat her on her back, but let her be desperate, desperate to seek You! Desperate to serve You, desperate enough to always serve You and give You the glory for every success and to give You praise even in the midst of failure! Lift her up now, God, that all people can see an anointed vessel of You. Lift her up even in this church, that we will see the hand of the Lord upon her! Oh, God, thank You Jesus! Satan, the Lord rebuke you! Baptize her with the Holy Ghost, fill her in her soul, and let the fire burn like never before! Do it now in Jesus' Name we pray, Jesus' Name we pray.

God, I pray for Little G. Help her, Lord, help her, Lord. There is a joyful personality which comes out, and peeks her head through the clouds that has come in her life, but there is a very real pain inside of her still. Oh, God, only You can remove that hurt only, You can remove that pain. Those disappointments, God, even in her young mind, questions why her life is how it is and others seem to be better. Set her free, let love abide, let the love of God come now and conquer ever evil and hurtful experience she has gone through. God, set her free. God, she is going into young womanhood. Set her free, God, as she goes through the stage of puberty that she will not turn away from people and become isolated in her emotions and her ability to make contact to trust people, God because, she has been let down. She holds things, God, and that is not good for her to hold things. Help her to let them go, God. For she will become embittered and never become successful as long as she holds these things in her heart. Move in her heart and remove the pain. You said, God, Your Son got up and quoted from Isaiah that He was anointed to preach and in that statement He said to bind the broken heart to mend the broken hearted, God; let her heart be mended for her heart has been broken. God, we ask now, oh, God, that You would protect her, protect her, Lord God, from hurtful and abusive situations. We ask that You would encourage her to use her brain to be excellent in everything she does. Take that fight, that repetitive fight and apply it to every area of her life, not just athletics, but everything she is in, she will want to be number one. She will want to be the number one smartest person in her school. She would want to be the class valedictorian, she would want to be the best athlete. She would want to be the best scientists or she would want to be the best lawyer. She would want to be the best child, the best daughter, the best child of God. Put it in her to want to be the best in everything. Move now God as only You can move. I pray now for her body that You would keep it injury free that she won't tear her body up before it is too soon. Her speed, her gifts that You have given her. God, challenge her mind and let her know she must train and work. There is dedication that must come; there is a sacrifice that must be given, in the area of athletics for females. God, we pray You protect her against any spirit that is not like You in the Name of Jesus. I pray now, God, You would give her the strength like David in her arms. For You anointed his arms as he slung that sling, God, so hard that it was like a missile being fired out of a cannon that took the life down. And anybody, male or female who touches her in any inappropriate way, You would anoint her, God, as she slings her fist that she would knock them out in the Name of Jesus! This world is sick and evil, the spirit of abomination is open now, God. I bind that spirit that will come against her because if she participates, she will have to face it. God, give her dad the strength to tell her the truth, not trying to sugar coat it. Strengthen his mind, God, to communicate to his daughter the very evil things which are happening in today's society, that she would not become a statistics or victim or a person that would turn to that abominable life style. God, keep her safe. She spends so much time by herself. Keep her mind, God from, wondering and thinking about getting into trouble and come up ideas to be disobedient. Let a spirit of obedience come over her now like never before as she obeys her dad, Lord God. That she would not break his heart any more with concerns or things to worry about. Let her, Lord God, see the news, let it touch her. People have been kidnapped with both parents, and both of their parents watch after them very good. Talk well, train them well how to avoid these predators. There are people who follow buses and wait for these kids who seem to be isolated or no parent will pick them up or seeing nobody is at the house and they prey on these children. And these children are not always found, more not found then more are. And those who are found most are found dead, so, God, we pray now that Your Angels will protect her and that You would touch her mind that she would hear her dad, Lord, and not be rebellious. I pray against the spirit of rebellion in her. I pray now for some joy in that house, let some joy come into that house, God, let joy come in that house! Let love come in that house love. The love that says we are family! Joy that we are family, we are alive! Joy and love, we are not homeless. Joy and love that things might not be the way we want them, but thank God somebody in this house loves me, Hallelujah! Let them realize this situation could be a lot worse; bring some love and joy, God, bring some love and joy into their lives, God bind the three of them closer together in this year that the chains of love will never be able to be broken. Bind them in the Word of God. Let Jesus be the One who sits on the throne in that household, God, in the Name of Jesus I pray these prayers! Every unclean spirit, every unclean act, and every sinful thing that has taken place, God, I come against now in the Name of Jesus! No peace, no peace, no peace, for every ungodly thing no peace! Break the will, break the stubborn will now; break the stubborn will, now in the Name of Jesus! These souls are very important to You, God, they are important to this church and we pray for their strength now in the Name of Jesus.

Oh, God, for every one of us in this place and as we pass the word out in this membership we ask now, God, that we would try something for this year. You have given in the word on tonight in Psalms 118 that we would praise You seven times a day. Seven times a day that we would take a minute to thank You for something. Every day for this year that there would be a seven times praises. Everyday seven times daily we would stop for a moment to tell You thank You for something for that day. Let it add up to seven things a day so that would be seven praises, God, seven times a day we would be grateful for something on that day, Hallelujah! On this day, God, we are grateful for prayer. We are grateful for the opportunity to pray, Hallelujah. Father, we will give You praise for Your Son Jesus! We will give You praise for life itself. We will give You praise for Your glory being in this place. We will give You praise, God, for hearing our prayers and answering them. We will give You praise for favor another day. We will give You praise for food You have provided for our bodies today. Seven things, God, we can go beyond seven, but we are grateful for those seven things. As we stretch out a little bit further we will grateful, God, for the Hope of Glory that is in the Word of God and in our souls! We will be grateful for the anointing of God that destroys every yoke! We grateful for the sixteenth day of prayer! We will be grateful for all that You have done for us. We are grateful, for You given us another day to tell You thank You, just to tell You thank You. Another day just to tell You thank You for those who are in the grave cannot praise You a praise cannot come out of the grave, but we are alive and we grateful enough to say thank You for letting us thank You Hallelujah! Thank You for letting us have another day to thank You God for being God!!! He is worthy He is worthy He is our God, He is our God Hallelujah!

Thank Him just for being able just to thank Him, Hallelujah! Dead people can't praise God, dead people can't thank God, and dead people can't give Him praises seven times a day. Dead people are dead. They are gone. They are on the other side. They cannot come back and tell us how it is, but we are in the Land of the Living. Will You give Him a praise? Will You give Him praise, will You give Him praise, will You give Him a praise! Hallelujah, Hallelujah, Hallelujah! Thank You, thank You, thank You, thank You, thank You, thank You, thank You, thank You, thank You, thank You, thank You, thank You, thank You, thank You, thank You, thank You, thank You, thank You, thank You, Hallelujah, bless Him. We are in the Land of the Living! A living dog is better than a dead lion and we are in the Land of the Living! A dead lion can't eat, a living dog still eats. A dead lion can't breathe but a living dog still breathes. Hallelujah! Thank You, God, thank You, God, thank You for this opportunity to begin during these 40 days of prayer the time of intercession for each member of this church. Bless us to live, God, that we can come in on tomorrow to continue to call out the Saints names. That we come to touch and agree in this place for how You would lead by Your Spirit. For strength and deliverance that it would come into all of our homes. God, that there will be joy and love in all our families and that peace would abide in every member's home. God, in our souls, God, thank You, Lord, thank You Lord, thank You, Lord, thank You, Lord. Thank You, Lord, thank You Lord, Hallelujah. We offer this time up in prayer in the covenant that You have allowed us to make and we know You will keep Your end. Help us to keep our end as we go forward in these 40 days of prayer. Signs and wonders and miracles will be wrought once again as we desire to be like Moses and the children of Israel to be witnesses to the hand works of God. Satan, we can't do anything but the God we serve can do everything! And Satan, the Lord rebuke you and we do have the VICTORY. Be it done in Jesus Name and the people of God say Amen, Amen.

Give God some praise in this place! Give God some praise in this place!

Closing Scripture: Psalms 126 (KJV)
"When the Lord turned again the captivity of Zion, we were like them that dream. Then was our mouth filled with laughter, and our tongue with singing: then said they among the [nations], The Lord hath done great things for them. The Lord hath done great things for us, whereof we are glad. Turn again our captivity, O Lord, like the streams in the [Negev]. They that sow in tears shall reap in joy. He that goeth forth and weepeth, bearing precious seed, shall doubtless come again with rejoicing, bringing his sheaves with him."

END OF DAY 16 PRAYER SERVICE

STEP 17/DAY 17, WEDNESDAY

"The Price Of Salvation Is Priceless!"

Personal Note:

What can we say to all of this, if God be for us who can be against us! On the seventeenth night we had another phenomenal experience. It was about 28 degrees and the building was cold but yet hot! Hot because the fire and God glory was great in the place! This was the second night that our Pastor was crying out for the individual souls at the church. It really blows our minds to hear the Holy Spirit pray. How do we know its God? Because when he is praying he prays directly for what is going on in that's person's life. How can a man know the unknown of another person? How can man know the mind of another, or what they are experiencing right now? Our Pastor is so yielded over to the Spirit of God that it like his words are being written on the wall. We are all waiting for our turn to hear what the Spirit will say to us and reveal in us. There are hidden treasures inside that must come forth, there are mighty ministries lying dormant waiting to erupt. Oh, how my soul cries out, Hallelujah! Oh, how I want the more of God in my life! Oh if I could only stay in His **PRESENCE** just a little while longer!

<u>If only, Lord, I can capture Your greatness and put it into words. If only, Lord, I can express Your glory that has filled my soul and the people of God, if only I could</u>

adequately use the right words to tell of Your majesty! Oh, God help me as I desire to stay in your PRESENCE.

On today I asked God to remember us, remember the church and He answered saying how can I forget anyone who stays before me? Wow! I could have fainted! I was just talking to God not expecting Him to answer immediately and what an answer it was! I guess the saying is true out of sight out of mind. I pray that you would stay in the face of God.
~ Evelyn

DAY 17 PRAYER SERVICE BEGINS

Opening Remarks:
This is the seventeenth day of prayer, seventeen days in this year, seventeen days for the month of January, and seventeen days of an opportunity to consecrate ourselves before God for these 40 days of prayer, believing God is going to instruct us and help us according to His Scriptures. Psalms 119:160 says: "Thy word is true from the beginning: and every one of thy righteous judgments endureth for ever." When God says something it is not going to change from Genesis to Revelation. This Scripture can make reference and can be applied also to our situations, the beginning of this year, New Year, and a new experience. God's Word is still true and cannot be changed because, as the Word says, it is forever settled in Heaven.

The number seventeen has its significance. As the sum of two divided numbers in order and perfection in God's system of Government seven and the number ten combined together make seventeen. Seventeen is one of the prime numbers that cannot be divided into and come out with a whole number. This is a number that God uses divinely for perfection and we ask God for perfection in our prayers, in our lives, in our thoughts and desires to serve Him believing that God will bless us.

In Romans the eighth chapter, you will find seventeen things in that Scripture for blessings. There are seventeen things that combine with ten things that whatsoever things that have been declared to separate us, it gives a list of things that cannot separate us from the love of Christ. We include the seventeenth division of Psalms in our prayers as we continue to intercede for others. This is the second night that we will pray specifically calling out names that God leads me and this leadership. We ask God as the Spirit leads us for the duration of prayer to move and to hear us, step in divinely and move on the behalf of our loved ones. When I say our loved ones I just don't mean our family members, but those who are a part of our church family. We should love them enough to pray for them and be concern about their welfare on this earth.

Opening Scripture: Psalms 17 (NLT)

"A prayer of David. O LORD, hear my plea for justice. Listen to my cry for help. Pay attention to my prayer, for it comes from an honest heart. Declare me innocent, for you know those who do right. You have tested my thoughts and examined my heart in the night. You have scrutinized me and found nothing amiss, for I am determined not to sin in what I say. I have followed your commands, which have kept me from going along with cruel and evil people. My steps have stayed on your path; I have not wavered from following you. I am praying to you because I know you will answer, O God. Bend down and listen as I pray. Show me your unfailing love in wonderful ways. You save with your strength those who seek refuge from their enemies. Guard me as the apple of your eye. Hide me in the shadow of your wings. Protect me from wicked people who attack me, from murderous enemies who surround me. They are without pity. Listen to their boasting. They track me down, surround me, and throw me to the ground. They are like hungry lions, eager to tear me apart – like young lions in hiding, waiting for their chance. Arise, O LORD! Stand against them and bring them to their knees! Rescue me from the wicked with your sword! Save me by your mighty hand, O LORD, from those whose only concern is earthly gain. May they have their punishment in full. May their children inherit more of the same, and may the judgment continue to their children's children. But because I have done what is right, I will see you. When I awake, I will be fully satisfied, for I will see you face to face."

Insight As We Prepared For Prayer:
Thank God for the reading of this seventh Psalms as we incorporated this into our prayer asking God to hear us. It had been sixteen days consecrating ourselves, proving ourselves to the Lord. Our language, our mouths and within our mouths, our thoughts and within our hearts should be pure so God can hear us. And our hearts have been proven. We don't want to transgress against God. On the previous night some shared that anything that is negative or contrary to building someone up, and anyone who goes against God's Word, those people fall into the category of transgressing with their mouths. The Bible says a fountain cannot bring forth sweet and bitter water at the same time. We cannot bring blessing and cursing out at the same time. If we are not in the blessing business then we are in the cursing business. What I mean by cursing is that I am not talking about language you know, when people say profane words. You can say bad words without saying profane words. When you tell people what they can't do and put people down and judge them that is not good. We do not want to transgress against God's people. When we speak anything we need to make sure God is telling us to say that concerning someone's life. That goes for everyone that says that they are saved. You know what happened to Moses for treating God's people wrong and disrespecting God. God required his life. I don't want God to require my life. Do you want Him to require your life before it's time? No David said "Lord let my soul live". I want my soul to live!

We admonished the people that when prayer is being made for someone and it's not their home or their family member each member should be just as intense as if it was your family. We never know what could happen in our family. I would rather pray in advance than after the fact. We should pray and bind sickness before sickness comes, pray and bind death before death comes. It's always good to have an umbrella with you just in case because you never know when it is going to rain. If you get caught without one it's too late, you are already soaked and wet. We don't want to get caught without the protection of God hovering over our homes. In the book of Exodus they put the blood of the lamb over the door post so the Death Angel could go by. Every day, every minute of the day whether we know it or not, people are dying and we are not so special that death cannot come to our door. If God has been kind and merciful and we have asked him to let us live, God has let us live!

Has anybody praised God seven times a day? Psalms 119:164 says "Seven times a day do I praise thee, because of thy righteous [ordinances]". That might seem like a lot to stop and for seven times a day to tell God thank you for one thing. That is all we have to do, not for seven different things but thank him seven times a day for one thing. Once we start the thank you system in our souls it will become easier and easier just to say "thank you."

We continued to pray for the members of the church, the entire congregation and as the Lord led I called out the members, name by name and lifted them up to God. We must fight in prayer for one another. We must stand spiritually and fight for what God has given us. God has given us our children. He has given us one another. If you are married, he has given you your husband or wife. If you are not married and you have brothers and sisters he has given them to you. We do not get to pick what family we want to be a part of, God makes those decisions. He knows all things. He only knows why he has put us in the families that he did. Some people wonder why they were not born in rich families or with a silver spoon in their mouth. I don't know, but I do know this the price of salvation like the commercial says "priceless"! With salvation comes the benefit to go boldly before the throne of God in prayer. And whatsoever you pray and don't doubt asking in Jesus name according to the Scriptures it will be done unto you. So why not ask God for life? Let us go before God asking for our daily bread. We asked God daily to supply our needs not just for food or clothing, but for safety.

Let Us Pray:

Oh bless your name, Hallelujah oh God, oh God we thank you for this day. We thank you for this seventeenth day of prayer. God, David asked that you would hear the cry and prayer of the righteous. God, we have made ourselves available to you all of this year God that you would sanctify us, each and every one of us God. That you would purify our thoughts; intentions, and our desires, God. We have made ourselves available so that you would crucify the flesh. Let self be crucified. Let us present our bodies as a living sacrifice to thee holy acceptable which is our reasonable service. Knowing God that we need You not knowing to what extent. Saying to You, God, that we are available to You to use us. We are available, not knowing what is going to transpire. But, God, now that these days are accumulating and we are seeing your handiwork right before us, You have been meeting us in our prayers and supplications that we make for all Saints. God we must be as David said, our heart must be tried and proved and found acceptable in thine sight because the things that we are now requesting God are just as serious as anything that we have ever prayed for. Often times God people pray for material things in life and those things only. Then they put those things at the top of the list and if you don't answer those things then they turn their backs on You. And they take away their prayers and oaths of commitments they gave to You. But God we are not praying in that manner this year, not just for these 40 days. We are asking that these 40 days be a stepping stone to point us God to a realm of prayer that we would ask for the spiritual. Knowing that the natural is taken care of when you said that you will supply all of our needs, all of our needs according to Your riches in glory.

We ask now God sincerely as we continue in our prayer God. Your Spirit lead us to specific interventions and intercession that only ultimately you God can bring to pass in the member's lives in this church. The enemies of this church, the enemies of each and every one of us in this place on tonight, the enemies of every human being whether they know it or not, it is not one another God, it's a spiritual warfare. Satan is the captain of those that come against us and we can't beat him and beat our adversary with conventional weapons. We must use the spiritual weaponry that You have given to us and prayer is included in that. God on tonight we just don't pray for our homes, we pray for each other's homes. We want to be sincere God for the different names that we have called out that You would touch and move in their lives God because it could be us one day Lord God needing somebody to pray for us, to love us enough to pray for us. To stand with us spiritually when the world is standing against us and it seems like we are outnumbered God, with more of them than it is of us. There are more sinners than those who are in the Body of Christ, but You said in your Word "What shall we then say to these things? If God be for us, who can be against us?" Therefore, God, we pray on tonight, for the strength of everyone in this room. As they begin to touch and agree with me as we intercede one for another Lord God the Devil unleashes his attacks on us! For standing in the gap for our fellow brothers and sisters in Christ, that if he could weaken the chains Lord God it feels like he causes the prayer not to be answered because of the lack of faith of someone in this room. But God we can't do at this particular time as Jesus did with the young damsel who they thought was dead. He asked everyone who did not have the faith to leave the room. He asked those to leave the room who laughed and mocked and scorned and gave their opinions that she was dead as He said she was only asleep. We pray now Lord God spiritually if there is anybody in this place under the sound of my voice that is doubting and fearful that falls asleep God, to know we didn't come into this place to sleep. Our lives and the lives of those names that we will be calling out are too valuable to fall asleep! To think about something else besides the fact that we are here to pray and to fight for the souls of our loved ones and our families God! For every soul that walks through those doors. For every soul that comes into our lives that we can give them hope and that hope is Jesus! It's got to be that serious God, just as the woman who was in here on last night testifying how her son is improving. But he is yet still in the hospital and it could be one of our children in a coma. They could be skate boarding, running, playing basketball and fall and bump their head and never regain consciences. Life is like a vapor and Your Bible says it can soon go away. So therefore God we are grateful for life on today right now. Before we say anything else as David said he praises you seven times a day. God this is beyond seven for some of us, but we want to take time to say seven things on this night. We are grateful God for salvation. We praise you for our natural lives. We thank you that there was no death in our families; our children lives. Our brothers and sisters, husband & wives they live God, parents they live! We are grateful Lord we are thankful God that none of us was wheeled into this place. We are not crippled but we can walk; we can move our arms and our hands. We might have pain, but we thank You, God, we add to the fact that we thank You that we have the ability to

A Call Into His Presence

feel! Because if we were paralyzed or paraplegic we would not feel a thing God but we are grateful! We thank You on this night that You have given us a desire and a burden to pray. Not just for ourselves but for the Saints God and to pray for the sinner man as well. We thank You God in advance for your glory being revealed on tonight taking us to another level in prayer.

Hallelujah and we thank you for answering the prayer God. By faith we know that it will be done, glory to your name, glory to Your name, glory to Your name God, glory to your name. Now God by your Spirit lead us in this prayer. We pray for "Brother Tormented" now God wherever he is. We pray for his strength God. We pray for the strength that he would stand up in the mirror of Your Word an examine himself honestly, We pray that You would show him a true picture of who he is in comparison to what Your Word says he should be. We pray Lord God that You would remove every excuse that he puts up, every barrier, obstacle that stops him from serving You in the manner of his own testimony. He said You called him to preach, and if it's true God then Lord give him no peace. Let him be like Jonah put him in the middle of a huge fish. Put him in a situation of uncomfortableness God that there are no outs. No exits and he will have to call upon You like Jonah did in the belly of the fish until deliverance comes in the name of Jesus. God touch that man's lips, his mouth God that the words that come out would no longer be untrue. Giving him a mind to speak the truth and live the truth. The Bible says we should be a pattern of good works. Paul said we ought to do what we say as preachers, as ministers, as saints of God lest we be a castaway. We can tell everybody else what they need to do, but we can't do what we are supposed to do. Help now in the name of Jesus God. We come against every demon that has attacked him and infiltrated his soul and his spirit Lord God. Because God there is a great call for everyone who accepts Your call to carry the Gospel and the Devil does not want them to be in position to win any souls! To help anybody be delivered so he keeps them under attack! And he keeps him God and his situations isolated from where his strength would be coming from. But God now in my mind I see scissors cut, cut away everything that has attached itself to his spirit! Every ungodly thing! Every ungodly thought! Every ungodly action! Every ungodly person, God. We pray for his soul Lord God! We pray for his soul Lord God! We pray for the well being of his life Lord God. We pray now for increase in his life Lord God. We pray now for the Spirit to move upon him like never before Lord God that he would yield whole heartily, because a double minded man is unstable in all his ways. A man who thinketh more of himself than he ought to deceiveth himself, that is your Word God! Those kinds of people cannot be used by You God; those kinds of people won't realize that they need You because it's the anointing that destroys the yoke! A gift is given without repentance but it's the anointing that makes the difference! Sanctify his mind. Sanctify his body. Sanctify his life and his thoughts God that he can be used as a vessel for you like he has never been used in his life God. Let him cut away the things of the past. Let him not relish in the things of yesterday. Let him not focus on the mistakes of yesteryear, if the tree falls from the north or the south according to Your Scripture there it lies. No man knows whether or not if the seed has been conceived or received in a woman that brings about conception. No one knows whether the bones are growing or how fast or at what rate or whether if there is life within the womb. That is your scripture, God. But oh, God, in other words he must give up the past and forget about what has happened and what has been done in order to move forward. Hallelujah. We pray now for progression in his life. We pray that you bring him closer to You, God in the Name of Jesus we pray! Satan, the Lord rebuke you in his life! Satan, the Lord rebuke you over his mind! Satan, the Lord rebuke you in his thoughts! Satan, the Lord rebuke you in his body! Satan, the Lord rebuke you in every ungodly, abominable thing that the Devil conceived! We bind the works of the enemy that comes against him. We bind the works that wants him to be a failure and not succeed, but we speak success and life in his life according to Proverbs 18:21 that life and death lies in the power of the tongue. We speak life now in the name of Jesus!

Satan, the Lord rebuke you, Satan, the Lord rebuke you! God, I pray for "Mother Weary" for consistency in her walk and in her faith as she is separated from her family, her husband and her church. She sees sick and afflicted battling with death every day trying to give them hope. Hope is being drained out of her at such a rate Lord God that she has become weary in her soul. Oh, God, we pray for strength now in the name of Jesus. Let her connect with a good godly person, a church, God. Connect with somebody that can speak life back into her regularly, Lord God, that it will be on regular basis that she would be able to speak life into someone else. But if there is no life in her she won't be able to speak what is not inside of her. We pray now God that you move; take the concerns and worries off of her heart concerning her children oh in the name of Jesus. A mother's love God as great as it is, it is not greater than your love. Let her place her children wholeheartedly in Your hands. I pray for her oldest son now in the name of Jesus. Oh God, how many young people have walked in those same shoes away from your family? Life seems fun and exciting giving up the path of righteousness for a season of sin and enjoyment. God where he is at, if he dies outside of the ark of salvation he will lose his soul, but we pray for his soul God for it is tied to his mother God and her heart is heavy, weighted down concerned about her son. Jesus we have no better sense but to believe the Word of God and you said whatsoever we ask, whatsoever we ask in your Name of the Father you would do it. So we are asking God that you would save her son, that you move in his life, and that you would give him a mind to re-enroll and get back in school God. Give him a mind Lord God to seek You and to serve you. Give him a mind to know God that his parents that it's not that they are trying to be strict or harsh they love him and want him to succeed in life. And they understand that there is no success outside of Christ. With Christ we can do anything. The Bible says we can do all things through Christ. He can accomplish any natural goal with you God, but without you he will experience failure even if he succeed it would be failure because life is empty without you. We pray now Lord God for the seeds that has been planted in his life and the upbringing and raising of him God that those seeds would grow. Those trees would break through the concrete of sin Lord God, as the Bible says let the tall Bay tree let it stand Lord God the Word of God in his heart let it keep him from being involved in illegal things God, that it would keep him from being involved in ungodly things. That it would keep him from being involved in things that are not beneficial to his soul, and his mother would have a peace that surpasses all understanding in the name of Jesus. David said and the light of your countenance would shine upon his face let the light of your countenance shine upon their faces right now God. There is nothing like the connection between a mother and a child God, connect now in the name of Jesus Hallelujah have Your way, God. Destroy every yoke in the name of Jesus. Bring rest in the mind of Mother X now God, bring rest in her body that she won't work herself into a frazzle, and her immune system would become weak and she become sick. Bring unrest to her son's mind God that he won't be able to sleep and all the plans that he has laid out would not come to pass God, and there would be no success in his life. Doors would be shut that he thought would be open. His so called friends would turn their backs on him and he would find himself like a prodigal son that he would have no other choice but to come to his senses and to come back home God, Hallelujah in the name of Jesus! And ask forgiveness of his parents and his family God, and more importantly he would ask forgiveness from you in the name of Jesus I pray this prayer. Whatever it takes to bring him to salvation God we pray that you move speedily, mightily in the name of Jesus and you send forth thine anointing that destroys every yoke now. Set him free in his soul! Set him free God, set him free from sin! Jesus name, Jesus name we pray. Move God, move God, move God. Lord God, we pray for Sister Low Self Esteem. We pray for her strength and her resolve not to give up. Give her a mind God, a mind like Hannah as Hannah took years of being laughed at, years of seeing Elkanah's other wife Peninnah bring forth children and she brought nothing. But yet he said he loved her more but there was nothing to show in the form of a child. We pray now Lord God that same burden and pain that Hannah brought to you in the Temple God, when she was so hurt and so serious in the desire what she placed before you in the desire and request for a son, that she prayed and her lips moved but her words didn't match. And the Prophet thought that she was drunk, she was not drunk off of drink she was drunk in her desire and her emotions and the pain and grief that she bore for you God. And before Jesus had come and said cast all our cares upon him for he cares for us she was a prime example of someone bringing all of their cares the weight of their world to you, and you did not fail her.

Oh God let our Sister take on the spirit of Hannah that she would take her burdens, her pains, her heartache, her desires, her wishes, her goals, her everything. Her past mistakes her up and downs of this life, she would take everything that is in her heart; things that she doesn't want to think about God that are still there. That she would take them all to thee and cry out of her soul like never before and ask you the desire that has been placed upon her heart God! Give her a spirit of Hannah that she would pray out of her soul until the breakthrough comes. She will pray out of her soul until there is a re-birth a new birth God that comes from out of this prayer, from out of her cry. The tears of sorrow the tears of joy we ask that you would bring laughter to her life. Those that laugh at her will no longer be able to laugh, but she will have true laugher from the joy and experience of the power of God, the move of God in her soul. God I pray now from your throne in heaven you would pour out your anointing over her life right now Lord God in the name of Jesus! Let the oil of the anointing come now and destroy every yoke, every excuse she has ever used God that keeps her from going 100% toward success in fear of failure once again, we bind that now and loose Lord God the spirit of success Hallelujah! Succeed God and I will succeed mentally! I will not quit mentally! I am confident of this: everything of he that has began a good work in me mentally! I can do all things through Christ mentally! Nothing can separate me from the love of God mentally! If God is for me I can care less who is against me mentally! And no weapon that is formed against me shall prosper mentally! Oh, God, as I feel you're anointing as I sit in this seat! God, overshadow her soul! That she will not wait for the manifestation to come! That she will praise you like she has never praised you! She will cry out of her soul thanksgiving God! She will cry out of her soul glory to the King of Kings! She will cry out of her soul Hallelujah God as you said in your Word you would take the foolish things and confound the wise. God in the name of Jesus we rebuke Satan in her home! We rebuke Satan over her home! We rebuke Satan that is coming into her life through other people with the negativity that they bring. The lies and the drama! The confusion Hallelujah! The broken promises but you will never break a promise God, Hallelujah and we thank you for your glory! Hallelujah no longer the same, no longer the same, no longer the same, no longer the same, no longer the same, no longer the same Hallelujah, Hallelujah, Hallelujah! I bind the drawback spirit, Hallelujah. The Lord is wanting to take you to a deeper dimension, but you cannot draw back. God wants to take you higher and praise is your vehicle. Learn to praise God like you have never praised him before my Sister. Cry until your eyes can't cry anymore. Holler until you can't talk anymore. Pray until you can't say anything but "thank you'. Hallelujah, Hallelujah, use the authority that God has given every believer in his Name. I don't care who comes into your life, into your home, family or friends I don't care who it is. I don't care if it is your mother, I don't care who it is! I don't care if it's the President of U.S. Don't let them speak anything of death or negativity into your life trying to kill what God has planted into your spirit. You bind it and cast it out in the name of Jesus. You use the authority that God has given you. And these signs shall follow them that believe! If you are a believer then begin using the authority that lies within your mouth. Life and death is in your mouth you can speak life! You can speak death! Speak death to those things that people try to climb up against to try to pull you down, and attach themselves to you and keep you in the same circle, but God said the circle has been broken! It is up to you to step outside the circle. There is a dispensation of time where God has given you liberty to walk outside the circle. And wherever you walk in your mind, wherever you walk in your efforts God is going to make that your circle Hallelujah! God is going to give you a broader vision where you will see more things than what you have ever seen in your life. And when you see these things you will speak these things and if you speak those things that are not as though they are they will come to pass in Jesus name give him some praise! Hallelujah! Hallelujah. Lord, I pray for Sister Weak & Worn now in the Name of Jesus. God, you said you will keep our minds in perfect peace only if we would keep our minds stayed on thee. God I come against every unclean spirit that has attacked her. I come against every unclean restless, angry, frustration, stressful spirit and situation that has attached itself to her mind to her body, to her hope that has poisoned her hope. Stifling out of her soul God when now things are appearing to be blasé, blasé, but there is no mediocrity in

God. There is no lowness that God cannot reach. There is no place where any of us can run where he is not already there waiting with his loving arms for us. God we bind every attack of the Devil that has come to destroy her life. Her soul and all that she has worked so hard for in getting closer to thee. God we come against every unclean spirit according to your scripture and we cast them out in the Name of Jesus! God weeping may endure for a night, but your scripture says joy comes in the morning. Well, God, she needs for the morning to manifest itself in her soul that You would give her joy back with a seventeen fold increase. Seventeen fold increase. Ten is another number we use to give your perfect law. Seven is the number of rest, God; seven is the number of completion, God. Seven is the number of manifestation of your perfect divine Will, therefore the number seven and ten combine together, the ten being the number of government of your laws perfect in its number in its own right. Seven being a number that you said was your perfect number and completion and weight, God. The number that there is no number that can divide perfectly into that number, combine to give us the number seventeen perfection, perfection, perfection of joy in her soul God, give her seven times the joy that she has never experienced in her life for the joy of the Lord is her strength! The joy of the Lord is her strength! The joy of the Lord is her strength! The joy of the Lord is her strength! Give her a praise God an eruption praise a volcanic praise that will cast every demon out of her belly! Out of her soul for there is no way God a fountain can forth life and death at the same time! It can't bring sweet or bitter at the same time. It can't bring hopeless and hopefulness at the same time, so God the hope that lays within her soul as she is on her knees before your throne right now reach out God from heaven and touch her with your glory! In her soul Hallelujah let the praise of Yahweh go forth in her soul now God! Remove the obstacle in her throat! Remove the chains that bind her tongue! Just as the prison gates opened up when you shook it where Paul and Silas was at, because they prayed and sang praises we sing praises and we are praying open up the gates that imprison her in her soul and let her come forth! Let the joy of God come forth. Now Satan the Lord rebuke you! Open up your mouth Sister and praise him for your life! A living dog is better than a dead lion, you are not

A Call Into His Presence

dead you are alive. There is hope for those who are the living! God loves you! Give him the glory for your life! God strengthen you from the inside out! God deliver you woman Hallelujah! Joy cometh now like the rivers of Jordan! Joy cometh now Hallelujah! Joy comes in your soul! Bless him! Bless him! Jesus, Jesus, Jesus, Jesus, Jesus, Jessssssusssss!!! Hallelujah sit her down, lay her down don't keep holding her up Hallelujah, Jesus, Jesus, Jesus, Jesus, no man will get the glory! No man will touch you the Holy Ghost lay hands on you! The Holy Ghost be inside of you! The Holy Ghost destroys the yoke! The Holy Ghost move in your soul be thou set free! As God's Son called Lazarus to come forth I operate in that same anointing Woman come forth! Woman, come forth! Woman, come forth in the name of Jesus!!!

Yes, Lord, yes, Lord, yes, Lord, yes, Lord, now, God, we plead the Blood of Jesus over this place. We pray a prayer of protection for every child in this room, God, that no unclean spirit would come and attack them. We pray that you protect their souls, God, that they would not be oppressed or possessed. As every unclean thing is cast out of this place be sent to the dry places that it could roam, but the souls of our children be not touched by any unclean thing in Jesus name. We pray for every soul in this place, God, that is not protected that they would not be susceptible to the attacks of the evil one in the name of Jesus. In the name of Jesus Hallelujah, Hallelujah, Hallelujah, Hallelujah. God, we pray for Brother Confused (teenager). Father, we thank you he could be a child on a milk carton or a poster. We could be praying for his mother now asking that a miracle would take place and that he would not be dead but found alive. For just a couple of summers ago Lord a man in this place where we live tried to snatch him, but he had enough sense to run. And you blessed him that he did not fall or trip. You anointed his legs to run and to get away. God, you didn't deliver him so he could live to be no good, or be not saved. To be killed by somebody, to not be a success in life, you could have allowed him to die then if that was the case. We believe there is a reason you allowed him to live, God, so we pray in conjunction, God, with your divine intervention on that situation you kept him alive that he might live to serve you. Now, God, we pray a prayer of protection as through their own testimonies their High School situations are becoming grim. And their lives have been played with a possibility, God, of even death as these gangs are forming and people are taking sides and sooner or later, God, if it has not happened they are going to try to force people to be a part of the gangs. We pray that you would give them the strength to say no, we pray that you would give him the strength if he has to fight God he would fight and not lose. We pray, Lord God, against every unclean influence that comes against his mind. High school can be a good experience, but it also can introduce you to some strange things. And we pray, Lord God, for the protection of his soul that he would not be caught up in what seems to be exciting. We pray against the spirits that come against him in the way of alternative life styles (Roman 1:24-28). We pray now, God, for those who have questions about their sexuality. We pray now against the young girls that are coming who have made themselves very available that he would not yield in no manner to none of those things, for his future is far more important than to be tied down to someone. Making a child and he is still a child himself, oh, God, or become involved in some ungodly relationship that will mess up his life forever. God, we bind every unclean spirit now, we bind the down-low spirit, homosexual spirit, we bind the effeminate spirit, we bind the fornication spirit, we bind the drug spirit drinking spirit don't let him experiment with taking a drink. Don't let him experiment on smoking something or sniffing something or crystal meth, no, God, not like what we are seeing in these High Schools no, God! His life and his future is too valuable! We pray that you continue to touch his health that seizures will not keep him from achieving his dreams. Touch his mind, God, that he would put his priorities in the right place that he needs to get his grades obedience is better than sacrifice. People his age no longer want to listen to their parents but those that love him, God, won't lie to him. They will tell him things that will help him not things that will hurt him. Open up his eyes that he will see that everybody that is smiling in his face is not his friend. God, you have gifted him creatively but in his mind, God, he can do things intellectually. In his body, God, maybe it's meant for him to be a basketball star, and, God, what you gifted him in is other things in life that is longer lasting then fleeting fame of sports.

You have gifted him with the arts, dance, choreography, web-sites, marketing, and putting things together what other people can't see because they are not thinking outside of the box, but he does. Those areas will open him up to people who do extremely specific things. We pray, God, that you would keep him safe that you're Angels would protect him. Let his mind not be one that would follow, but let his mind be one of a leader that he won't be lead to ungodly things. Use his gifts to be brought forth before great people do it, God, I pray. Now touch him, God, out of all these things save him. Fill him with your Holy Spirit and open up your Word to his understanding. Give him a desire to seek you because there a ministry gifts inside of him that only you can bring out. God we ask now that you move in his soul and have your way in him. Lord I am not asking that you take his joy and youth away, I am asking that you add to the joy of his youth. Keep him protected from the things that adults have to deal with. Oh God don't let him worry about money. Don't let him worry about food. Don't let him worry about if his clothes matches somebody else's clothes God. Let him learn now that a man is not judged by the things that he have, but he is judged by the content of his character. Let him grow up to be a honest man not lying, not stealing, not envious or jealous of others, but to help anybody that ask for help showing that he is a true man. Even at his young age teach him how to be a man. Place men around him that will show him how to be a man. Help us in this church every man in this church, God, to stand in these young men lives and show them how to be a man. That every day is not a day of laughter, and every day is not a day of playing games! Everyday doesn't go our way but we can't stop being men! We can't give up, because somebody is attached to us! Men cry! Men feel like quitting! Men fail, but a real man gets up! A real man says Lord Help me when we can't help ourselves! A real man will say I don't know what the answer is, but I know who the answer is. Jesus is the answer! A real man will not be ashamed to praise God! A real man will not be ashamed to cry out of their souls and say, Lord have mercy and help me! Help us as men in this church to teach them that, not by the words we say, but by the actions that he sees! A real man is not ashamed to say I am sorry I made a mistake. I said the wrong thing, I did the wrong thing please forgive me. A real man is not ashamed to say I love you. A real man is not ashamed to love God, love his family and love his self. Help us to show him and many other young men in this church that you can be a man and love God and still be a man. God made all us men differently we don't have to be envious of any man's gift. Help now God to teach him and other young men that the number of girlfriends that you have and the girls you sleep with does not make you a man. Keeping yourself makes you more of a man than anybody could ever think, and it pleases God and God will honor anyone that keeps themselves and the anointing will be poured out upon their lives that they would do signs & wonders out of the Bible would take place because of their sacrifice they laid out before God keeping their vessels clean before the Lord. I pray that prayer for our young brother in Jesus name I pray. Amen

Now, God, as I close this segment of prayer, I ask now, Lord God, that you would help us. Help us, God, not to come off the wall of prayer. Help us, God, because the more we pray the harder we pray the more fervent our prayer and desire is for you to help us all the more the Devil is going to attack us and try to get us to quit praying one for another. And, God, if you don't help us he will win, if you help us he will never win. So we pray for your help for each person in this room. For every member of this church, God, that has been praying one for another that we will not stop praying for each other even after these 40 days are up. As long as we think about each other, as long as we see each other, God, we will always pray for each other until the day we die. We will count on one another to pray for one another and not to look for the bad in each other, but to look toward the good, God, and if anyone of us falls, sin or make a mistake, get caught up, that we won't laugh at the other one, God. The Bible says those who are meek, those who are humble, those who are loving, those who are spiritual let them go to such a one in the spirit of meekness and love and share with, God, that they are making mistakes that are hurting them and their souls are on the line, and to restore that brother or sister not to kill them, restore them. Not to judge them, restore them and bring them back to the house hold of faith where the Saints can pray for them and encourage them not to give up. Not to give up. There is hope for the living and a living dog is still better than a dead lion. We thank you for this time of prayer. We thank you and us give you praise. We give you glory, God, now Lord as I close this prayer I pray for someone that is not on this membership list.

I pray for our visitor on tonight as your Spirit has led him into this place. I pray for his strength and his soul, God, he is battling with so much within his soul. The war is raging Hallelujah, no peace. I speak peace to the raging storm inside of him. I speak peace in the Name of Jesus. God, oh God, I bind everything inside of him that is battling your Word and your Will for his life and I cast it out in the name of Jesus. Let a settling come because there is an unsettling in his life. Let a settling come, let a settling come, God, it is hard for anybody to think clearly when things are in a uproar going, going rapidly. I speak a settling in his life that he can think clearly, that he can hear exactly what you are saying. Give him a mind of obedience a willingness to say yes to your Will and whatever instructions you give him regardless of how hard the decision is going to be cut loose, cut loose, cut loose. God, is saying to you young man cut loose you have attached yourself to some things that have taken you away from, God, cut loose. Have faith because these things appear that they will benefit you, but just as a rocket engine is attached to the space ship the rocket engine does not have a life of its own. It's job is to help the space ship get into space and when it disconnects people no longer care about it, because it disintegrates as it re-enter back into the earth's atmosphere. God is saying you are like that rocket engine except the difference is He cares about you. And he will not let you disintegrate as you re-enter back into God's atmosphere. And it seems impossible that a rocket engine can develop wings and the ability to fly because its only job is to get the rocket into space, but if there is a malfunction and the rocket engine can't disengage it stays stuck and then it is taken on a course that it has no control over for it is only a engine. But if God says disconnect then you disconnect then God will turn your rocket engine into a space ship. Where you will have the ability to fly where ever you want to go under God's direction, but you have to disconnect. It is going to be painful, some people are going to criticize you, a lot of people are not going to understand, but it is for the benefit of your Soul. I also perceive in my spirit to share with you do not be like the Bible says some people fall in the category of having a form of godliness, but denying the power thereof. This is a new beginning for you God do not move by accident or co-incident everything happens by God divine providence. You have the opportunity to re-commit your life back to God the past is over with. God holds no grudges. He does not hold our past against us. If we ask him to forgive us he is faithful and just to forgive us of all our sins and cleanse us from all unrighteousness. Joy, praising the Lord like you experience tonight is nothing to be compared to what God is going to do for you inside of your soul.

Salvation takes place a Soul Saved!

God, as this man takes your oil symbolic of your blessing, as he rubs it over his head and his hands, give his mind clearly on what he needs to do in his life. God he has a strong desire for success. He has tried different avenues and he is still not happy. The drive is in him, but there is no peace. But God as he has anointed his head and poured the oil into his hands let the yoke be destroyed from the crown of his head to the soles of his feet. No longer having the same mind as before, as he anointed his hands God and rubbed his hands together God let his mind work and his hands work that whatsoever he put his efforts in God bring success to it in the name of Jesus. In his mind God obedience, yielding to your Will being submissive to your Word, no longer a wild running spirit, but peace, peace in the name of Jesus. Father God be it done now we pray for this young man. God give him an understanding in his mind even now, that there is no success without a 100% commitment to serve you. In that God, you have promised that you would meet all of our needs. You said you would give us these other things if we would seek ye first the Kingdom of God and your righteousness and all these other things you would add. Well God let him have a mind to seek you first like never before with the same passion and desire that he sought after every other thing let him seek you God, give him a 7-fold increase in his desire to serve you and to praise you. To be real for you God, to submit himself to you. Lord God, destroy every yoke, Lord God that comes against him. Satan, the Lord rebuke you,

Satan, the Lord rebuke you! We speak wholeness in his spirit! We speak divine intervention into his life! God, in the name of Jesus you will get the glory and the victory be it done now in the name of Jesus! Give him some praise in this place! Give God some praise in this place! Hallelujah! As Jesus told the man at the pool of Bethesda, Jesus eliminated every excuse that the man gave. Finally, he said "rise take up thy bed and walk" young man rise. No longer no more excuses, a day of excuses, a day of your past, no longer. No longer, you have a clean slate with God even right now be it done in Jesus name. Father God we thank you for this time of prayer. We love you and we appreciate you and ask Lord God that you would strengthen everyone in this place for it is godly serious the work that you have called us to do, PRAY. We give you glory for the victory is ours. The victory is ours over the Devil in Jesus name, we pray thy Will be done and the people of God say Amen.

Closing Scripture: Psalms 34 (NLT)
"A psalm of David, regarding the time he pretended to be insane in front of Abimelech, who sent him away. I will praise the LORD at all times. I will constantly speak his praises. I will boast only in the LORD; let all who are discouraged take heart. Come, let us tell of the LORD's greatness; let us exalt his name together. I prayed to the LORD, and he answered me, freeing me from all my fears. Those who look to him for help will be radiant with joy; no shadow of shame will darken their faces. I cried out to the LORD in my suffering, and he heard me. He set me free from all my fears. For the angel of the LORD guards all who fear him, and he rescues them. Taste and see that the LORD is good. Oh, the joys of those who trust in him! Let the LORD's people show him reverence, for those who honor him will have all they need. Even strong young lions sometimes go hungry, but those who trust in the LORD will never lack any good thing. Come, my children, and listen to me, and I will teach you to fear the LORD. Do any of you want to live a life that is long and good? Then watch your tongue! Keep your lips from telling lies! Turn away from evil and do good. Work hard at living in peace with others. The eyes of the LORD watch over those who do right; his ears are open to their cries for help. But the LORD

turns his face against those who do evil; he will erase their memory from the earth. The LORD hears his people when they call to him for help. He rescues them from all their troubles. The LORD is close to the brokenhearted; he rescues those who are crushed in spirit. The righteous face many troubles, but the LORD rescues them from each and every one. For the LORD protects them from harm – not one of their bones will be broken! Calamity will surely overtake the wicked, and those who hate the righteous will be punished. But the LORD will redeem those who serve him. Everyone who trusts in him will be freely pardoned."

END OF DAY 17 PRAYER SERVICE

Personal Note:
    The Word of the Lord is so powerful! That is why Satan doesn't want you to read it. He knows the Word. He has seen the Word and the Word is Jesus! He knows the power the Word has so don't let him stop you from reading it and praying it back to God. The Word of God is so great that it tells us that heaven and earth will pass away before one jot or tiddle of the Word would. Hold on to it and never let it go! Read it, pray it, believe it and receive all that it says you can do and have! Praise the Lord for the Word!
~ Evelyn

STEP 18/DAY 18, THURSDAY

"I Love You, Oh, Lord, With All of Who I Am"

DAY 18 PRAYER SERVICE BEGINS

Opening Remarks:

We join in this prayer with David as we pray for manifold manifestation of His marvelous blessing. We pray God would do as He did for David. He said, "[He] loved God with all [his] strength, for the Lord is [his] rock, [his] fortress, [his] deliverer; [his] God in whom I will trust. I will call upon the Lord, who is worthy to be praised" and when he called upon the Lord, so shall I be saved from mine enemies. God is worthy of the praise and we shall be saved from our enemies. When we call on God to make His **PRESENCE** known, He is our strength, our rock and buckler and He is our high tower. We pray God would help us with our families as we called for the help of God on this eighteenth night.

Opening Scripture: Psalms 18:1-19 (KJV)
"I will love thee, O Lord, my strength. The Lord is my rock, and my fortress, and my deliverer; my God, my strength, in whom I will trust; my buckler, and the horn or my salvation, and my high tower. I will call upon the Lord, who is worthy to be praised: so shall I be saved from mine enemies. The sorrows of death compassed me, and the floods

of ungodly men made me afraid. The sorrow [cords] of hell [Sheol] compassed me about: the snares of death prevented me [came upon me]. In my distress I called upon the Lord, and cried unto my God: he heard my voice out of his temple, and cry came before him, even into his ears. Then the earth shook and trembled: the foundations also of the hills moved and were shaken, because he was wroth. There went up a smoke out of his nostrils, and fire out of his mouth devoured: coals were kindled by it. He bowed the heavens also, and came down; and darkness was under his feet. And he rode upon a cherub, and did fly: yea, he did fly upon the wings of the wind. He made darkness his secret places; his pavilion round about him were dark waters and thick clouds of the skies. At the brightness that was before him his thick cloud passed, hail stones and coals of fire. The Lord also thundered in the heavens, and the Highest gave his voice; hail stones and coals of fire. Yea, he sent out his arrows, and scattered them; and he shout out lightings, and discomfited them. Then the channels of waters were seen, and the foundations of the world were discovered at thy rebuke, O Lord, at the blast of the breath of thy nostrils. He sent from above, he took me; he drew me out of many waters. He delivered me from my strong enemy, and from them while hated me: for they were too strong for me. They prevented me in the day of my calamity: but the Lord was my stay. He brought me forth also into a large place; he delivered me, because he delighted in me."

Let Us Pray:

Oh, God, we come to You in this place, humble, God, before Thy **PRESENCE** but boldly, God, which we are instructed by Your Word that we can come boldly before Your throne to make our prayer request known to Thee. God, we honor this eighteenth day of consecration this year. We are blessed to be alive for eighteen days in the first month of this year. Time, God, doesn't mean anything to You. Time means so much to us as human beings because we have so little time and we don't know how much time we have here on this earth. God, we are grateful for life today for what You have done and we thank You seven times today for something, God, worthy of praising You. For each of us are willing to do so, God, as we are asking for greater explanation in our minds, God, to obey Your Word and to do like these people we read in these scriptures. You have allowed for segments of their lives to be recorded that we might take from there example and see how they waited for Your **PRESENCE** and You showed up and blessed them. We come before Your **PRESENCE** that You might bless us. On tonight, God, we need a blessing like we've never needed before, for this new day has brought new challenges, this new day has brought new problems, trials and tribulations, successes as well as failures. We cannot go back to yesterday or the day before, we can only live for this moment. We pray today to see the next. God, You have granted us life and You have proven throughout our lives You will always be there to protect Your children; we are Your children and we believe we are Your children, we are Your children.

David was brave. He said when we call and cry out for help, as any loving parent, God, would come to the aide and rescue of their frightened child, You would come to the rescue. Therefore, God, we ask that You come to our rescue because if we look at what we face in our lives then we can become fearful. Only because our faith is rooted and planted grounded in the Word of God to go beyond our fears and perfecting love, we place at Your altar, God, the love we have for You. Perfect love casts out all fear. We love You Lord God we love You. We will serve You, and we will praise You and pray. We will magnify You, we will be obedient to Thee, God, and we will honor Thee. We will intercede for our brothers and sisters. God, when we call their names out, we will ask for mercy for their lives. We will ask for intervention and Your Will. We will ask for Your help, not just for our individual family, but also for this church family, and every family of this church. We need Your help on today, this eighteenth day we need Your help. David said, "I will call upon the Lord for he is worthy to be praised so shall I be saved from my enemies." God, we call upon the Lord on tonight, to the Lord God of all Gods that we would be saved from our enemies who attack us, who want to see us fail. Want to see our families torn apart, happy when tragedy comes our way. The world is pleased to see the church struggle, the church be torn apart, the people in the church give up and turn back, but God we have come into this place because we have not turned back. We are praying for everyone in this church, every member who we will never turn back.

Oh, God, oh, God, oh, God, help now, Lord, help us now, Lord. If we, God, try our best to be judicious in our statements and careful on what we ask openly in prayer. Oh, God, help this church, help this church look upon our Sister wherever she might be, God, and keep her mind together. Oh, God, bring her focus back to Thee. You spared her life last year and we pray You spare her life once again. Oh, God, put a hedge of protection around her. The Devil can only go so far and when You speak and say enough is enough, he must freeze, stop, leave, and let go. We speak now, Lord God for the issues of our heart. God, even in her young age, let her not forget the seriousness of life and how fleeing it is that we can die at any moment at any instance. I just pray, Lord God, You remind her on what You have done for her by keeping her safe and that will be enough, God, to light the fire inside of her soul once again to come crying to Thee, to present her body a living sacrifice holy unto You, God. We pray now, God, You keep her safe. Move, God, move in her soul strengthen her, strengthen her, Lord, strengthen her now, God, as she goes through this life trying to find her way, find her niche in life; find where she fits, God, strengthen, trying to do things right but, oh, God. Let her never forget You have to first, know Christ is to be the center in everything otherwise, success will never be obtained. God, we pray now against every demonic force that comes against her, that You would bind it. We cry out of our souls for our Sister, God, help her, God, help her, Lord, help her, Lord, help her, Lord, Jesus, Jesus, we plead the Blood of Jesus. Oh, God, oh, God we plead the Blood, we plead the Blood, we plead the Blood of Jesus, Hallelujah. Satan, the Lord rebuke You. Take your hands off her mind; take your hands off her mind. Be thou set free in your mind, my Sister. Be thou set free in your mind, liberty comes from the Spirit of God. Over shadow now, Lord God, wherever she might be, let her feel Thine **PRESENCE** and the prayers of the Saints. Let her feel the burdens of the hearts of these people who are concerned and care about her soul, God. Let her feel Your love, the warmth of Your mercy, God. Jesus, we pray to Your Father in Your Name. Do it now we pray, God. Move now, we pray, God, move now, Hallelujah.

A Call Into His Presence

God, we pray now for another one of our Sisters. Oh, Lord, oh, Lord, separate her from what pulls her down. Her and her children, God, let her turn back toward You and cry out for repentance. Let her see where You have shown her mercy throughout her life and kept her alive, God. Remove any fear or doubt, any skepticism and let her know You are real and true. Give her an experience, God, out of the Bible; one as David had such an experience that he compared it to riding a chariot, riding the wind speaking, God with the voice of thunder! Lighting stepping off Your throne and coming down to this earth with the darkness under Your feet. You gave him a revelation God, which no human being could give. Give her revelation, God, no other human being can give, that You are God and there is none else. Move in her life we pray, Jesus, Jesus have Your way. Satan, the Lord rebuke you, we plead the Blood over her life, over her children, in her home. Move now, God.

We pray for Sister now. God, touch her and strengthen her, God, she is holding on. Oh, God, she needs Your help, even now, she needs Your help, and she needs Your help, God. Ooooh, the everyday battles, they are hard. It's almost like a magnate drawing her, drawing her, drawing her away from You. We come against the effects of this world; we come against the enticements that the Devil has set forth in her life. We come against weakness and mediocrity, God, and the spirit of just settling for how she is not. Place inside of her a hop, God; no one can pull out, a hope that lies within You, her help. Help her, God, strengthen her, God, and move in her life, God, deliver, God, in the Name of Jesus. Satan the Lord rebuke You, Satan the Lord rebuke You. Satan, the Lord rebuke you. Take your hands off her life, take your hands off her home, and let her mind set her free everywhere, everywhere, everywhere. Look on her grandson now in the Name of Jesus, God. Touch that little boy's mind, ooooh, God, help him, help him now as he grows up. Keep him safe, God, keep his mind innocent and pure from the things he has seen which will bring about contamination, God. We send Your Word his way, send Your Word, God, send Your Word, God send Your Word, God. Let Your Angels protect him. Keep him alive, God; keep him safe, God, oooh in the Name of Jesus.

Look on his father, Lord God. You have looked after his soul; You have looked after his life. There is a calling upon him, God. Don't let him look away. Let him yield to Thee in the Name of Jesus; don't let him ever forget what You have done for him in his life, God. Help him now to understand to yield to You to pray like never before, because he needs You. Give him clarity in his mind, God that he will understand the instructions and he won't sin. Oh, God, remove any desire to go back into that old life style in the Name of Jesus. Set him free and sanctify his mind, God, sanctify his mind, God. Bind the Devil who comes against him who wants him to fail and not succeed, but we speak success in his soul, God. Through the Word of God, send and dispatch Your Angels to minister to him, God, in the Name of Jesus. Break him down, break every yoke, and destroy every yoke that is inside of him, every strong hold by the power of the Holy Ghost. Be it done that You might build him up upon the rock of the Word that is life would never be the same. His countenance would be changed, God. People would not recognized and know who he is because of the change You would bring about in his life. We pray for these things by faith, God, believing it is done.

Touch his Sister now, God, oooh, God, oooh, God. We bind and cast out the drawback spirit, we bind it now. Give her a boldness not to be afraid how her friends, how people will perceive her as she yields her life 100% to Thee, God. Help her, Lord God. There is a kind spirit inside of her wanting to come out, God, not knowing how, not knowing how, God, but teach her. Help her, Lord God. Teach her how to pray, teach her how to call upon Thee. Teach her how not to be afraid to open up her mouth and praise You, teach her how not to be afraid to open up her emotions and let You come in; let You sweep over her soul, God, that You have Your way in her life, God. Teach her how not to be worried about how she would look or how she would appear, Lord God, as she yields to You. Help her to yield in her soul that wholeness would come to her life in the Name of Jesus! Moves now, move now, move now, God, move now, Jesus, Jesus have Your way. Disconnect the things of the past from her life, Lord God, Hallelujah, bless Your Name, bless Your Name. We plead the Blood over their home, God, over that entire home, God; the Blood of Jesus cover them. Squish the works of the enemy that

A Call Into His Presence

is trying to bring death to their lives, God, the curse one, Hallelujah but Your Word is true from the beginning.

We speak the truth of the Word in her life as we call upon the Lord God. As David said, "When I called upon Him," meaning our personal selves would only be saved from our enemies, but we call for this Church Family, that as a Church we would be saved from our enemies. He attacks us. The Devil has unleashed his demons, Lord God, upon us that we might give up, but You are our strength. You are our Rock! You are our everything. We will not give up, Lord God, and we will not give in! Thank You, Jesus, thank You, Jesus, thank You, Jesus, Hallelujah, Hallelujah, Hallelujah!

God, I come against the spirit of witchcraft and idolatry, Hallelujah. Those who are casting spells and praying games. Those who are trying to test Your Spirit, God, to try Your anointing to see if the people are real, see if I am real, God, see if the gifts You have given is real. I come against that now in Name of Jesus; bring these people to the forefront, God. Make them an open shame; those who are playing games, lying in there testimonies, lying in their statements, God, oh God. We come against the works of the enemy that is trying to discredit Your servant, discredit this ministry, and discredit these people, Lord God. We come against it now in the Name of Jesus! Send Your arrows from Your throne, God. We know You never miss a target. Send Your arrows from Your throne, God. We rebuke this in the Name of Jesus. Have Your way, God, have Your way, and have Your way as we yield ourselves to Thee 100%. God, we yield ourselves to You totally. By faith we make this journey, by faith word our mouths and our prayers, God, by faith lead and guide us, God!

Jesus, Jesus, oh, God there is a great weight in this place on tonight. There is a great weight inside of my soul, oh, God, oh God, help us now, help us now, Lord God, and help us now in the Name of Jesus. Jesus, Jesus, Jesus. I will call upon the Lord Jesus! Help us now, help us right now I pray, help up right now, I pray, help us right now. Send Thy help from the sanctuary, God. Zion, hear us when we call upon Thee. We need You in this place, God, cover us under the Blood. Cover every child under the Blood in this place, every child be covered under the Blood in this place. Lord, we bind forces that will attack our children in their minds, that they will not have any bad dreams, oh, God, see anything that they should not see, Lord God. Experience anything they should not experience, we plead the Blood of Jesus right now in the Name of Jesus cover them, cover them! Cover them, Lord Jesus, oh, Sweet Wonder, ooooh, Sweet Wonder, Sweet Wonder have Your way in this place. Have Your way in this place, my God, have Your way in this place, my God.

Oh, Jesus, I pray for a bold spirit for one of our Elders, Lord God, a bold spirit of faith. A bold spirit for his wife, faith she leans and depends upon blindly, whole-heartedly, God. Oh, God, don't let fear creep in. We bind the spirit of fear that can creep in; we bind the spirit of fear. Oh, God, give her peace in her decision-making; she trust You to make a way. Make a way, Lord, make a way, strengthen her body, strengthen her thoughts, strengthen her in her mind, strengthen her in her gifts, strengthen her in her faith, and strengthen her in her walk. Help her to be obedient, God. Help her to obedient to Thee, Lord; help her to be obedient to Thee, Lord. We bind the fearful spirit and cast it out in the Name of Jesus. We loose a warrior spirit, God, a strong spirit of servitude, a strong spirit of faith, anointing, God, anointing fall fresh upon her life in the Name of Jesus. Take her to a new level of worship, God, and praise, Hallelujah, a desire to serve You the more, and a reality of knowing heaven has been promised and there is nothing to be afraid of here on this earth. Oh, God, get the glory in her life, get the glory in her life, give her wisdom, Lord God, and the application of wisdom, Lord God, in the Name of Jesus I pray. Help her, God, to yield. Give her a spirit of submitting that she would yield, God, a spirit of yielding to Your will, a spirit of yielding, God! We bind the strong hold in her temper, in her anger, God, frustrations; things she holds on to in the inside. Let it go, let it go, let it go, in the Name of Jesus, let it go, let it go. Replace it with love, God, a love that can only come from You, oh, Jesus. You provide for the sparrows the lilies in the fields, provide forever in her life, forever I pray, forever I pray, forever I pray in the Name of Jesus.

God, look on our Sister right now (a member we haven't seen in months). Help her, Lord God, in her mind. Help her, Lord God, not to be so concerned and carried away with trying to help others when she is not able to help herself spiritually. Help her now, Lord God, to look unto Thee, call upon Thee, and cry unto Thee with all her soul as David cried unto Thee God. Let her cry unto to Thee and ask for help. Let her cry unto Thee, God, and ask for strength, let her cry unto Thee, God, and be strong enough to cut the ties of the weights of people who are pulling her down, God. Let her call unto Thee, God, until every excuse has been carried away. Let her call upon Thee, God, until every excuse has been erased out of her life. Let her call unto Thee, God, until she does nothing but praise You and look forward to having communion and fellowship with Thee. Look upon her children, God, and keep them safe. We rebuke death over their home; we rebuke death in the Name of Jesus. Oh, God, separate her from the people who have spoken death. And death is now slowly creeping into her life and pulling her down, God. Let her break free as Lazarus broke free from death, God. Let her break free from the people who are negative God, let her be strong enough to stand and not hear, not allow them to speak negativity into her life. Give her a bold spirit, Lord God, to tell the truth and shame the Devil. Give her a bold spirit to call upon You when she does not know how to respond. Help her and lead her and direct her in her life, God, in every avenue she goes down, will not be one of a dead end, or one of a curse or failure, God. But it would be one of success because You have already granted permission that the victory would be hers, Lord God. Let her recommit her life back to You in this year, God. Let her not have that same mentality of inconsistency and instability, God, but we speak a stable spirit to her mind, not a lukewarm spirit but a hot one or cold spirit, for You would spew out the lukewarm person, God. Help her now to be hot or cold for You, God, help her now to have a desire to serve You, God. Lift her up now where she has been broken down, and beaten down by so many incidences. Strengthen her now in her walk in her resolve to serve You. Give her a praise on the inside of her soul that even in the worst times she will tell You thank You. When things don't add up, she will tell You thank You, when she finds herself alone, she will tell You thank You. Help her now and lift her in her spirit, this I pray. Have Your way in her life, this I pray, destroy every yoke in the Name of Jesus! Do it, Lord, do it, Lord, do it, Lord, do it, Lord, please, Lord, please, Lord, please, Lord. All that You have placed in Your hands, You never lost one, God. Don't let this one, don't let this one be lost, help her now, God, help her now, help her now. The spirit of error that is in her life, God, I bind the spirit of error. Let the truth come and make her free. Let the truth come and destroy every yoke. Let the truth come, let the truth come, let the truth come, come now, come now, the spirit of truth, come now which the World cannot know. The spirit of truth that the world will never recognize; the spirit of truth, come now and set her soul free! In the Name of Jesus, Hallelujah, thank You, Lord, thank You, Lord, thank You, Lord!

God, I pray for one of our Deacons who is in training. A man who spent majority of his adult life in and out of prison, God, I pray for him in the Name of Jesus. God he is doing his best trying to keep his commitment to Thee. Move in his mind, God, expand his understanding of the Word. Let him hear clear instructions You are speaking into his life. Oh, God, he wants to go higher in thee, but there is a sacrifice, which is required, God. Is he willing to give the sacrifice? Is he willing to cut loose everything that is not like Thee? Is he willing to cut loose the habits, God, is he willing to cut loose, God, the conversations, thoughts and different things and people, God, that who trying to play games with him? Oh, God, as he recognizes them, let him stay away, and if he doesn't recognize them, open up his understanding spiritually and his discernment, God, that there are people trying to set him up and pull him down, Lord God, in the Name of Jesus. Open up his understanding, God, give him a boldness to be a warrior to be like David, displaying his sling shot to throw his stone and knock the giant down. Take the sword and cut the head off! I don't care who it is, God, I don't care how close they are to him, God. I don't care who it is on his job, God. He needs Your strength. He needs the spirit of discernment, God, to be enhanced, God, as he is going to be a great soul winner among those who are on the street. God, he will come under many spiritual attacks, God, as those spirits that he is dealing with, as he is dealing with will try to jump on him, attack him and take him over. For he will literally wrestle with these spirits at night, but I speak strength in his soul now by the power of the Blood of Jesus! Strengthen his soul, God, let peace abide in his home, God; let peace abide in his home, God, Hallelujah, Hallelujah. Bring a oneness in his home,

God, bind he and his wife stronger and tighter than they have ever been in their life with any other human being. Give them a tie that can never be broken, God by any lies, any deceptions anybody trying to get over on them, anybody trying to split them up. Anyone who comes to break them up, God, I don't care who it is. Anyone who comes against that home, God, let that same destruction that they try to bring in their home come upon them, God. Anyone who digs a ditch for them, God, let them fall in the ditch! Let the enemy fall into the ditch, God, for every lie that is told upon them, God, let it be cursed seven times in their life, God, in the Name of Jesus! Satan, the Lord rebuke you now! Give him the boldness to stand, give him the compassion to love his wife. Give him the compassion to love his enemies, give him the compassion to love everybody, God. Give him the compassion to be kind, God, give him the compassion he needs to be a great man of God. Help him now, God, in his struggles, help him in his struggles, God, a just man can fall seven times, but You will get him up every time, God. A wicked man fall once and never recovers. God, let him try his heart as David said on last night prove his heart give him a desire to really love You! Give him a desire to yield to Thee! God, in the Name of Jesus, I speak a spirit of realness like never before in his life! Touch his wife now, God. Many things she doesn't understand, but she is yielding herself to Thee, God, Hallelujah! Do an uncommon thing in her life. God, every gift anoint it now, oh, Jesus the spirit of discernment is great in her soul; bring about a seven fold increase, Hallelujah, as she stands with her husband, God. Help them both to know when to cut off the assistance. They help people who don't want to be helped. You cannot help the Devil; he is cursed from the beginning. People are coming in their lives who mean them no good under the disguise of trying to use them as they reach out to help them. But let them be strong enough as You told the Disciples, shake the dust off your feet, remove your blessing from that home and go to the next one. God, let them remove their blessing from people who are trying to use them, take advantage of them, use their lives as an excuse. Oh, God send forth Thine anointing, send forth Thine anointing, baptize and fill them with the Holy Ghost, God, with the evidence of speaking in tongues. Move in their souls that there will be no doubt in their minds the reality of an awesome power of an ever-living God! Move in the Name of Jesus; let the holy wind of God blow! Hallelujah! Do it now, God, reward them for their faithfulness. Give them their promise land just as You gave the children of Israel. They had to go through Jericho. God, we are saying if we have to go through our Jericho Hallelujah, anoint them, anoint them, anoint both of them now in the of Jesus, that they stand like Joshua, Rehab and Caleb. God, even in the mist of the other spies who said it could not be done. They believe, they believe, they believe and it came to pass, God, in the Name of Jesus. Give them a warrior mentality give them a mountain mentality. Caleb wanted the mountain; he wanted the high land, he didn't want the valley. He was a warrior. He wanted to build his nation on top on the mountain; he wanted his family strong and tough. God, make them strong and tough in Your Spirit now. Make them strong and tough in Your Spirit now, open up their understanding to the revelation of the Word like never before, Hallelujah. Satan, take your hands off their home, Satan, take your hands of their finances, oh, God, give them an increase; give an increase, better jobs. Give an increase, promotions, God, open doors so that money can come in, Hallelujah! Revaluate the mind God; revaluate the mind for entrepreneurship, do it now in the Name of Jesus. Let the connections, God be in a straight line that they can connect with the people who can assist them in making their dreams can come true in the Name of Jesus, be it so! Be it so now and we praise You and we praise You, and we praise You, Hallelujah, Hallelujah, Hallelujah!

God, I pray for one of our teenagers who is not from America in the Name of Jesus, God, a quietness has come out of him. He has come out of his shell by being in this country. I pray that this country, God, does not have a negative effect on him, that he would not take on the bad things of this nation and act like some of the teenagers, disrespectful, losing their minds, giving up hope on academics, but strengthen him in his walk with Thee, God, as he puts You first. We know there is no perfect kid, God. We are not praying for a perfect child in any of these homes. We ask our children have a spirit of obedience and willingness to listen to people who are older who know more about life then they do. Let him listen, God, to the godly advice that would be shared with him. God, don't let the sin that is going on, even in his school, infiltrate his mind or his desires. He is a young man, God, tempted like any other young man. Oh, in the Name of Jesus, even as these young girls in the school make themselves so easy and available, God, let him say no, let him say no, let him say no, God, don't let him mess up his life. Don't let him mess up his life, God, please in the Name of Jesus, please don't let him mess up his life, God. Help him in his grades, God, help him in his studies, and help him to be serious about You, help him not to give his family any problems, God. Help him to be a help in the home, Lord God, teach him how to be a man, God. Help us in this church, as we prayed on last night for every young man growing up, that we could help him, teach him, and show him how to be a young man. How not to make the mistakes we made growing up, God help him now, God to have a spirit to listen in the Name of Jesus! Don't let him lose his focus and become caught up in things that are not important for his age. God, let him remain focused, that if he completes the task, which is laid out before him, God, the desires he has in life, give him the drive to never quit until he achieves the goal, God. Let him always be goal oriented, God, that he would never be satisfied with just being nothing. Satisfied with just barely making it, satisfied with just saying forget it I quit, satisfied and say I failed I cannot make it. However, if he falls, help him to get up. If he feels like he cannot make it, help him to look up, look up to Thee, God, from which cometh his help; all his help will only come from You, God. Help him to realize he is not gifted, special, or different from anybody else. God, only You can give gifts. God, touch him that he would give those gifts back to You, and that he would forever always recognize and praise You for the one who is the gift giver! Help him in his life, God; help him now because one day he will be a man. One day he will be a father, one day he will be a husband, he will have reasonability greater than anything he could ever imagine. Help him now to understand as a young man the serious nature of life and how precious life is, God. We rebuke the addiction spirit that comes and challenge our teenagers trying to get them to try this and try that, to smoke this or drink that, or to shoot this or snort that, God, or to huff that. We bind that addiction to prescription drugs, we bind it in the Name of Jesus, keep his mind stayed on Thee. Keep his mind focused on school, keep his mind focused on his family, and keep his mind focused on the positive wholesome things of life in the Name of Jesus. Satan, the Lord rebuke you, Satan, the Lord rebuke you, Satan, the Lord rebuke you! Satan, the Lord rebuke you!

We bind the effeminate spirit that attacks our young men; not one of the young men in this church grows up to be a "Down Low Brother" we bind that in the Name of Jesus, Hallelujah!

God, we pray for one of our teenagers (young ladies) now in the Name of Jesus. Help her to stretch out even the more in faith, God, in You, in her service to You. Help her not to be afraid, God, to use the gifts You have placed in her. Help her never let fear conquer her again, God, and stop her from doing things boldly, which You have given her to do, God. Let her seek and pursue the things she has not even shared with her mother; the things she hasn't shared with anybody that is in her heart, things she really wants to do. Things she desires to do, things she believes she can do, God. Open up a stage where she can show that she can do these things. Open up a stage, God, where You will bring out these gifts inside of her. Help her academically, God, that she would have a spirit of excellence to get good grades, to let her know college is a reality; she can go to college, she can go to any school she wants, God. Help her now God. It is not too late, it is not too late in her grades, God, it is not too late, God, help her now in the Name of Jesus. God, even now, separate even more. God, there are still sinful and negative influences in her life she needs to cut loose. Help her to cut loose from things and those people who are going to bring her down, those people who are not going to help her go any higher in her life, God. The things they talk about, the idle chit chat, oh, God, give her a busy spirit, give her a busy spirit that she would be busy doing Your work, busy studying, busy doing things that are going to enhance her life, not things that are going to take away from her life. Let her be so busy, God, she won't be concerned about young men, she won't be concerned about who likes her, who loves her, who dislikes her. Help her now, God, for there is much greatness in her mind. There is money in her fingertips, God, but if she is not busy doing anything, God, she will never realize the truth of that statement. She will never realize the truth of the potential that is inside of her, God, as she will be bogged down with child after child after child, chasing after different men, God trying to find love. But let her find this love in You, God, and as she seek ye first the Kingdom of God and Your righteousness, God, all these things, other things, will come in time, God. She will be a self-independent woman being able to have her own home, pay for her own car and not have any children, God, out of wedlock, and then, God, Hallelujah the godly man will be so attracted to her, God, because she will not be a weight, she will not be a typical women. She will be a woman, God, Hallelujah a different kind in this day and age. A virtuous woman, a Godly woman, a holy woman, a woman who has dedicated her life to You and because of her dedication to You, God, if she does this tonight, in her soul You will forever reward her. She will never want for anything, materialistic thing here on this earth in the Name of Jesus. Satan, loose her mind, loose her desirers, loose her mind, loose her mind in the Name of Jesus! Loose her mind from the past in the Name of Jesus. Loose her mind from the hurts in the Name of Jesus! Let her stand strong in You in the faith that You have given everybody, the measure of faith, God. Now water it with the Word. Anoint it and bring great increase, God, in the Name of Jesus, in the Name of Jesus, in the Name of Jesus. God, give her a mind for holiness in the Name of Jesus! Give her a mind for truth and sanctification, Hallelujah, which is a setting yourself apart from the world; let her set herself apart from the ungodly music. Let her set herself apart from the ungodly friends, success is here now, God! Success through Jesus Christ is here now! It is here now, God, all she has to do is say "YES" to You, God, yes, to You, God, yes, to You, God. Ministry gifts, ministry gifts is inside her soul, oh, yes, Lord, I feel a strong anointing over her life in the Name of Jesus. Hallelujah! Bless her, God, bless her, God, and teach her how to praise You, give her a praise, God. Give her a praise, God, in the Name of Jesus. Don't hold back young woman, praise the Lord. Victory is yours even on this night; open up your soul, let a praise come out!

Thank God, for deliverance is here! Your deliverance is here. You had better give God some glory! Hallelujah, Hallelujah, Hallelujah, give the Lord some glory. Step out and give God some glory, step out give God some glory, the oil of God be poured over your soul, the oil of God be poured over your soul; never the same, never the same. you don't have to fake anything; you don't have to impress anybody; you don't have to please any friends. You don't have to please any adults in this church. God is your God; Jesus is your Savior; love and serve Him. The Lord will never let you be without love and serve Him. God will always supply for you; love and serve Him. Don't be ashamed of your gifts; you are multi-gifted; don't be ashamed of your gifts, give them to God. If other people don't want to use their gifts, let them laugh at you, but you will get the last laugh. God, is going to bless you and anoint your gifts! Lay your hands on her First Lady, increase, increase, increase, increase, increase, and increase in your gifts! Increase! Hallelujah, Hallelujah, thank You Jesus, thank You Jesus! Thank You Jesus!

A peculiar people we are; a peculiar people. The same anointing that was on John The Baptist, that made him peculiar, that made him a wild man in the wilderness, that same anointing be on thee, which makes you peculiar; no longer like your friends, no longer like other young ladies. Don't dress like them, don't act like them, don't talk like them, Hallelujah! Hallelujah.

Where is the oil? Where is the oil? Give me the oil in the Name of Jesus, oh bless His Name, oh bless His Name, bless His Name. Now rub this over your lips, rub this over your lips! Your mouth be purified, every dirty and unclean thing be thou gone! God give you the Word inside of your belly, inside your mouth, you will carry the Word, and you will take the Gospel to this World in the Name of Jesus! Hallelujah, Hallelujah, bless Him in this place. Bless Him in this place! Bless Him in this place, give Him some praise in this place, bless Him in this place, Hallelujah! Bless Him in this place, bless Him in this place, the Lord be praised! The Lord God be praised, the Lord God be praised, and the Lord God be praised! Bless Him, bless Him. The fire of the Holy Ghost be upon your cup now. Remove your hands from your mouth and praise Him from out of your soul! Praise Him out of your soul! Praise Him out of your soul; yield to His Will, let the Holy Ghost have his way, Hallelujah!

Bless Him, bless Him, bless Him, bless Him!!! Jesus! Glory to our God.

Now we pray for the strength of this church once again. Every day, God, we are under attack as we go forward in intercession for the saints, as we pray one for another, God, desiring the blessing of God to be in every home upon every child, upon every adult, every parent, God, upon every loved one; Your hand be upon us now. Deliver us from the evil one who attacks us and literally tries to kill us, Hallelujah. We pray now for the strength of this church, the strength of the body of Christ everywhere, touch Your Saints everywhere; strengthen them to pray like never before and call upon the Name of our Lord God for He is worthy of the praise. As we call upon Your Name, so shall we be saved from our enemies and we close this prayer by calling on the Name of Jesus! Jesus, Jesus! Ring it out of your souls Jesus! Jesus, be it done now we pray and the people of God say Amen and Amen.

Closing Scripture: Psalms 18:20- 50 (NLT)

"The LORD rewarded me for doing right; he compensated me because of my innocence. For I have kept the ways of the LORD; I have not turned from my God to follow evil. For all his laws are constantly before me; I have never abandoned his principles. I am blameless before God; I have kept myself from sin. The LORD rewarded me for doing right, because of the innocence of my hands in his sight. To the faithful you show yourself faithful; to those with integrity you show integrity. To the pure you show yourself pure, but to the wicked you show yourself hostile. You rescue those who are humble, but you humiliate the proud. LORD, you have brought light to my life; my God, you light up my darkness. In your strength I can crush an army; with my God I can scale any wall. As for God, his way is perfect. All the LORD's promises prove true. He is a shield for all who look to him for protection. For who is God except the LORD? Who but our God is a solid rock? God arms me with strength; he has made my way safe. He makes me as surefooted as a deer, leading me safely along the mountain heights. He prepares me for battle; he strengthens me to draw a bow of bronze. You have given me the shield of your salvation. Your right hand supports me;

your gentleness has made me great. You have made a wide path for my feet to keep them from slipping. I chased my enemies and caught them; I did not stop until they were conquered. I struck them down so they could not get up; they fell beneath my feet. You have armed me with strength for the battle; you have subdued my enemies under my feet. You made them turn and run; I have destroyed all who hated me. They called for help, but no one came to rescue them. They cried to the LORD, but he refused to answer them. I ground them as fine as dust carried by the wind. I swept them into the gutter like dirt. You gave me victory over my accusers. You appointed me as the ruler over nations; people I don't even know now serve me. As soon as they hear of me, they submit; foreigners cringe before me. They all lose their courage and come trembling from their strongholds. The LORD lives! Blessed be my rock! May the God of my salvation be exalted! He is the God who pays back those who harm me; he subdues the nations under me and rescues me from my enemies. You hold me safe beyond the reach of my enemies; you save me from violent opponents. For this, O LORD, I will praise you among the nations; I will sing joyfully to your name. You give great victories to your king; you show unfailing love to your anointed, to David and all his descendants forever."

END OF DAY 18 PRAYER SERVICE

Personal Note:

Thought: The flesh is like a virus that kills the spirit. If you take your daily injections of God's Word, His Holy Spirit, His love, His power and His anointing, it will kill off everything that is in you, which is an offense to Him. Let your daily shots be the first thing you do to add years of life to your soul.

~ Evelyn

"Lord, teach me how to pray the prayer of victory!"

STEP 19/DAY 19, FRIDAY

"Stay on the Wall: the Wall of Faith & Belief!"

Personal Note:

The nineteenth night was phenomenal! I cannot explain the glory of God! The Lord took our Pastor higher up the mountain. That day Satan tried to overpower him with bad news. However, God! The Devil is a liar and we have the victory! In the midst of all of life's problems, the light will always shine. God knows how to lift our spirits.

As we were getting ready for service, Pastor's youngest brother walked in from Chicago and surprised him! When he saw him, his soul was strengthened! On this nineteenth day, God, allowed me to come into His **PRESENCE**! I praised Him from the depths of my soul and all that is within me; I blessed His Holy Name! I praised Him with all of my understanding, with all of my being! I love my God with everything I have, with every breath I take. I love Him! On this night, I disappeared in the cloud! The cloud of Glory! We thanked God we were able to experience His **PRESENCE** in such a way words cannot explain. As members, God takes us so far, but for the Pastors, the Moses'; they are led further as He takes them. Pastor Johnson was dressed in the Ephod as he dwelled in the **PRESENCE** of God for 40 days and 40 nights.

~ Evelyn

DAY 19 PRAYER SERVICE BEGINS

Opening Scripture: Psalms 19 (KJV)
"The heavens declare the glory God; and the firmament sheweth his handy-work. Day unto day uttereth speech, and night unto night sheweth knowledge. There is no speech nor language where their voice is not heard. Their line is gone out through all the earth, and their words to the end of the world. In them hath he set a tabernacle for the sun, which is as a bridegroom coming out of his chamber, and rejoiceth as a strong man to run a race [his course]. His going forth is from the end of the heaven, and his circuit unto the ends of it: and there is nothing hid from the heat thereof. The law of the Lord is perfect, converting the soul: the testimony of the Lord is sure, making wise the simple. The statutes of the Lord are right, rejoicing the heart: the commandment of the Lord is pure, enlightening the eyes. The fear of the Lord is clean, enduring for ever: the judgments of the Lord are true and righteous altogether. More to be desired are they than gold, yea, than much fine gold: sweeter also than honey and the honeycomb. Moreover by them is thy servant warned: and in keeping of them there is great reward. Who can understand his errors? Cleanse thou me from secret faults. Keep back thy servant also from presumptuous sins; Let them not have dominion over me: then shall I be upright, and I be innocent from the great transgression. Let the words of my mouth, and the meditation of my heart, be acceptable in thy sight, O Lord, my strength, and my redeemer."

Insight As We Prepared For Prayer:
Let us go to God on tonight asking that our words of our mouths and the meditations of our heart will continue to be acceptable in His sight, for the things we are asking God for, are crucial and only God can help us and bring these prayer request to reality.

Let Us Pray:
Oh, God, we thank You, we thank You for allowing us to come into this place and pray. We ask now, once again, as we come on this nineteenth day, consecrating ourselves before Thy **PRESENCE** seeking Thine Will an instructions, asking for understanding and

wisdom that we might do what You have instructed us, God, that men should pray and not faint; we should always pray, Lord God. We come, Lord God with an understanding as limited as it might be with the fullness of the capacity that we have as human being asking that our capacity would be expanded that we might come into a greater understanding God of the importance of prayer and who You are. We know, God, from what we have been told down throughout the years, passed from generation to generations, knowing that the Word of God tells us, God, we need to pray in order to pray to You. We love You, Lord God, and we thank You and we bless Your Name, God, bless Your Name. We need You, God; we need You now in the Name of Jesus. God, David made such a wonderful, wonderful exhortation about Your glory and about Your magnificence. He also shared how beautiful You made the sun, the heavens, and the creation. David talked about how Your judgments are true and righteous and laws and how we should seek them more then gold, more than fine gold for they are more precious then any materialistic thing we could have in this life. We pray on tonight, God, that our minds and hearts be turned toward the words that David said in the nineteenth division of Psalms. God, we really are intent with Thee oh, God. We desire to seek Your Word and seek You. We know if we find anything in the Word, it is more precious than any gold or money or silver or any jewelry, God, more precious than fame or glory popularity, God, more precious than power and prestige on this earth, that we fine something in the Word of God. A revelation, God, illumination, something that would enlighten our lives and help us to become more like the servant Jesus, You created us to be. God, we love You, we want to be like Your Son, Jesus more and more everyday God.

God, we come before You resisting the Devil, binding his works, pulling down the strong holds, pleading the Blood of Jesus. God, we ask now for You strength, help us to stand. God, we need Your strength to help us to stand for what is right, to stand on the rock; the scripture says it is higher than we are, that rock is Your Word. We ask now, Lord God, that Your anointing be mighty in this place, that it will destroy every yoke, God, in the Name of Jesus. We freely call upon that Name, Jesus, God. We have prayed before, leading up to these nineteen days and we include this in our formula of prayer, God, even the more that self be crucified as David has said he didn't want anything, Lord God, to stop Him from getting closer to You, and hearing from You, seeking Your help, being used by You, God. He said let the words of my mouth, now let the words of our praise, the mediation that's in our hearts, if they are not acceptable and received by You, God, then we are wasting our time and we are not here to waste time. We don't have time to waste, God. You have all the time, we don't. God, we have wasted enough time in our lives; we acknowledge and realize that, therefore we have a great urgency.

We come before You asking You would expedite the answers to our prayers, speed the answers up, the manifestation of what the answers are in our lives. Time is so valuable and precious yet it is running out. There are souls that are at stake, God, souls in our very homes, souls in our school systems, souls in the hospital, God souls in the jails, prisons, souls in the rehabilitation centers, God. Souls, God, that are in some place trying to rehab themselves from drugs and alcohol addictions. Souls, God, that are battered and bruised that are walking in the streets like zombies because they are emotionally detached from society. Souls in the corporate world, God, where money, fame and seeking a position are so important, God, that they will stab one another in the back, climb up on somebody else in misery. Help us now, God, because there are souls everywhere in every walk of life, in the race of life that needs Jesus. God, we want to be a part of the great solution of taking the Word out to the world, God, that people might hear the Gospel. You are the Word and You said the Word would not return void. We pray somebody would receive salvation, somebody would be delivered, somebody would receive encouragement, and somebody would receive the Hope of Glory, which is Christ. Somebody, God, would make a change in their life and be converted through the gospel, God, that they might continue to denounce the sentence of Hell. We need Your help. God as we give You a very sincere praise; there are sick people everywhere, God, we want to pray for somebody to be healed. We want to pray for somebody to be delivered, God, but we need Your power, we need Your help, we need Your encouragement, we need You to lift up every bow down head in the Name of Jesus.

Have Your way in this place, have Your way in our lives. Have Your way in this service, God. When we start the service off, we start if off we prayer every Friday night. God, this is a part of our 40 days of consecration; therefore, God, we ask for something special to take place on tonight. God, we are not picky or choosy on what it is, we just ask You move, and You do something, God. You make Your **PRESENCE** known. You help us, God, You deliver somebody, God, You save somebody on tonight. We thank You for the testimonies that have gone forth, God, throughout these nineteen days of prayer. God, but we are looking for greater as we are climbing up the mountain step by step, inch by inch, God, centimeter by centimeter; it's a fight, it's a struggle on some days, God, but we are not coming down off the mountain. We are climbing up God into Thy **PRESENCE** we are. Help us and teach us how to be in Thy **PRESENCE** for an extended period of time, God. How to keep our minds stayed on You as the Word instructs us to do, God. Teach us how to minister unto You instead of You always having to minister to us, how to be servants of the Most High God, to worship You in spirit and in truth. Help us to do as David said to have a praise seven times a day, God. We will praise You and magnify You and thank You for all You have done, for that day, God, for is a day we will never see again. God, that is a day that we cannot relive, that was a day not promised; that is a day somebody did not have an opportunity to see and we are grateful, we are grateful, we are grateful, God! Let the words of our mouths, God, everything that is inside of us, sanctify us holy, God, that when we speak, we will speak with understanding; we are talking to the true and Living God. He is Holy!

We don't want to bring any mess, any junk before Thy **PRESENCE**, God. We don't want to be half stepping, we don't want to have three quarters of our heart fixed on You, but let our hearts be fixed on You 100%. We don't want to have 98% faith. Help us, God, in our unbelief help us, God! Strengthen us in our faith as a church! Strengthen our faith, God, that we would pray confidently knowing You hear us and You would help us. For You have promised us, You would never leave us nor forsake us. Let the words of our mouths, God, the meditations of our hearts, the thoughts and the secret place of our souls, God, let them be pleasing in Thy sight. The things we don't share, the thoughts that come across our minds daily, God, let them be pleasing in Your eye sight, God, as we mediate and concentrate our thoughts on Thee, God, and think about Your goodness and think about Your glory think; about Your characteristics which are holy and immutable. A God who never changes for anyone or nothing, for You are God and God alone! You are God in every situation; You are God over every situation; You are the only true and living God, the God of the Bible! We pray to You, the God of Abraham, Isaac and Jacob; the God of the Old Testament; The God of the New Testament Saints; the God of the body of Christ everywhere. We pray, we pray to that God. The God who put the sun up in the sky, the God who created everything seen and unseen, the God who speaks and His voice is like thunder. The God that when He moves and when He walks upon this earth, darkness will flee, according to Your scripture. We believe that, we believe that. The God who sits high and looks low, nothing gets pass Your eyesight. The God who already knows every thought that comes into our minds, the very thoughts before they even come into our minds. The very God who knows every number of everyone's hair follicles, God, the hair on their heads, on their bodies; You already know the number of them, God, for every human being. Your knowledge, Lord God, is far superior then anything our feeble minds could ever imagine, God. Your love far surpasses anything or anyone. What people could do to bring about pain, Your love can bring about joy in an instance. That joy that will last forever; this is the God we pray to on tonight, God.

    Help us now; help us now in the political system. In this country it is falling apart, help us now, God as so many homes, God, are going through crucial experiences of pain and turmoil. Transition is not good, changing and moving off the foundation of the Word of God, help us now in the Name of Jesus we pray. We call on the God of heaven, shine the light down from heaven in this place, on this night bring joy into this service, God. Let a praise ring forth from Your people and we will praise the Lord for Your mercy endureth forever. As we will praise the Lord for His mercy will endure forever, as we will praise the Lord for his mercy will endure forever! Help us now in the Name of Jesus, as we are not ashamed to call upon the Name of the Most High God in this place, God, Hallelujah! Shake the very foundation of our trials and tribulations with Your **PRESENCE!** Shake the foundation of our souls with Your glory! Manifest Yourself in somebody's life on tonight like never before, God; give them an experience they have never had before, as they would only open up their souls, open up their mouths and begin to praise and magnify the true and Living God! For He is God alone, He is Holy. We talk about the characteristics of our Savior, Holy is He! Righteous is He, magnificent is He, His Name alone is worthy of all the praises heaven and earth can bring forth for He alone is God. Great is our God and greatly to be praised! Praise Him, praise Him for the firmaments of His power, praise Him for his excellent greatness!

Praise Him, praise Him, praise Him, praise Him, praise Him in a dance! Praise Him with the timbrel and harp, praise Him with the psaltery, praise Him on the stringed instruments and organs, praise Him with the cymbals with loud cymbals & high cymbal, praise Him, praise, praise Him, praise Him with Your voice! Lift up Your voice and shout unto the Lord with a praise. Give Him glory for He alone is worthy He is worthy! He is God, He alone is God, He is worthy, He alone is worthy! No trial or circumstance can take away the fact that our Lord is glorious! Magnificent is He! He is worthy of the praise, He is worthy of the glory. We will praise Him in this place! He has blessed us nineteen days to be alive in this year, Hallelujah. A dead person cannot have trials and tribulations. A dead person cannot be sick, a dead person never needs help, a dead person doesn't need help, a dead person can't eat, a dead person can't sleep, but God has blessed us to be in the land of the living and He is worthy of the praise! If nothing else, praise Him for Your very life on tonight! Praise Him for being alive on tonight, glory to the Name of our God! Glory to the Name of our God! Glory to the Name of our God! He is worthy, He is worthy, He is worthy, He worthy! He is worthy, He is worthy, God is worthy! Worthy is the Lamb! Worthy is the Lamb, He is worthy, He is Jehovah, He is God all Mighty, He is Jehovah-Jireh the all mighty God, our provider! He is Jehovah Shalom, the very God of peace! Hallelujah, Hallelujah, He is El Shaddai; He is our God the shekinah glory be in this place!

We welcome Your **PRESENCE**, we welcome Your **PRESENCE**, we welcome Your **PRESENCE**, we welcome You! We welcome You with outstretched hands, holy hands. We lift them up and we give Him glory in this place! Out of your, soul worship the Lord in the beauty of holiness, He is worthy, worthy, worthy of the praise! He is God! God we declare Your handy work among the Heathen, among the Nations, among the Congregation of the righteous, among the Heavens You are worthy!!! Worthy is the Lamb, glory to His Name, Hallelujah, bless His Name, bless His Name, bless His Name! **Remember: "NO PRAISE – NO PRESENCE"**

Closing Scripture: Psalms 148 (KJV)

"Praise the LORD! Praise the LORD from the heavens! Praise him from the skies! Praise him, all his angels! Praise him, all the armies of heaven! Praise him, sun and moon! Praise him, all you twinkling stars! Praise him, skies above! Praise him, vapors high above the clouds! Let every created thing give praise to the LORD, for he issued his command, and they came into being. He established them forever and forever. His orders will never be revoked. Praise the LORD from the earth, you creatures of the ocean depths, fire and hail, snow and storm, wind and weather that obey him, mountains and all hills, fruit trees and all cedars, wild animals and all livestock, reptiles and birds, kings of the earth and all people, rulers and judges of the earth, young men and maidens, old men and children. Let them all praise the name of the LORD. For his name is very great; his glory towers over the earth and heaven! He has made his people strong, honoring his godly ones – the people of Israel who are close to him. Praise the LORD!"

Stay on the wall of praise! If you want to get God's attention, praise Him!!!

END OF DAY 19 PRAYER SERVICE

STEP 20/DAY 20, SATURDAY

"Spirit of the Living God, Fall Fresh On Me!!

Personal Note:

On the twentieth day, you will read Psalms 20, a very significant Psalm in my life. This is one I really became quite dependent upon during the time of my son's birth and during the difficult experiences during the first three years of his life. I leaned upon this scripture and cried many times asking God to honor this Psalm of David as I applied it to my own personal life. It's not that God's scriptures don't work because they all work, but I know this one has worked. I am very confident and my faith is even strengthen as we are able to read this 20th division of Psalms before we go into prayer. We just believe God as I look back over my own life knowing what God has done through this scripture.
~ *Evelyn*

DAY 20 PRAYER SERVICE BEGINS

Opening Scripture: Psalms 20 (NLT)
"In times of trouble may the Lord respond to your cry. May the God of Israel keep you safe from all harm. May he send you help for his sanctuary and strengthen you from Jerusalem. May he remember all your gifts and look favorably on your burnt offerings. May he grant

your heart's desire and fulfill all your plans. May we shout for joy when we hear of your victory, flying banners to honor our God. May the Lord answer all your prayers. Now I know that the Lord saves his anointed king. He will answer him from this holy heaven and rescue him by this great power. Some nations boast of their armies and weapons, but we boast in the Lord our God. those nations will fall down and collapse, but we will rise up and stand firm. Give victory to our king, O Lord! Respond to our cry for help."

Insight As We Prepared For Prayer:
We know that the Lord saveth his anointed and He will hear him from His holy heaven with the saving strength of His right hand. He will deliver us; we are not trusting in anything but God Amen. The last verse says "Save, Lord: let the King here us when we call." We want the King of Glory to hear us and we call upon the name of our Lord and ask God to help us.

Let us Pray:
We are grateful on this twentieth day to come back into thy **PRESENCE** once again. We are grateful, God, you have granted us life to make it back to the house of prayer. God, it has been twenty days of this year that we have come to sacrificed our time, sacrifice ourselves to bring you, God, a sacrifice that is holy and expectable unto you. Your Word tells us it's only reasonable for us to obey you. We thank you, Lord God, for a transformation and a renewing of our minds. We have been strengthened through your Word even on today. God, we are not taking a break from being encourage on this week to praise you seven times a day and to give you glory for something wonderful! We give you glory for just being God in our lives our Savior, Lord and King.

God, we pray and we will continue to pray with all our strength and our might one for another. We pray, Lord God, that you would keep our families safe. Keep us from becoming statistics for tragedy that strikes homes. Keep death from coming to our doors through murder and different violent acts. Keep the perpetrators away, God, we pray. We know that one day according to your scripture we all will see you. God, we have no foreign knowledge of how or when that time will come. God, we are not praying for a life or ease. When trouble comes our way, we know that if Christ suffered we have to suffer.

We understand that while we are serving you, while we are in your army that our life might be required. Christ gave his and so some many other Disciples and Patriots gave their life for the service of the Lord. We are not saying, God, that will run away and turn our backs on our commitment to you if that day come, but until that time, God, if that time ever come so let it be. You said to bring all things to you. We can ask you anything so we are continuing to ask you to protect us. Protect our homes and protect our children, God. We are asking, God, that they have an opportunity live to become adults. Give them a chance in this life, God, to let your glory shine through their souls that other people would see salvation. Let the hope of glory shine through them that they will lead others to Christ. There might be Preachers, Pastors, Apostles, Evangelists, Prophets, Teachers, Musicians, Praise Leaders, Praise Dancers, Secretaries, and Administrators in one of our children that will be work in your Kingdom. God, we need them, as they are the future to keep the church running. Use them to be a blessing and edify the Body of Christ. God, we pray that their lives would give you all the glory in Jesus Name.

We pray that very earnestly and sincerely, God, on this night as it seem like, God, your Word is becoming more edible, communicated and made known. Your Word is more visible than ever before as we see the signs of the end times are upon us. The media has made mockery of the end times "The Great Apoplectic" as they call it. The Bible promises that time as we know it, is going to come to an end. Jesus is going to return and He will be crowned King of Kings and the life that we live now is making preparations for that day. God, we pray our life will match your Word that we will be able to attend and be there and witness for ourselves the Inauguration of the King! We want to be in that number to give him glory! We want to give him glory for the wonderful things he has done. Father the gift of Salvation that is enough! God, we are grateful that you give us a mind to be like Christ to intercede. We take our example from Jesus who is at the right of you, Father, right now interceding for us. Jesus never stops. He never gets tired. He never gets weary. Help us, God, even in our tiredness and our weariness of this life as human beings and the sadness that is so pervasive in our society, God that we will press our way through and continue to intercede for our brothers and sisters here in this church and all over the World. We are praying for the Christians everywhere. We don't know them by names. We don't know them by face but you do, God. We know the Christians here, God. We know each other because we attend the same church. We live in the same city. We live in the same areas so we pray for the Christians we don't know. Please don't let tragedy to come to their homes. Continue to rebuke the Death Angel for Christ sake! Keep him away from our homes and keep him away from our children. Keep him away from our loves ones and us. Keep him away, God, this we pray in the name of Jesus.

Oooooh Savior, Savior, Savior have mercy, have mercy on us in this place. Have mercy, have mercy prepare us on this night as we prepare ourselves, God, to carry the saints to you before your throne. We ask that you help us, God. Help us, God, to press through humanity. A segment of humanity, God, that drains and pulls and take away from us, that pushes the church into a corner, ridicules the church and the laws that you have given us to live by. Humanity criticized the church for not doing enough but what do they say when the churches do too much. God, we are truly here not to please anybody but do our best to please you. Lord, let the words of my mouth and the meditations of my heart let it be expectable in your sight.

On this night, we pray through the unction of the Holy Ghost with every word and every thought that we have lifted up in this place and lifted before your throne. Oh, God, we want to be pleasing and expectable in your sight. We are not here to waste time, God, because it's not ours to waste. We are not here to impress anybody because nobody can reward us or punish us the way you can do. We are here out of love. We are here out of obedience. We are here out of a burden a <u>"call to pray"</u>. God, we are not just here praying and asking that you take us into Thine **PRESENCE** so, we can take it easy and rest for 40 days. God, we have been "**<u>Called Into Your PRESENCE</u>**." A call has been made to come and hear what you have to say. We want to come out of your **PRESENCE** working harder like it is the last 40 days of our lives! We want to pray, God, until every yoke be destroyed for every person that is a part of this ministry. We want to pray, God, until every sick person be healed. We want to pray, God, for those that are to the point of death be brought back to life! Bless your name! God, we want to pray until every unsaved love one becomes saved. We want to pray, Lord God, unto those who have no idea no clue that they are holding back their own progress and blessing because of the limitations that they place upon you by trying to be conceptive, and visualize and think of you with a human mind. Our minds are not capable to understand you, God, or your ways. We are here on tonight saying once again, God, crucify the flesh. Kill self and the will of I. It's our greatest hindrance, God, from seeing you how you really are. It is the greatest hindrance and fight that we have for the rest of our lives, which keep us here on this earth, God. The flesh hinders us from letting our spirit sore high into thy glory to sit in heavenly places before thee, God, that you would give us something that words would never be able to explain to another human being unless they experience it themselves, God, being with thee Hallelujah! Bless your name! Bless your name, God! Bless your name now in the name of Jesus!

    God, if I ever needed your anointing, if I ever needed the power of the Holy Ghost, God, I need it now. If this church ever needed you before we need you know! David said now I know the Lord saveth his anointed! He will hear us from his Holy Heaven and with the strength of this right hand he will deliver some trust in chariots, some trust in the strength & wisdom of men but we will trust in the Lord he is our banner! He is our deliver! He is the Savior! He saves! Lord let the King hear us when we call!

    On tonight, we place a call on behalf of the Saints of the most high! Look on one of our Deacons now in the name of Jesus. Bind every strong hold and principality, God, which has locked him up in his spirit. Oh, God, you take no pleasure in anyone who draws back. Who looks away and takes away their hands working on the Gospel plow. God, you don't take any pleasure in a drawback spirit the Bibles said. We bind that spirit now in the name of Jesus and we speak liberty and freedom in his souls. God, let him take his worries to you and leave them there. Let him leave them and not turn around and say, "give back". God, let him yield over to you and give over to you one hundred percent. Bind the works of the enemy that has come to pull him down. Oh, God, as he is in a moment of vulnerability we speak strength in his soul. We speak strength to his mind. We speak strength in his life. David asked "Lord would you let his soul live"? David said let my soul live. We are asking on behalf of our Brother let his soul live, God. Let his soul live, God. Let his soul live, God. Oh, God, I hear the words of Jesus speaking to the Devil saying, "man should not live by bread alone but by every word that preceded out of the mouth of God." God, bring him to a point where he would hear your Word. Bring him to a point in his life where he would desire the sincere meat of the Word. God, bring him to a point where he would be desperate to come to church. Desperate to pray, desperate to read the Word! Desperate to praise you as he look over his life and realize a living dog is better than a dead lion! Help him now God, help him now to open up in his soul. God, I bind that masculine old tough spirit in the name of Jesus. Let a heart of compassion be move within his soul and a yielding and a gentleness that he would yield to thee. Don't let him hold back the tears any longer, God. Let him release! Let there be a release. Let there be a release, God, right now in the name of Jesus. Touch his body, Lord, the pain that he deals with, God, touch his body now and bring about complete healing. The suffering that goes on inside his body he doesn't complain. He is keeps everything on the inside, God, but he needs to give it to thee. It's not a complaint when we say," God, I can't take it." It's not a complaint when we say "Lord have mercy". It's not murmuring when we say," God I am only human I can't make it without your help"! That a statement of reality, God, sometimes the pain is so great we cannot take it. Sometime life is so miserable we don't know what to do except say "have mercy God." We are asking for mercy for his soul. Mercy for his home move now in the name of Jesus! Let the anointing of God destroy the yoke right now, destroy it right now! Let the yoke be destroyed and we plead the Blood of Jesus!

    The Devil wants to attack, God, those who have stepped out on faith. He is trying to cripple this church by crippling us one by one. The Devil is attacking us trying to make us feel isolated and alone.

God we will never be alone for your Word says, "you will never leave us nor forsake us." Wherever we try to go if we make our bed in Hell, you said you are already there. If we take the wings of the morning and try to fly to the uttermost parts of the world you said you are already there. There is no place in life that you cannot go. You are already there preceding us, God, waiting to meet us. There is no pain, no emotion that we can experience that Jesus haven't experience on this earth Hallelujah! He overcame everything that Thy Will would be done. Help us to have the spirit of hope that we will overcome everything, God that you're Will; will be done in our lives in the name of Jesus Hallelujah, Hallelujah.

I pray for one of the Sisters in the church in the name of Jesus. She is young and in love with you, God, a twenty-two years old woman that has given over to thee. Oh, God, touch and refresh in her mind Hallelujah. Just the way, God, we understand with computers that sometime we have to refresh the last page Hallelujah. We pray now that your anointing would come and refresh her mind for she is doing so much, God, that it can become an over load. The mind can pop. The mind can crack. The will and desire can be weakened to the point that we give up. Our bodies can become so run down that we become more susceptible to colds, virus, and sicknesses all because we are running, running, running, and never resting. Let her soul rest in you, God, that with all the running there will be no stressful activities. There is much pressure is placed on her, we pray that it will not bring any stress because the field in college that she desires to go in is loaded with stress. It is loaded with pressure, lack of sleep, lack of being able to take care of oneself, God, for always looking after someone else. Let her know, God, that she has to place her life her very natural life as well as her soul inside your hands and know that you will always look after her. You will never leave her nor forsake her, God. Reward her according to her faith. God, you have given her the gift of faith for she has made statements bold statements, God, that can only be given by you in her spirit as she leans and depends upon you and you have not fail her yet. Oh, God, continue to back her up. Continue to stand up in her. Continue to let her have a Caleb spirit he had another spirit. He didn't have the same mind as the rest of the spies. He had another spirit. He had another mind he had another type of faith! A faith that relies solely on what You have said. A faith that would not look on what he sees with his natural eyes but a faith that will believe the report of the Lord. God, let her continue to believe the report of the Lord God. Speak to her soul and bring increase in her spirit Hallelujah, Hallelujah, God! In your Bible, you said don't give your pearls to swine. God, every ungodly young man that is after her, chasing her talking to her pursuing her, God, let the line be cut. Cut the lines of communication now, God. They mean her no good, God. They desire nothing but something from the flesh, God. They don't have a clue what a real relationship is because they don't have one with you, God! They don't know what real love it because they don't know about you, God. Bring somebody godly in her life. Bring somebody saved in her life. Lord, up until that point let her shut down the communication lines. Lift her up away from things and sinful influences, God. You said let us present our bodies a living sacrifice. The first characteristic you said was "holy" holy, holy, God. If we want to be in your **PRESENCE,** we have to come holy before thee because you are a holy God. The things that she ask for, God, she is going to have to step out of the realm of carnality and step in the realm of holiness in the name of Jesus. Give her a spirit of humility and obedience in her soul, so much so God, that she would yield herself like Hannah did and whatever you bless her with she will say this is not mine it's yours, I give it back to you, Lord. Every blessing, every gift, every talent, every reward, every good and perfect thing that you give to her let her say God; I'm not going to horded it. I'm not going to keep it to myself. I'm going to give it back to thee. My time, my service, my mind, my dreams, my thoughts, my life, and my further I place it in your hands. Give her the mentality, God, which she will yield herself as a servant of God. Let her know she can be a servant of the Most High God Hallelujah! Lift her spirit up, God. Lift her spirit up, God. Send some joy and laughter into her life and in her soul. God, put some swing in her step physically, Lord God, because of the joy that lies in her soul. As she begins to commune with you more this year than she has ever done in her life let joy be just that great, God, Hallelujah. As she, talks to you, God, talk back to her. Talk back to her mind and let her hear your voice. Let her see your glory. Let her experience your Spirit in her soul! Baptize her in the Holy Spirit, God! Fill her with Thy **PRESENCE**! Fill her with Thy anointing! Fill her with Thy glory! Fill her with Thy loving power! Fill her with Thy kindness and Thy mercy. Fill her, God, with goodness, God! Hallelujah, open up your good treasure according to your scripture, God, Hallelujah. Fill her baskets. Let her be blessed in the city and outside of the city. Let her be blessed everywhere she goes, God. Let her be blessed! I pronounce a blessing upon her life now in the name of Jesus. Do it now, Father we pray. Bless your name. Bless your name. Bless your name!

    God, David said "save Lord, save Lord" I pray for another one of our Sisters. Save, Lord, you are the King of Glory, let the King of Glory hear her when she calls. God, save her from herself. Crucify the flesh. Touch her tongue, God, Hallelujah with the hot coals off the altar as you did for Isaiah. Let her eyes be opened to see your glory everywhere she goes. Let her see your train fill her temple. Fill her home with your **PRESENCE** as her soul is filled the more with Thy Spirit. Let everywhere she goes, God, people see the difference from this moment forward in her. Give her a quirt spirit, Lord God, which she will be able to take whatever is done to her correctly and not say a mumbling word. Hallelujah, God, don't let her worry about defending herself for you are a defender. At the time she needs to speak let her wait on you to give her what to say, God, Hallelujah. God, her very home depends upon it! Her children and her children's children they look up to her, God. Let her live, God, for if she dies that home and not just her home but her family would be split down the middle, God. They need her to live, God, in her right mind. The Devil is attacking her like never before, God; he is bringing all kinds of thoughts to her mind that are ungodly, thoughts that bring about depression. He is bringing thoughts of doom and gloom, God, thoughts of anger and frustration, questions and confusion. Let no thought come to her mind questioning your power and your glory. Wondering or not if you are God. Let her know you are God and there is none else! Satan's workshop is the mind. He worked on John the Baptist until he asked the question about Jesus was He the Savior or do he look for another. Jesus response was sent back to him that He is still working miracles! God, let the response go to

A Call Into His Presence

her soul and remind her that You are still sitting on the throne. You are still God and you created everything. You rule and super rule as the old Saints would say everything is in your divine order. No one can touch her! No one can put their hands on her life! No one can do these things unless you ordain it to be so. Let her know that all things work together to them that love You who are the called according to your purpose. God, as she yields herself, the Devil doesn't want her to yield, God, because he doesn't want her home to be saved. The more she yields, the more power and authority You will give her. Bless him, bless him, bless him!

Take authority over every demon that walks in her home. Hallelujah, that she doesn't have to raise her voice but when she gets tough let her just say, "Peace, in the Name of Jesus." Give her the power to stand strong and say, "Satan the Lord rebuke you!" Fight woman and tell the Devil not here! Not in my house! Not in my children! Not in my grandchildren and anywhere we go! At the store, on my job, at the mall, anywhere the Devil follows her she will be able to use the power that has been given to every believer. At the name of Jesus, she will be able to stand bold to tell the Devil "I'm not afraid of you because the God that is in my soul has all power. No weapon formed against me can prosper. There is nothing you can do to me unless God gives the say so." If you have to suffer then He will bring you out like he did for Job. If it is not my time to suffer then Satan get away, get away! Resist the Devil and he will flee. That doesn't mean not sinning only, that doesn't mean yielding to temptation. Resisting means stand up when you see the Devil and let him know I see you. I recognize what you are doing you are trying to bring evil to my life. You are trying to steal, kill and destroy but I am going to call on Jesus and he is going to bring life! I speak an anointing a Prayer Warrior anointing over her life, God, that as she prays, as she calls on the name of Jesus people will think it is foolish but you said "now I know the Lord saves his anointed"! David wrote it down "now I know" let her know she is anointed of God Hallelujah! Let her know she is a child of God. You will save your anointed! Guard her life it is her bloodline, God. We rebuke every curse over that bloodline in the name of Jesus. I rebuke very generational curse in the name of Jesus. I rebuke every curse the

Devil has brought in that family tree, God, through the bloodline I rebuke it now Hallelujah. Not only that I rebuke it, God, I cut off the faucet of everything that is sinful and ungodly. Now, God, we ask by the move of your Holy Spirit that you take the vein of that family blood line, God, and remove the fleshly mind, the fleshly heart and attach it God Hallelujah to this woman for she is the vein that is connected to thee. God, they need a transplant. Take a vein from the leg and put it into their heart! She has the transplant, God, a godly vein that is connected to the Holy Spirit so the blood of Jesus can flow into her family bloodline! Save her family, God. Give them a blood transfusion the only blood that can transform, revive, restore and bring life to a soul that will never die! The Blood of Jesus Christ the blood that has never been contaminated and indeed cannot be! Save, God, save we pray in the name of Jesus! Bless his name! Bless his name! Bless his name!

The **PRESENCE** of the Lord is here! He has come to see about his Saints! He has come to see about his Saints! Hallelujah! We might be praying for somebody else but God has come to see about everybody in this place! Tell the Lord thank you because his **PRESENCE** is here! You can make your prayer request known God is here! God is sitting on the throne in this place! Can't you see and hear the Lord breathing upon this place Hallelujah, Hallelujah the breath of the Holy God is in this place! The cloud of glory is sitting upon this place! Give God some glory in here! Give God glory in here! The Lord be magnified! The Lord be lifted high above the heavens! He is God, the manifestations of His **PRESENCE** is here! Let your soul be filled with his glory! Thank you God, thank you for your **PRESENCE**! Thank you for coming to check on the Saints thank you Lord! Thank you, thank you, thank you, thank you! Jesus, Jesus, Jesus Hallelujah, thank you Lord, thank you Lord, thank you Lord, thank you Lord, thank you Lord, Jesus bless your name God, bless your name God bless your name God!!!

God, I pray for my Sister X now. I pray for the joy of the Lord to give her strength. I pray the prayer of power into her life, God. A power, God, a power that she has never experienced before a power God, an uncontrollable power that power is you, Lord, no one controls you. No one can control you. No one can dictate to you. No situation can dictate to you. No circumstance, God, can tell you rules and regulations when to be God and when not to be God. No trial or circumstance, God, could define you. You surpass any of those things your Will supersedes anything connected to the human experience because you created us, God, Hallelujah. Move in her soul, God, destroy every yoke; destroy every yoke of the past, God. Destroy every yoke of the past, God, a new thing, a new thing, a new thing, God, pour out some fresh oil.

Pour out a fresh anointing in our souls, God, Hallelujah! Let a yielding take place like never before. Let praise come forth, God, like never before. Satan the Lord rebuke you. Satan the Lord rebuke you in her body. Lord, strengthen her physically. God, there is a great strain placed upon her life, God, that is taken a toll. This toil is taking away from her emotionally. It's taking away from her physically, God. It's taking away from her spirit there is a sapping a sapping, a sapping, a sapping, God, Hallelujah like someone is sifting the very life and hope out of her, God! Every time she is charged up, something comes to take away from her. Somebody, God, is coming to rob her strength right. Help her now in the name of Jesus. God, as her natural eyes are shut closed praying to you, open up her spiritual eyes that she will see every enemy that is placed around her, God, which appears to be a friend. Everyone that is out to use her and misuse her, God, give her the strength, the power to stand against them. God, thank you. Jesus, thank you. Jesus thank you. Lord God Hallelujah! Speak to her mind right now, God, which she would yield herself 100% to you. Hallelujah! I pull down every veil in her life, God, everything that she has placed to try to hide who she really is pull it down now in the name of Jesus! God, because of the things that have happened in the past she has put up a wall, God, Hallelujah pull it down now in the name of Jesus that she would commit her soul to thee 100% not worrying about what has happened. Let her commit herself to the point that she will see who is jealous, God, who is envious or whatever the situation is, God. People cannot lift her up as you can. If they lift her up, they can bring her down. Nevertheless, if you lift her up, God, nothing will take her down. No one will bring her down if you lift her up. We pray that you lift her up, lift up her soul in the name of Jesus! Satan the Lord rebuke you.

Satan the Lord rebuke you. Hallelujah! Satan the Lord rebuke you no more ciphering, sifting off hope. No more sapping her strength. No more shifting that bring about misdirection in her understanding. God, Hallelujah just like a button that is played on a video tape or video we push the stop button now and let it be erased. The things, God that run across her mind that has happen in the past erased now that she can go forward.

Paul said forgetting about those things that are behind me let her forget about the things that are behind her God. The past is over. The things that have been good we cannot relive them. The things that have been bad thank God we cannot relive them either Hallelujah.

Let her press toward the mark of the high calling it's a high calling, it' a sacrifice to climb up to the high call! It's a sacrifice to climb up this mountain Hallelujah. If you are willing to make the ultimate sacrifice, if you make a 100% sacrifice unto the Lord God he will never in no wise ever make you ashamed of your decision Hallelujah! Hallelujah, don't be afraid, don't be fearful, don't be bashful, don't hold back no more! Give your all! Step out on faith and give God your all like it is the last moment of your life! Give him your all in your praise. Give him your all in your worship. Give him your all in your soul Hallelujah! God wants to take you higher in him, and as he lifts you up, he is putting a hedge around you Hallelujah. No demon is going to be able to put their hands on your life! There will be no more compendium of blood Hallelujah. A signification now. A purification of your Spirit the Holy Spirit come and sanctifies this woman. We pray the Word of God come which is the Word of truth to sanctify you the more in Jesus name.

If you want great things gives something great of yourself to God. If you are the only one in church that will step out of the box step out the box! If you are the only one in church that will cry while everybody else is laughing cry! If you are the only one in church that will lift up your voice and shout unto God with a voice of triumph then shout unto God! Give him whatever he moves upon you to give him yeah Hallelujah! If you do, if you do said the Lord God of hosts, He has something that you cannot imagine according to the Scripture "Eyes have not seen ears have not heard nor has it entered into the heart of man the things that God has prepared for those that love him". The question is being asked on tonight from your soul do you love him? How much do you love him my Sister? Do you love God and how much do you love him? Do you love him enough to forsake mother, father, sister, friends love ones jobs! Do you love him enough to forsake yourself, your thoughts, and your ways? Do you love him enough to forsake yourself and place yourself as a sacrifice on his altar? Do you love him enough to say God "here I am?" This is the way you made me. I'm not going to complain and whoever likes it good and they that don't like me, too bad, because you made me this way, God!

Paul said it is a blessing to be single and for those who are single there first priority should be to love and serve God. My sister let that be consumed a consuming word in our soul on tonight that you must love God like nothing else. You must love God like no one else. You must love God first! If you hide yourself in God, if you hide yourself in the anointing Hallelujah the Lord knows your heart yes he does and if you want someone in your life, if you want a husband the Lord is saying in due season Hallelujah. If you sow your seeds now with him, you won't have to worry about happiness God has not forgotten about you. The tear you cried on the inside of your soul the Lord has seen them. He will send you a strong man. He will send you a blessed man, but first you must submit your mind, your soul and your will to God. Happiness is over the horizon. Give God some glory in this place for happiness! Bless him, bless him, bless him, Hallelujah!

The Lord says you can fool everybody else, you can put on a front of toughness but he knows your heart my sister he sees the YOU! You are not tuff in his eyesight you cannot put up a wall that he cannot penetrate. You cannot put up a façade that he can't read through. God knows your intentions. He knows your thoughts a far off. He said stop being afraid whatever you want from him just make it plain ask him with no pretence. Ask him and don't put a time limit on it and after you have laid it before him in prayer he said leave it alone and go serve him like you have never done before in your life! Be stable stand still I hear him say and watch him move. Stand still and see his salvation if you would stand still in your soul and settle yourself no wind will blow you Hallelujah! When the one comes and presents himself like an angel of light the Lord will let you see right through him Hallelujah. Don't yield, don't yield and don't go back don't turn and look back you will be like Lot's wife. Don't turn and look back on last year it is over Hallelujah! Yesterday is over. Will you bless him in for a new day? Will you bless him for a new dawning a resurrection in your soul right now! Give God some praise my sister. Give him some glory Hallelujah! Bless him. Bless him in the name of Jesus Hallelujah! Hallelujah, glory, glory, glory, glory! Thank you God, thank you!

God, move now on (another sister) have your way destroy every yoke Hallelujah, Hallelujah! A fresh anointing in her soul, the tree has fallen! Many trees have fallen thank you God, thank you Lord. You have caused those trees to fall in your life my sister because of your disobedience your stubbornness you have caused obstacles in your own life but the resurrection power of God is here, Hallelujah, bless Him! God is saying don't worry about what has happened the tree is down. Don't waste any time trying to move the tree or reset it. It is over with. God has given a fresh clean slate, start from this moment forward except it! Except a new anointing Hallelujah, thank you Jesus. No more pretences, no more carnality, no more hypocrisy give God a real praise out of your soul, an unusual praise Hallelujah! He is turning your tears of sorrow and your tears of misery into tears of joy!

God said settle yourself. Hallelujah, Hallelujah, Hallelujah. I hear the Lord saying He is going to do for you like he did for John the Baptist's Father he is going to shut your mouth for a period of time Hallelujah! Don't get stuck into conversations. Don't get sucked into trying to defend yourself and don't get sucked into trying to defend your God. Don't get sucked into things people are trying to draw you in. You don't have to prove that you are godly. God is going to prove that you are godly he is going to give you some godly fruit. Don't give any more advice. Don't try to council people it is a waste of time! Shake the dust of your feet that's wasted energy the Lord is saying you need a healing! You need to be rebuilt from the inside out! God is going to take you for the rest of these 40 days, twenty days if you will be obedient and dedicate your life like you have never had before. My sister all of your life you have had a few problems one is inconsistence Hallelujah. One is not being able to be committed for a long period of time and a bad judge of people. God said he has a remedy for all of that, the remedy is prayer! The more you pray and just praise him your deliverance is coming through praise! Because of your praise, my sister your praise has not be hypocritical. Because of your praise, God has shown you great favor and mercy. Now if your heart be proved for these 20 days as Paul went away to be instructed by the Holy Ghost before he came back to do ministry God is going to take you in the spirit to the hidden treasure trove of his Word! Read it like you never have! Read it, read it and God is going to let the Word that you read become a reality in your life and to your soul, Hallelujah give him some praise!

The anointing of God is strong in this place! The anointing of God is strong in my soul! Oh, God, I thank you, I thank you! I thank you for your Word God Hallelujah! Bless the name of the Lord! Bless the name of the Lord! Bless the name of the Lord! A humble spirit God is going to give thee. Not a fake humble spirit but a true humble spirit. Your very physical countenance is going to be changed. People are going to see a different in your soul if you yield yourself, if you yield yourself, if you yield yourself to God's power and authority. Sanctify your thoughts, sanctify your mind Hallelujah, I bind every unclean thought that comes your way. I bind every unclean spirit that has infiltrated and has attacked your soul Hallelujah! Don't worry about a man he will come. Skip the dating stop chasing after men and settle your soul. You have to make a choice do you want God's anointing? Do you want to be an anointed vessel of God you said the Lord has called you to preach Hallelujah, but a preacher has a greater reasonability you cannot serve God and mammon! You can only serve God or the Devil! God is not going to bless you to be anointed with the Word. You cannot bring blessing and cursing at the same time. God does not reward disobedience! A gift can only take you so far your gift have brought you to this point but your gift will not destroy the yoke for the anointing destroy the yoke Hallelujah! Thank you Jesus, thank you Jesus, thank you Jesus!

A bit, a bit that is placed in the mouth of a horse. A bit has been placed in your mouth Hallelujah my sister! A bit and the Holy Spirit is the one who control what direction you will be taken and what words you will say. Hallelujah in your spirit, Hallelujah! I call for a "Yes," a submitting in her soul, God, have your way like never before God!

A VISION IN THE MIDST OF THE PRAYER

Great warriors God is going to bring forth from this ministry! Great warriors, great warriors, great warriors, great warriors, great warriors, great warrior's Hallelujah! I see the hands of the Holy Ghost reaching inside the belly of this church and pulling out every malignant, every cursed thing Hallelujah! I see God opening up our mouths and the mouth of this church. I see the hand of God placed over the mouth of this church. I see the power the fire of the anointing coming out of his hand going down the throats of everyone who has their mouth open like a suckling that has their mouth open. Like a baby eaglet that is ready to be fed. I see the empowerment the indwelling power of the Holy Ghost Hallelujah flooding the mouths of the people in this place that will say yes to God Hallelujah bless him! Bless him!

I see the fire of God coming forth in tongues. In tongues in people who have never spoken in tongues like on the day of Pentecost (Acts 2:1-4) thank you Jesus! Bless him! Bless him! On tonight if you want the Baptism of the Holy Ghost, if you want it with the evidence of speaking in tongues you better open up your mouth tonight, you better praise him tonight! You better get yours tonight thy anointing is in this place the Anointer is here! It is God himself! Jesus the Lord he is baptizing and anointing with the Holy Ghost if really want it! If you want it with the evidence, stand up! Get up off your knees if you know you don't have it you begin to praise him out of your soul and tell him thank you! Give God a glorious praise Hallelujah! God wants to set fire! Fire, fire to your soul! Now I know what it means when the Prophet said it's like fire shut up in my bones! Can you feel the fire! Can you feel the fire in your soul ooooooooohhhhh!!!! The fire of God!!! Oooooooooh in your belly, in your belly the fire of God is in here how bad do you want it! How bad do you want it! I can't get if for you! How bad do you want it! How bad do you want it? The glory of the Lord is here! How can you let the glory of the Lord come and you not get what you want? How can you let the glory of the Lord come and not be taken higher! How could you let the glory of the Lord come and not be baptized in the Holy Ghost! If you never had it, receive it! If you've never been baptized, be thou filled! If you never spoken in tongues just believe! God said yes, he didn't say no he said yes! He said yes, he confirms his Word! He said in the last days he would pour out His Spirit upon all flesh are you alive! Are you alive? Then don't let the Devil get the victory. Open up your mouth talk to your God! Praise your God! He is God! Do you really believe in your soul he is God? Then press your way up the mountain! Press your way up the mountain don't let the Devil shut you up! Don't let the Devil shut you up. Open your mouth and give God glory! That's it cry out somebody in here really want the Holy Spirit down in their soul! That's it cry out, somebody in here really want it! That's it yield, yield, yield to the Holy Ghost yield! Let him have his way let him do whatever he wants to do. If he want to roll you, if he want to knock you out, if he want to flip you, if he want to lift you through the ceiling if you feel like your soul is exposing don't stop him let him have his way! Don't try to understand it, don't try to understand it just yield. Don't try to understand it yield. Step out of your comfort zone! Step out of your mind, your mind is earthly; your mind is not like God! Give him your mind, give him your will don't worry about how you have seen things before. Don't worry about how what you have experience things before. A new thing God wants to do a new thing! Do you really want the newest of God? Do you want a fresh anointing? Do you want some new wine! You better stretch out of your own soul! Bless him, bless him, bless him, bless him, bless him, bless him, bless the Lord oh my soul and all that is within me bless his Holy name! Bless the Lord oh my soul, thank you, thank you, thank you! Hallelujah Jesus, Jesus, Jesus, Lord we thank you in this place for allowing us to call on thy name once again. Thine will be done in our souls. Thy will be done in our homes. God we love you and we submit ourselves to thee now, God.

Now God we have sacrificed on this day giving you all from our souls. We want you to be please with the sacrifices of praise we your people have given on this night. We stand firm on your Word we know the Lord saveth is anointed, the King hears us when we call. We have done this boldly let a proclamation of the Word you have given we receive it now. We give you praise and glory in Jesus name the people of God say Amen, Amen.

<u>Closing Scripture: Joel 2:1-29 (KJV)</u>
"Blow the trumpet in Jerusalem! Sound the alarm on my holy mountain! Let everyone tremble in fear because the day of the LORD is upon us. It is a day of darkness and gloom, a day of thick clouds and deep blackness. Suddenly, like dawn spreading across the mountains, a mighty army appears! How great and powerful they are! The likes of them have not been seen before and never will be seen again. Fire burns in front of them and follows them in every direction! Ahead of them, the land lies as fair as the Garden of Eden in all its beauty. Behind them is nothing but desolation; not one thing escapes. They look like tiny horses, and they run as fast. Look at them as they leap along the mountaintops! Listen to the noise they make – like the rumbling of chariots, like the roar of a fire sweeping across a field, or like a mighty army moving into battle. Fear grips all the people; every face grows pale with fright. The attackers march like warriors and scale city walls like trained soldiers. Straight forward they march, never breaking rank. They never jostle each other; each moves in exactly the right place. They lunge through the gaps, and no weapon can stop them. They swarm over the city and run along its walls. They enter all the houses, climbing like thieves through the windows. The earth quakes as they advance, and the heavens tremble. The sun and moon grow dark, and the stars no longer shine. The LORD leads them with a shout! This is his mighty army, and they follow his orders. The day of the LORD is an awesome, terrible thing. Who can endure it? That is why the LORD says, "Turn to me now, while there is time! Give me your hearts. Come with fasting, weeping, and mourning. Don't tear your clothing in your grief; instead, tear your hearts." Return to the LORD your God, for he is gracious and merciful. He is not easily angered. He is filled with kindness and is eager not to punish you. Who knows? Perhaps even yet he will give you a reprieve, sending you a blessing instead of this terrible curse. Perhaps he will give you so much that you will be able to offer grain and wine to the LORD your God as before! Blow the trumpet in Jerusalem! Announce a time of fasting; call the people together for a solemn meeting. Bring everyone – the

elders, the children, and even the babies. Call the bridegroom from his quarters and the bride from her private room. The priests, who minister in the LORD's **PRESENCE**, will stand between the people and the altar, weeping. Let them pray, "Spare your people, LORD! They belong to you, so don't let them become an object of mockery. Don't let their name become a proverb of unbelieving foreigners who say, 'Where is the God of Israel? He must be helpless!'" Then the LORD will pity his people and be indignant for the honor of his land! He will reply, "Look! I am sending you grain and wine and olive oil, enough to satisfy your needs. You will no longer be an object of mockery among the surrounding nations. I will remove these armies from the north and send them far away. I will drive them back into the parched wastelands, where they will die. Those in the rear will go into the Dead Sea; those at the front will go into the Mediterranean. The stench of their rotting bodies will rise over the land." Surely, the LORD has done great things! Don't be afraid, my people! Be glad now and rejoice because the LORD has done great things. Don't be afraid, you animals of the field! The pastures will soon be green. The trees will again be filled with luscious fruit; fig trees and grapevines will flourish once more. Rejoice, you people of Jerusalem! Rejoice in the LORD your God! For the rains, he sends are an expression of his grace. Once more the autumn rains will come, as well as the rains of spring. The threshing floors will again be piled high with grain, and the presses will overflow with wine and olive oil. The LORD says, "I will give you back what you lost to the stripping locusts, the cutting locusts, the swarming locusts, and the hopping locusts. It was I who sent this great destroying army against you. Once again you will have all the food you want, and you will praise the LORD your God, who does these miracles for you. Never again will my people be disgraced like this. Then you will know that I am here among my people of Israel and that I alone am the LORD your God. My people will never again be disgraced like this. "Then after I have poured out my rains again, I will pour out my Spirit upon all people. Your sons and daughters will prophesy. Your old men will dream dreams. Your young men will see visions. In those days, I will pour out my Spirit even on servants, men and women alike."

Closing Remarks:

Hallelujah thus said the Word of God therefore, you are blessed. Every Sunday at the Temple of Prayer, the affirmation of faith is read stating we believe the Bible to be the only infallible written Word of God. We say that, but do we really believe it? I believe it God's Bible. I believe what the scripture said in Joel. As I read it, I prayed it back to God. It's not so much, what I have to say; it's God honoring what He has said. God has to honor His Word. It's His Word. When you pray your own words, He doesn't necessarily have to honor that, but He has to honor His own Word. God will not let His Word fail. I hope you are trying to do what this chapter is telling you to do. If you do these things, then you will find out what God will do for you. What was done in this chapter is what you should want God to do for you and that is for His Spirit to come.

Do you really believe that if God said He would pour out His spirit on all flesh that He will do it? If so you should give him some praise! Hallelujah, Hallelujah, Hallelujah! Bless Him, bless Him, bless Him! I'm not made out of steel; I'm not made out of plastic; I'm made out of flesh! God said in the last days He would pour out His spirit upon all flesh, after the call had been made for prayer (verse 28) after the call has been made for a solemn fast, a solemn assembly. If you meet the requirements of God; God will always meet and do or backup whatever He said He would do if something is contingent or based upon it. God is not going to do anything you spoken unless you do the "if." If you do the "if," God has what He says covered. You need to make sure what you need to do is covered. Why? Because I want God to pour out His Spirit. God will pour out His spirit on those who say "Yes" to Him. I want God to pour out his spirit on me not just one time, but on as many times as He wants! I am saying "Yes" to God, I am available! Have Your way, pour it out on me! For those who may not have ever experienced it before, I am telling you now that there is no way that you will sit still. There is no way you can govern or control yourself. You may not yell or shout out as loud as someone else shouts but you will cry, or move, rock, bend over, fall out, you will do something! There is no way the power of the Holy Ghost can be inside of your soul and you act like you are just sitting somewhere waiting for someone to call your name and you are tired of sitting there all day. When God pours out His spirit! I'm talking about for those of you who have had that experience again and again. You know when God pours out His Spirit on you; you don't know what to do! You don't know how to handle the greatness of God's power! God might have poured it out on you yesterday and yesterday you could not shut it but today you cannot stop crying! You don't know how you are going to act, but you know you are going to act some kind of way! Because you cannot hold the power of the Holy Ghost inside of your soul and not have some kind of human reaction!!!

Is there a witness that God has poured out his Spirit on any flesh in here!!! Bless Him, bless Him! Flood my soul! Somebody say flood my soul with thou Spirit, God!!! Flood my soul!!! You said You are going to let it rain the former and the latter rain moderately. God is not going to send a flood that you cannot handle. If He sends a flood, you can handle it! Whatever measure of rain He sends, you can handle it. He said He is going to restore. This is a new year. The scripture said in that first month; this is the first month for our calendar year. God said He would do all the things listed. I believe Him to do it this month! I'm looking for deliverance this month! I'm looking for a miracle this month! I don't know what your miracle is but I have one miracle I need for God to do; He said all that the locust, the cankerworm, the caterpillar and the palmerworm; He said He was going to restore that back! This month, this month, the first month, this month and the only thing God asks me to do is pray and lay before the porch and alter and call on His name and ask God to spare His people. He said, "pray and say spare the people." That's all the elders had to do! You mean we come and pray asking God to spare the people, and the people had to be there in prayer with them with the elders and in agreement with the elders. And God was going to bless the whole Nation!?! Moreover, not just pour out His spirit on the elders but that He was going to pour out His spirit on all flesh!!! The ladies ought to be passed out! God didn't just say He was going to pour out on just the men, He said all flesh!!! Sons and daughters! Sons and daughters!

Do you want God to pour out His Spirit on you! Somebody say, thank You, Lord! Thank You, Lord! Thank You, Lord! Thank You for Your Spirit! Thank You for Your outpouring! Thank God for it! Thank

Him for the outpouring of the Holy Ghost! Thank Him for it! Thank Him for it! I thank You for it, God! I thank You for the anointing! I thank You for the outpouring and the indwelling! Hallelujah! Hallelujah! Hallelujah! I'm trying to contain myself in here for the people's sake! Oh, but I want the more of You, God, in my soul! I love You, Lord! My soul surrenders to Thee now and forever more!

END OF DAY 20 PRAYER SERVICE

Personal Note:
Oh, I cannot stop writing. Just listening to the tape of this prayer, the anointing fell in my room as I was writing. Have you ever seen the fire of God or felt it? Tonight my body was on fire! My hands were so hot that I could not touch my own face! Oh, what an experience I will never forget. My soul longs for God. When you are in the **PRESENCE** of God, everything is made clear. Nothing is out of place. Nothing can harm you. There is a peace and a love that we cannot define that takes place. Every night as we get closer and closer to the top of the mountain, it's get harder and harder to leave. Oh, how we desire to stay in the church and just commune with God. Our hope is in Him. God is so real. Once you experience Him, no one or nothing can make you doubt Him! Have you ever seen the praises come out of your mouth like music notes dancing in the air! Have you ever experienced a shedding, a part of you drop off like clothes. That is what it was like for us on the twentieth night and one day we will be free from the flesh. The flesh will no longer have us as a prisoner and at that time; we will be able to praise God with the very existence of who we are.
~ Evelyn

Dear Reader,

We are half way up the mountain! Hold on because the journey is worth it! In the next volume we will experience the day the "Earth Stood Still," "I Am Helped!" and "The Battle We Fight Everyday Is One of Life & Death" just to name a few. I'm excited as we travel together getting closer to the top of the mountain where God is waiting for us. Also in volume 2, we will experience a "shut out." What is a shut out? It is when we went into the church and shut everything out! We shut out our problems, sickness, and our way of thinking. Anything, which was attached to the flesh that would hinder us from being in God's Presence! It's like a sleep over without sleep! We called it a "Soul-Over." The experience was phenomenal!

I look forward to connecting with you in the spirit in volume 2 of "A Call Into His Presence: When the Spirit Prays" as we pray for one another and the World!

Thank you so much for purchasing my book and partnering with me in prayer!

I love you and may God, continue to bless and strengthen you!

Evelyn A. Johnson
Please visit me at www.evelynajohnsonbooks.com!
Email: evelynajohnsonbooks@yahoo.com